OPEN-BOOK MANAGEMENT

Creating an Ownership Culture

Thomas L. Barton
University of North Florida

William G. Shenkir
McIntire School of Commerce, University of Virginia

Thomas N. Tyson
St. John Fisher College

A publication of Financial Executives Research Foundation, Inc.

Financial Executives Research Foundation, Inc.
10 Madison Avenue
P.O. Box 1938
Morristown, NJ 07962-1938
(973) 898-4608

International Standard Book Number 1-885065-12-4
Library of Congress Catalog Card Number 97-77705
Printed in the United States of America

First Printing

Financial Executives Research Foundation, Inc. (FERF™) is the research affiliate of Financial Executives Institute. The basic purpose of the Foundation is to sponsor research and publish informative material in the field of business management, with particular emphasis on the practice of financial management and its evolving role in the management of business.

The views set forth in this publication are those of the authors and do not necessarily represent those of the FERF Board as a whole, individual trustees, or the members of the Advisory Committee.

FERF publications can be ordered by calling 1-800-680-FERF
(U.S. and Canada only; international orders, please call 770-751-1986).
Quantity discounts are available.

ADVISORY COMMITTEE

Robert J. Schuler (Chairman)
Senior Vice President
Med3000 Group, Inc.

Dawn Mahoney Cottrell
Vice President of Finance
Plow & Hearth, Inc.

James C. Horsch, C.M.A.
President, IMA Foundation for Applied Research, Inc.
Director of Electric Business Planning
Consumers Energy

J. James Lewis
Executive Vice President
Financial Executives Research Foundation, Inc.

G. William McIntyre
Director of Finance and CFO
ComSonics, Inc.

Larry E. Pearson
Senior Vice President, Finance
GE Fanuc Automation North America, Inc.

William M. Sinnett
Project Manager
Financial Executives Research Foundation, Inc.

Rhona L. Ferling
Publications Manager
Financial Executives Research Foundation, Inc.

CONTENTS

APPENDICES

1

Introduction

> You can resist an invading army; you cannot resist an idea whose time has come.
>
> Victor Hugo

The approaching millennium offers business managers and owners the opportunity to reflect on how competitive pressures and new market opportunities will shape the way they do business into the 21st century. Business leaders have already experienced the upheavals and massive reallocation of resources brought about by rapid technological change and the opening of markets in the former Soviet Union and the People's Republic of China. Who would have imagined 20 years ago that in 1997 the fifth largest company in market capitalization in the world would be a computer software firm—Microsoft—that was started only in 1975? Who would have envisioned that the richest man in the world in 1997—Bill Gates—would be a computer techie and Harvard dropout who was cranking out primitive computer code in 1977? Who would have had the foresight to imagine a McDonald's restaurant situated on prime Moscow real estate, with 50,000 Russians waiting to order Big Macs on opening day?

As the saying goes, "There is nothing permanent except change."[1] The businesses that will survive and prosper into the next millennium are those that adopt the management practices and tools that give them the needed competitive edge and an effective, rock-solid management infrastructure capable of keeping pace with change. Business will only become more complicated and less predictable with each passing year; change will not go away.

It is ironic that with the many sophisticated resource management tools available in the late 20th century, the one resource that has the highest potential to help many businesses cope with change is the one most underutilized—the human resource. Inside every business and in every unit within the business are people with experience, insight, and know-how who are paid to perform a well-defined task and often nothing more. Surely there must be a way to tap that tremendous store of human capital and, in so doing, make the almost-certain upheavals of the future infinitely more manageable and profitable. Simply put, how can business leaders align employee goals with company goals to create a world-class organization that can compete successfully in a global economy?

To be sure, a number of management methods have been suggested in recent years to deal with this problem. Among them are total quality management (TQM), the balanced scorecard, reengineered company processes, self-directed teams, leadership with vision and values, the learning organization, and customer-focused management. But a new approach has taken root over the past several years that may be the most promising of all. It is called open-book management, and it has received a surprising amount of attention in the business and popular press. Open-book management can provide a framework for aligning employee goals with those of the organization—for making employees think like owners—and the method is credited with many successes. But while some have made extravagant claims about the potential of open-book management, others have considered it with great skepticism—wondering if it is a passing fad that might even be dangerous to their companies.

This research study provides an analytical view of open-book management and its benefits for a company. The study is built around the case stories of seven companies that have successfully adopted open-book management. The stories have been analyzed to suggest lessons for others—especially financial managers—who might be interested in implementing open-book management in their companies.

As corporate America faces unremitting pressure to reduce costs, add value, and improve financial performance, business leaders must consider breakthrough management methods with the potential to significantly improve the bottom line. Open-book management is one of the newest candidates, and, like activity-based costing[2] of the 1980s, it challenges some basic assumptions of doing business.

What Is Open-Book Management?

Open-book management is a management philosophy that:

- Shares a broad array of financial and other information with employees.
- Trains employees to become more business literate.
- Empowers them to use the information in their work, trusting them as partners.
- Rewards them when the company is successful.

The four essential elements of open-book management are shown in figure 1.1. As shown in the diagram, open-book management must contain all elements to achieve the necessary alignment of employee and company goals. Table 1.1 displays a matrix of the consequences if one of the four elements is omitted. In each case, the remaining three elements are affected negatively, and the open-book management system itself is fatally flawed. In effect, the four elements—share, train, empower, reward—are the *STER steps* to open-book management.

Open-book management is more than an accounting phenomenon (although accounting plays a major role); it is a fundamental change in the traditional way most managements have operated their business. Open-book management requires that business leaders be committed to teaching their employees to *think and act like owners*. Employees are likely to share company goals when they (1) understand how the business makes money; (2) possess a basic understanding of critical information about the business; (3) regularly receive reports and explanations of company operations; (4) use their knowledge about the company in their jobs to improve operations; (5) celebrate exceptional performance together; and (6) receive bonuses when the company does well. Table 1.2 contrasts the new paradigm with the old in terms of management's perspective on employees, employees' access to information, employees' level of training, and management's overall focus for the business.

Figure 1.1
Open-Book Management

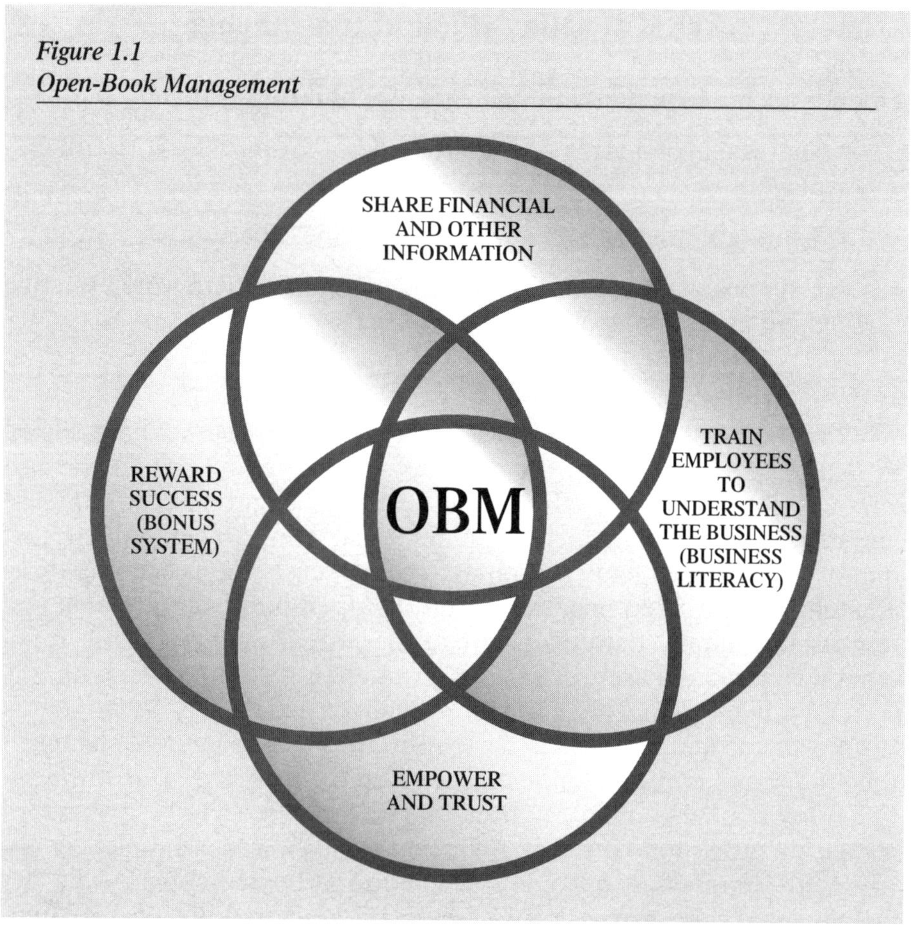

Not surprisingly, some financial executives may be reluctant to open company books to employees and to explain the intricacies of accounting and finance. Financial executives who believe the typical employee dislikes work, avoids responsibility, rejects organizational values, works only for pay and security, and needs to be closely monitored and controlled are probably not going to be favorably disposed to open-book management. Financial executives who have risen through the ranks of command-and-control organizations may very well want to "close the book" on open-book management.[3]

Table 1.1
STER Steps to Open-Book Management
Share-Train-Empower-Reward *Effect of Missing Element on the Other Three*

Element Missing	Share	Train	Empower	Reward
Share		No need for training if no sharing; training in *what*?	No feedback; decisions will be uninformed.	Reward will appear arbitrary; management will appear untrustworthy.
Train	Will not understand or will misunderstand information; possible chaos.		Will not know how to use information.	Will not understand how to increase reward.
Empower	Can't affect numbers; satisfies curiosity only.	No need for training if no empowerment; empty.		Can't affect bonus; passive recipient.
Reward	No stake; satisfies curiosity only.	No stake; no need for training.	No stake; no incentive for action.	

Table 1.2
A Paradigm Shift

	Old Paradigm	New Paradigm
Perspective on Employees	Hired hand	Businessperson
Access to Information	Limited	Open
Level of Training	Limited	Continuous
Focus of Management	Primarily financial	Financial and nonfinancial

Adapted from Shenkir, William G., and Thomas L. Barton. "A New Small Business Order." In *Performance Management in Small Businesses*. New York: International Federation of Accountants, 1996:120.

1

What Open-Book Management Is Not

Open-book management is not a quick fix for a business facing some major difficulty, such as financial problems, declining markets, or increasing competition. The seven study companies have put forth an extraordinary effort over a number of years to build their open-book cultures. The effort takes much time on the part of company leadership and a sustained commitment to training employees about business operations and financial statements. A company's leadership should decide to create an open-book culture only if it is committed to the concept for the long term.

Among the seven study companies, only Springfield ReManufacturing Corp. (SRC) adopted open-book management while it was having financial problems. In that case, the leadership credits open-book management as a primary reason for the company's survival. In the other six study companies, open-book management was the outgrowth of some other management initiative or of the owner's personal business philosophy.

Open-book management is not uncontroversial. Sharing sensitive financial information with employees is risky because such information might fall into competitors' hands. Although those who question the value of open-book management often raise this issue, the study companies were not overly concerned about it. Certainly, they preferred that their competitors not get the information they were sharing with employees, but they felt the benefits of harmonizing employee and organizational goals exceeded the costs (or risks) of competitors' obtaining sensitive financial information. Also, at least two study companies felt competitors had little to gain from knowing company financial information.

Another controversy centers on the belief that employees can and must learn how the business makes money. To do that, they must understand financial information. Those who question the value of open-book management point out that most businesses are complex, and financial statements are difficult to understand, particularly for people with no prior training in accounting and finance. Accordingly, they view open-book management as an extreme and naïve method. It is unrealistic and very idealistic, skeptics say, to believe management can organize training courses that will enable employees not previously schooled in finance to become literate about business and financial issues. Interestingly, the study companies are committed to doing just that, and they have established formal and informal training to accomplish the goal.

Origin of Open-Book Management

Although open-book management is widely attributed to Jack Stack, CEO of Springfield ReManufacturing Corp., the foundation for the approach was laid decades earlier. Stock purchase plans for employees date back to the 1920s; some of the benefits of these arrangements were improved worker morale, better productivity, and greater loyalty to the company.[4] In the 1950s, Joseph Scanlon, union leader turned MIT lecturer, recognized the value of joint labor-management participation by devising a model plant-wide bonus system that focused on reducing costs, improving productivity, and eliminating waste. Although the Scanlon plan was used successfully by a number of companies in the 1950s, its use never was widespread because "few managements wished to involve the workers to the degree contemplated in the plan or were willing to make the sustained efforts to maintain the plan over time."[5] Nevertheless, Scanlon plans are still used to a limited extent in the 1990s; there is even an organization called Scanlon Plan Associates dedicated to maintaining interest in the plans.

In the 1950s and 1960s, motivational researchers McGregor, Maslow, Argyris, and Herzberg proposed theories that by the 1980s and 1990s had become widely accepted in the business community. As a result, the cultures at many organizations are more receptive to a revolutionary idea like open-book management. For example, McGregor contrasted two polar positions: Theory X posited that people dislike work and need to be told what to do; Theory Y posited that people like work and are more productive when they are given responsibility and have greater job satisfaction. McGregor's Theory Y provides a rationale for sharing financial information with rank-and-file employees because (1) they will use it appropriately, (2) they are responsible, and (3) they will resist disclosing the information outside the company.[6] According to McGregor, "The central principle which derives from

Theory Y is that of integration: the creation of conditions such that the members of the organization can achieve their own goals *best* by directing their efforts toward the success of the enterprise."[7] Two of McGregor's assumptions seem especially fitting to open-book management programs:

1. "The average human being learns, under proper conditions, not only to accept but to seek responsibility."
2. "The capacity to exercise a relatively high degree of imagination, ingenuity, and creativity in the solution of organizational problems is widely, not narrowly, distributed in the population."[8]

As Jack Stack was building on the open-book management foundation in the early 1980s, two of the study companies, ComSonics and Physician Sales & Service (PSS), were creating their own forms of open-book management. Notwithstanding the existence at the time of various practices related to open-book management, Stack's creative contribution was to implement and sustain an entire system involving employees from all levels in the organization, not just key managers, that includes teaching them how the company makes money and sharing financial information with them. In addition, he designed a system that gives every employee the opportunity to participate in the economic rewards of a successful organization by aligning total compensation with the organization's performance.

Stack's story is discussed in more detail in chapter 9. But briefly, his company, Springfield ReManufacturing, was established through a leveraged buyout from International Harvester in 1983. Faced at that time with interest rate payments of 22 percent, the loss of its major customer, and possible employee layoffs, Stack made a decision to share the company's precarious financial situation with employees and to seek their help. Stack called his approach "The Great Game of Business." (The term "open-book management" was coined later.) He regularly shared financial information and operating data with employees, teaching them to view business as a game in which the financial statements were the scorecard and expenses were the enemy. Employees learned how the game was played and how their work affected the company's bottom line and other people in the organization. For about 15 years, SRC has been successfully practicing The Great Game of Business or open-book management. In an ongoing Cinderella story of shrewd and successful risk taking, SRC has been transformed into a $100-million network of manufacturing and service businesses that serve as a model for open-book management. Stack's fame has spread to the point that his company is able to market open-book management programs and instructional materials through its Great Game of Business® subsidiary.

The term "open-book management" is attributed to John Case, a senior writer with *Inc.* magazine, who in 1990 published an article entitled "The Open-Book Managers."[9] The experience of SRC was described in a 1992 book, *The Great Game of Business*, by Jack Stack with Bo Burlingham.[10] In 1995, Case published *Open-Book Management: The Coming Business Revolution*, which drew more attention to the movement.[11] At about the same time, *Inc.* also published a lengthy article based on Case's book.[12] All of these publications have popularized the open-book management approach.

Some might ask why it took so long for someone to develop the essentials of open-book management if the approach has so much potential for dramatic change. Clearly, many other companies have faced conditions similar to those that confronted SRC and have attempted to engage workers' support by tying portions of pay to performance or by sharing financial information. But it took a variety of social and economic factors converging in the 1990s to give open-book management the growing popularity it currently enjoys.

One factor is that the basic health and safety needs of most American workers no longer preoccupy labor-management relations. Another is that the growth of small business, which parallels the decline of labor unions, has resulted in a wider acceptance of profit sharing and employee stock ownership plans (ESOPs).[13] Managers and workers alike have experienced corporate downsizing and clearly recognize that uncertainty is now the norm: No jobs are guaranteed for life. Furthermore, everyone agrees that organizations must change and continually search for ways to reduce costs and increase value just to remain viable in the face of unrelenting competition. Thus, programs—such as open-book management—that challenge conventional thinking and prove successful now receive serious consideration rather than being rejected out of hand, as they might have been before.

Changes within organizations also account for the growing popularity of participative programs like open-book management. Stereotypes based on class, race, and gender, which may have justified restricting access to information, tend to disappear in corporate structures that rely on teams of workers and managers. As organizations flatten, hierarchies disappear, and personal interactions increase, sharing financial information with people who can affect the bottom line becomes less threatening and eminently sensible. In open, trusting, participatory, and democratic work environments, the logic of open-book management becomes nearly irrefutable, especially when significant portions of pay and the opportunity for equity are tied to financial performance. Few, if any, reasons support *not* providing employees with an understanding of how their actions affect the measures (i.e., financial statements) that outsiders use to evaluate the company.

Objectives and Approach of the Study

The objectives of this Financial Executives Research Foundation project are as follows:

- To provide practical guidelines for companies and financial executives planning to implement or contemplating open-book management.
- To examine the role and responsibilities of financial executives in open-book management companies.

With these objectives in mind, the researchers identified seven companies that had successfully adopted open-book management[14] and conducted in-depth interviews with the CEO, the CFO (or a comparable financial executive),[15] and a variety of other managers and employees. When possible, employees were interviewed in the factory, on the shop floor, or in the warehouse. An interview protocol containing a list of questions guided the visits and interviews (see appendix A). Each company was visited at least once, and several were visited a second time. Telephone interviews also were conducted as needed to clarify information obtained during the visits. The case stories are based on the transcribed interviews as well as on other materials provided by the company.

In selecting the companies, the researchers sought a cross-section of successful users of open-book management. The seven firms chosen include four private companies, one public company, a subsidiary of a public company, and a joint venture between a Japanese company and a subsidiary of a U.S. public firm. The group represents the manufacturing, service, distribution, and retail industries. Brief profiles of the companies appear in table 1.3. (Figures 1.2 through 1.8 display timelines for the seven companies and indicate key events in their histories, especially those related to open-book management.)

To gain additional background on the implementation of open-book management, all three researchers attended The National Gathering of the Games V, the fifth annual meeting of companies that have adopted open-book management or are considering doing so. The meeting was sponsored by The Great Game of Business, Inc., and *Inc.* magazine. It was held in St. Louis on September 22–23, 1997, and attracted more than 600 attendees to its 60 workshops and concurrent sessions. Topics explored included the following:

- Designing business games.
- Establishing an ESOP.
- Training in business operations and financial literacy.
- Designing variable compensation plans.

Table 1.3
ComSonics, Inc.

Founded:	1972 by Warren L. Braun
Industry:	Manufactures and repairs cable television (CATV) equipment for cable system operators
Location:	Plant in Harrisonburg, Virginia; sales reps nationwide
Revenues:	$11 million
Employees:	154

Other information:

- Became ESOP in 1975; 100% employee owned by 1985.
- Started practicing open-book management in 1985.
- Instituted pay-for-performance in 1991.
- Integrates ESOP, open-book management, and pay-for-performance.
- Received quality awards in 1984 and 1990.

Table 1.3 (Continued)

GE Fanuc Automation North America, Inc.

Founded: 1987; joint venture between GE and FANUC Ltd. of Japan
Industry: Manufactures programmable logic controllers (PLCs) and computer numerical controllers (CNCs)
Location: Headquartered in Charlottesville, Virginia; extensive operations in Asia/Pacific, Europe, and the Americas
Revenues: $515 million
Employees: 1,600
Other information:

- Jack Welch launched Work Out in 1989.
- GE Fanuc launched Vision-Powered Management in 1989, followed by High-Involvement Workforce initiative.
- Open-book management uses monthly report card with grades.
- Instituted bonus system.
- Certified for ISO 9000.

Mid-States Technical Staffing Services, Inc.

Founded: 1986 by Steve Wilson
Industry: Places temporary engineering and drafting staff and offers contract engineering and design services
Location: Seven offices in Iowa, Indiana, and Kentucky
Revenues: $12 million
Employees: 105
Other information:

- Operates as a division of a public company.
- Practiced open-book management from start-up, but changed approach in 1992.
- Sold in 1993 to AccuStaff, which went public in 1994.
- Offers bucket bonus plan.

North American Signs

Founded: 1934
Industry: Manufactures outdoor signs
Location: South Bend, Indiana
Revenues: $11 million
Employees: Just under 100
Other information:

- Owned by two brothers.
- Shop is unionized.
- Open-book management evolved piecemeal.
- Open-book management supports owners' personal philosophy.
- Instituted gain-sharing program in 1989.

Table 1.3 (Continued)

Physician Sales & Service, Inc.

Founded: 1983 by Pat Kelly
Industry: Distributes medical supplies, pharmaceuticals, x-ray supplies, and equipment to doctors' offices, nursing homes, and hospitals
Location: Headquartered in Jacksonville, Florida; nationwide distribution
Revenues: $1.3 billion (projected 1998)
Employees: 4,000
Other information:

- Company became public in 1994.
- Open-book management grew naturally out of PSS culture.
- As public company, only reveals "sharing piece."
- Employees purchased stock early on.
- Uses bonus system.

Plow & Hearth, Inc.

Founded: 1980 by Peter and Peggy Rice
Industry: Primarily mail order; one retail store
Location: Madison and Charlottesville, Virginia
Revenues: Almost $32 million
Employees: 72 full-time; 50 part-time; 350 during holiday season
Other information:

- Company is closely held.
- Open-book management evolved out of total quality management program.
- Bonus plan instituted in 1989.
- Bonus plan formalized in 1996.
- Received quality award in 1994.

Springfield ReManufacturing Corp.

Founded: Leveraged buyout by Jack Stack in 1983 (previously a division of International Harvester)
Industry: Remanufactures heavy-duty diesel engines and automotive engines; several subsidiaries, including The Great Game of Business
Location: Springfield, Missouri
Revenues: $100 million
Employees: 900
Other information:

- Company is an ESOP.
- Stack is credited with originating open-book management (called Great Game of Business).
- Started open-book management when in financial difficulty.
- Coined term "huddle meetings."
- Instituted bonus system.

Figure 1.2
Timeline, ComSonics, Inc.

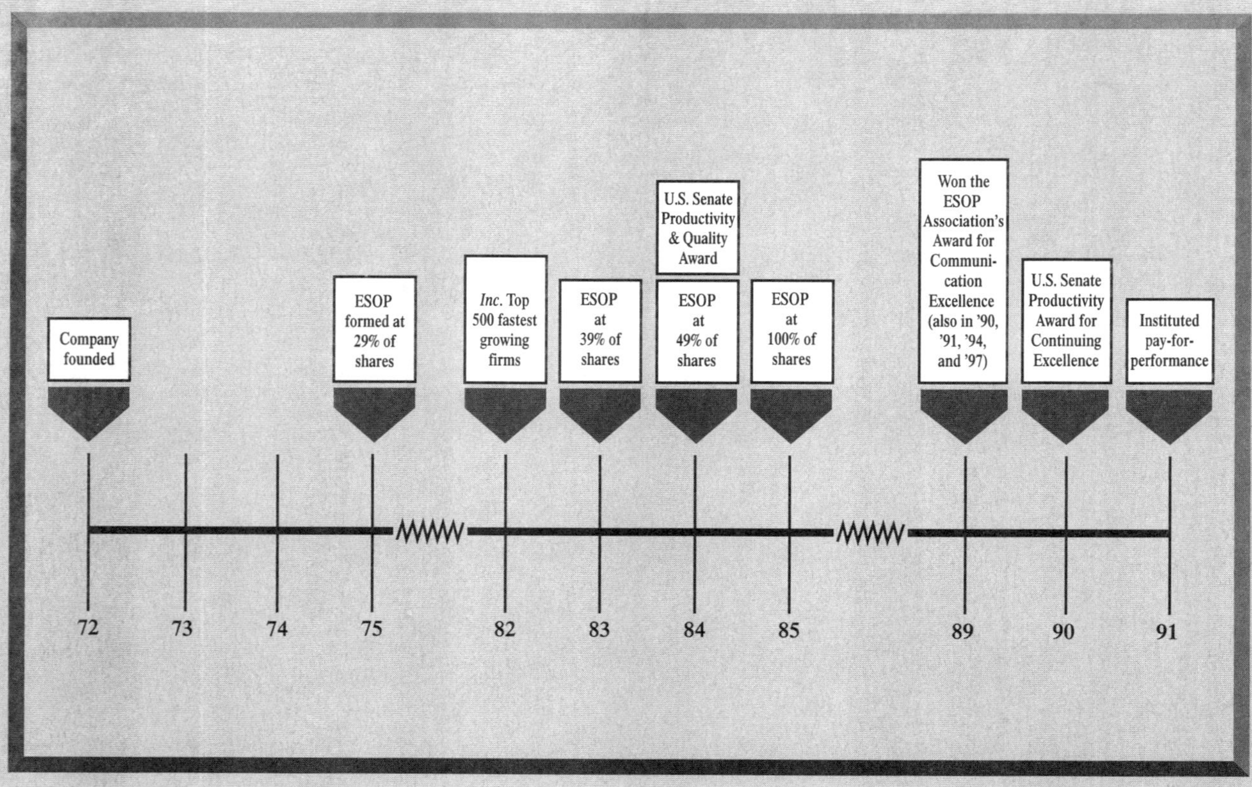

Figure 1.3
Timeline, GE Fanuc Automation North America, Inc.

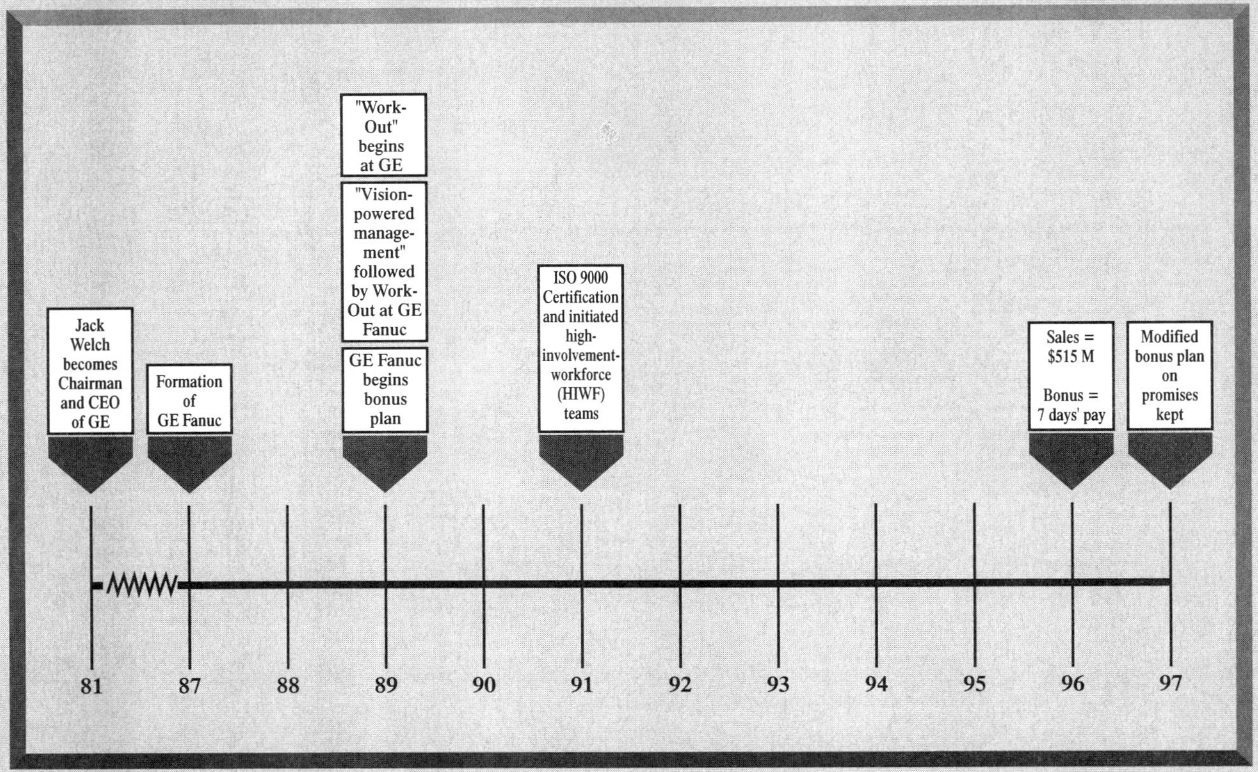

Figure 1.4
Timeline, Mid-States Technical Staffing Services, Inc.

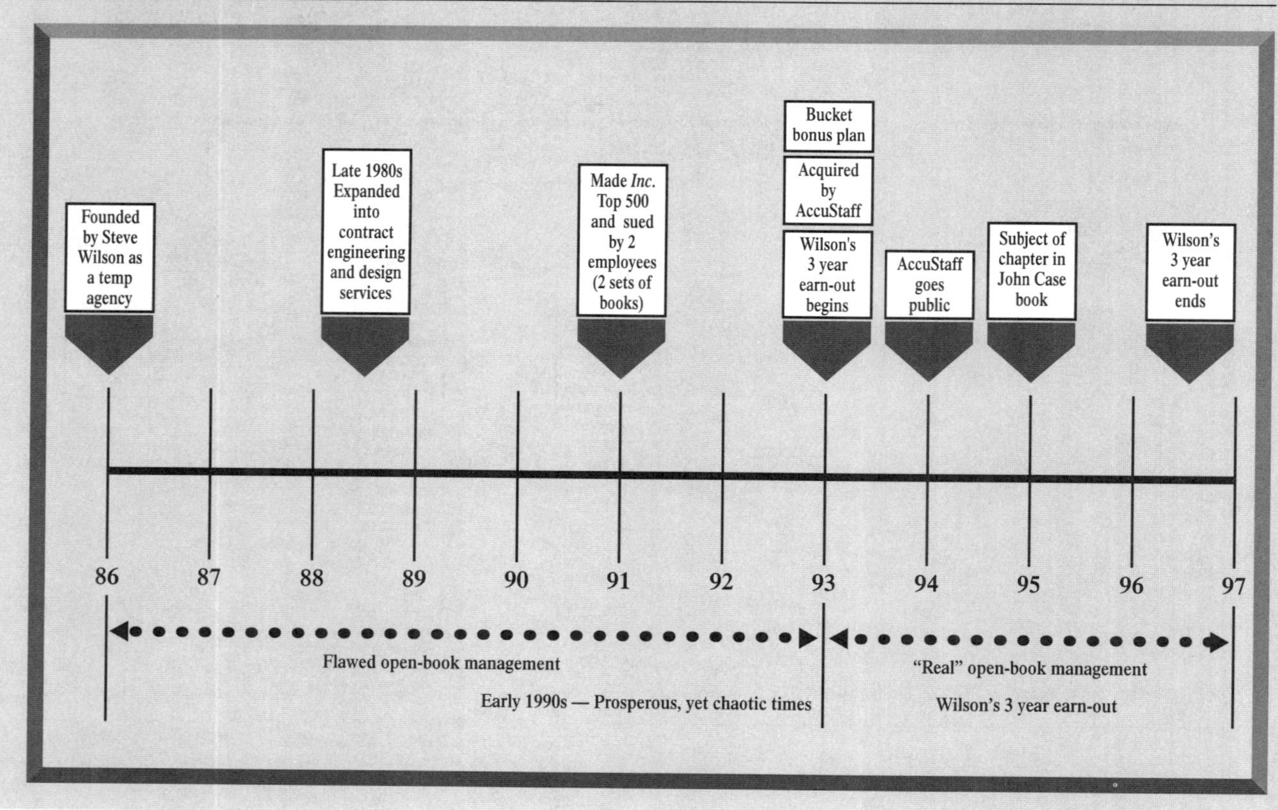

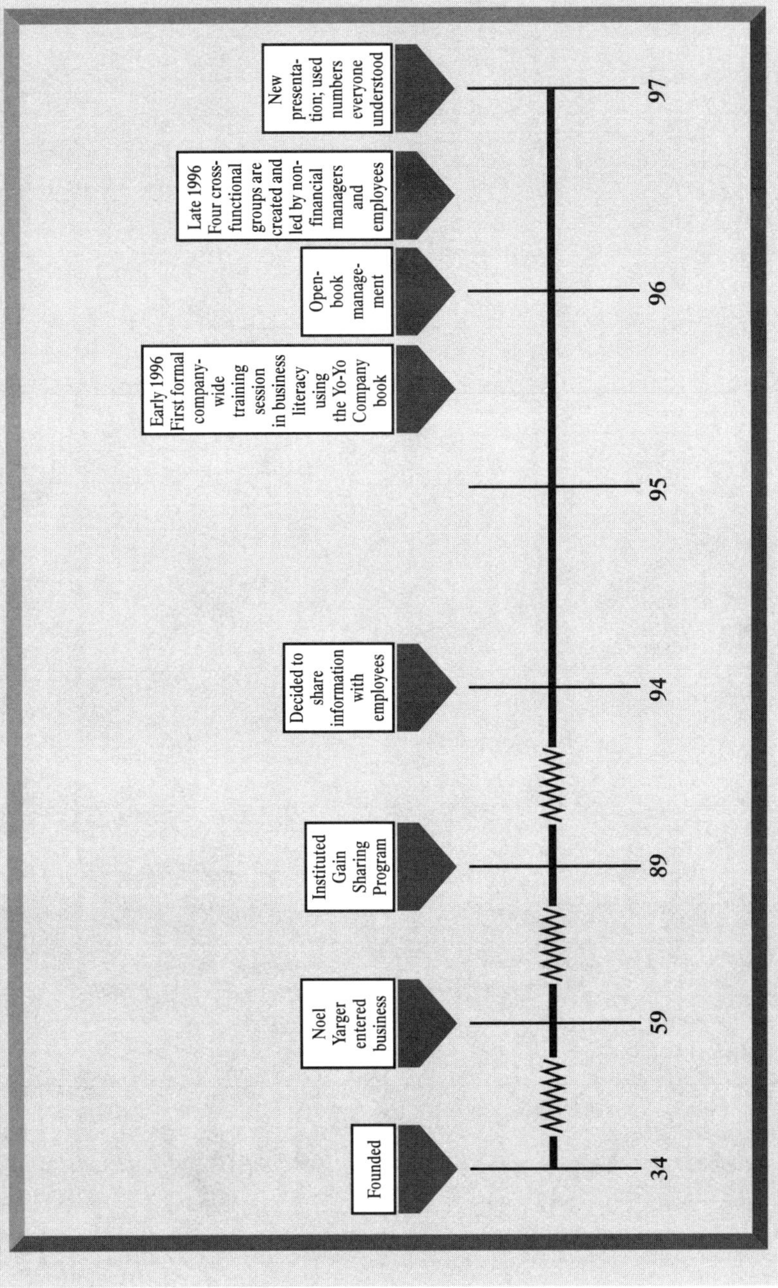

Figure 1.5
Timeline, North American Signs

34 — Founded

59 — Noel Yarger entered business

89 — Instituted Gain Sharing Program

94 — Decided to share information with employees

95

Early 1996 First formal company-wide training session in business literacy using the Yo-Yo Company book

96 — Open-book management

Late 1996 Four cross-functional groups are created and led by non-financial managers and employees

97 — New presentation; used numbers everyone understood

Figure 1.6
Timeline, Physician Sales & Service, Inc.

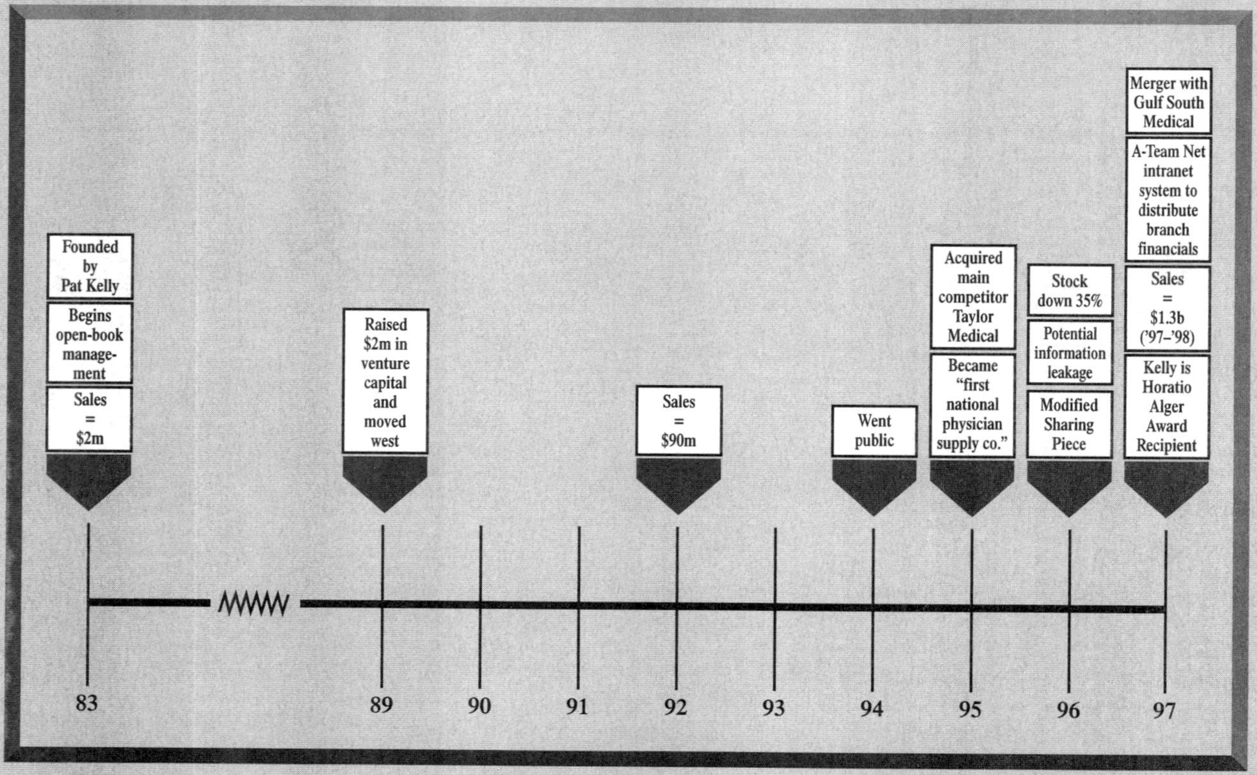

83
Founded by Pat Kelly
Begins open-book manage-ment
Sales = $2m

89
Raised $2m in venture capital and moved west

90

91

92
Sales = $90m

93

94
Went public

95
Acquired main competitor Taylor Medical
Became "first national physician supply co."

96
Stock down 35%
Potential information leakage
Modified Sharing Piece

97
Merger with Gulf South Medical
A-Team Net intranet system to distribute branch financials
Sales = $1.3b ('97–'98)
Kelly is Horatio Alger Award Recipient

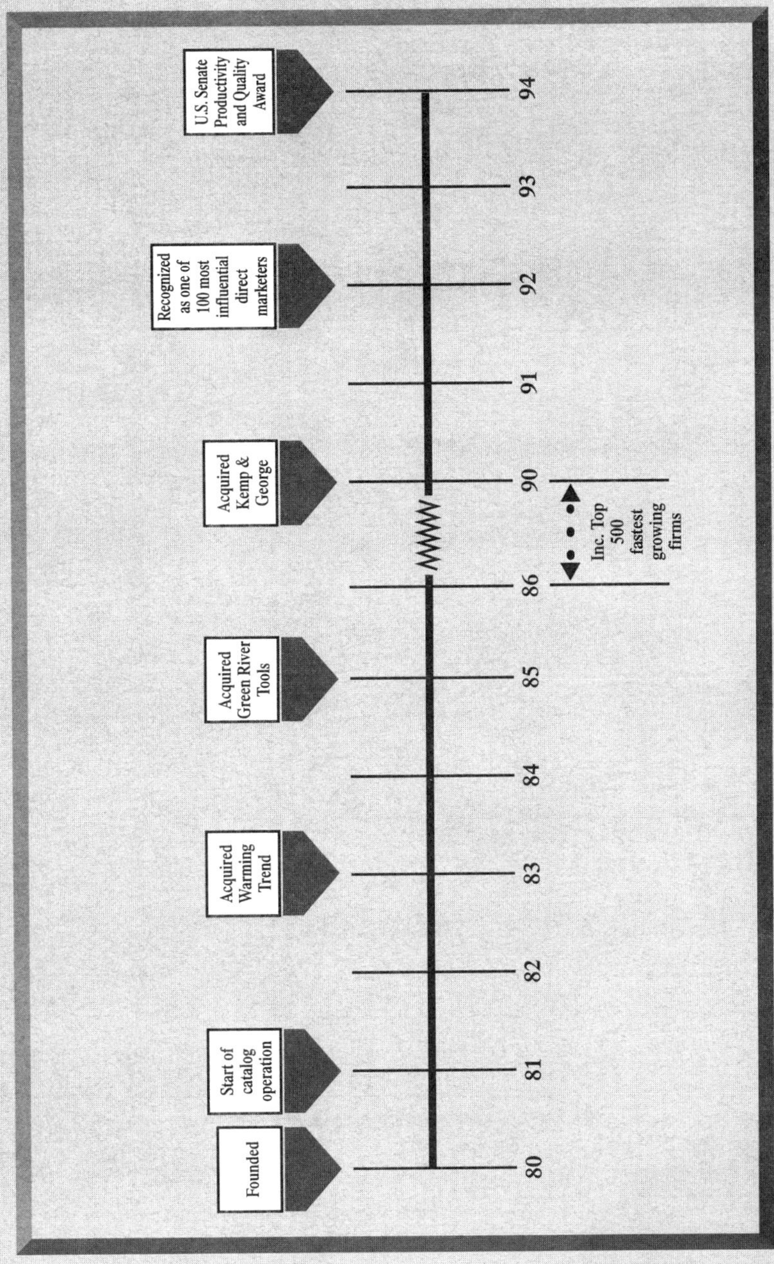

Figure 1.7
Timeline, Plow & Hearth, Inc.

80	Founded
81	Start of catalog operation
82	
83	Acquired Warming Trend
84	
85	Acquired Green River Tools
86	
90	Acquired Kemp & George
91	
92	Recognized as one of 100 most influential direct marketers
93	
94	U.S. Senate Productivity and Quality Award

86–90: Inc. Top 500 fastest growing firms

Figure 1.8
Timeline, Springfield ReManufacturing Corp.

74	SRC founded as the International Harvester ReNew Center
83	Jack Stack (JS) initiates private leveraged buyout and renames co. SRC
84	SRC's ESOP is set up
89	*Inc.* features SRC in cover story
90	
91	SRC launches 2-day monthly seminars to observe huddle process
92	JS publishes the Great Game of Business with Bo Burlingham
93	First Gathering of Games is held in Springfield, MO Denise Bredfeldt publishes the Yo-Yo Company book
97	The 5th annual National Gathering of Games is held in St. Louis, MO and draws over 600 attendees

In addition, one researcher attended the popular Two-Day Great Game Overview Seminar, conducted at Springfield ReManufacturing, which enables outsiders to see how SRC practices open-book management.

Organization of This Report

The next chapter discusses the lessons learned from the seven case stories. Then the seven cases follow in alphabetical order. The report ends with a chapter on the conclusions drawn from the research.

Endnotes

1. It turns out that this saying is very old indeed. It can be traced to the Greek philosopher Heraclitus, fifth century B.C. Subsequent versions are attributed to the poet Percy Bysshe Shelley and 19th-century British prime minister Benjamin Disraeli.
2. Activity-based costing identifies multiple cost pools and multiple cost drivers to provide a more realistic assignment of costs to cost objects such as manufactured products.
3. Robert R. Falconi, "Too Many Cooks Spoil the Books," *Financial Executive* (November/December 1995): 15-16.
4. Robert N. Stern and Philip Comstock, *Employee Stock Ownership Plans (ESOPs): Benefits for Whom?* (Ithaca, N.Y.: New York State School of Industrial and Labor Relations, 1978) 5. According to Stern and Comstock, 389 American corporations had instituted employee stock purchase plans by 1927.
5. Milton Derber, *The American Idea of Industrial Democracy, 1865–1965* (Urbana: University of Illinois Press, 1970) 479.
6. Douglas McGregor, *The Human Side of Enterprise: 25th Anniversary Printing* (New York: McGraw-Hill, Inc., 1985) 47–48.
7. *Ibid.*, 49.
8. *Ibid.*, 48.

9. John Case, "The Open-Book Managers," *Inc.* (September 1990).
10. Jack Stack with Bo Burlingham, *The Great Game of Business* (New York: Doubleday/Currency, 1992).
11. John Case, *Open-Book Management: The Coming Business Revolution* (New York: HarperBusiness, Inc., 1995).
12. John Case, "The Open-Book Revolution," *Inc.* (June 1995): 26–43.
13. When a company sets up an employee stock ownership plan, it establishes a trust fund to acquire shares of its own stock. The company's contributions to the ESOP are generally tax deductible. Shares held by the trust are assigned to individual employee accounts and will vest over time. A private company must buy back an employee's vested stock at fair value when the employee leaves the company.
14. "Successful" adoption of open-book management means that the company's system included the four basic elements (share, train, empower, reward) and was in place long enough to show positive results. In addition, prospective study companies were informally evaluated to determine whether their culture was consistent with an open-book culture; in other words, whether information was freely available with few restrictions and whether a trusting, open relationship existed between employees and management.
15. The CFO of Springfield ReManufacturing was not interviewed for the study.

Lessons Learned from Case Studies

> The corporation is being hurled about, shaken and transformed by the Third Wave of change. And a good many top managers do not know what has hit them.
>
> Alvin Toffler, *The Third Wave*[1]

> The new source of power is not money in the hands of a few but information in the hands of many.
>
> John Naisbitt, *Megatrends*[2]

We have seen that open-book management represents a paradigm shift in the way businesses are led and managed. Open-book management is about treating employees as owners—sharing information with them, training them, and building a culture in which they are encouraged and motivated to act like owners. It relates to the "third wave" corporation of the information age. These corporations are characterized by information technology, knowledge workers, multiple bottom lines, flatter organizations, and employee empowerment. CEOs and CFOs who cling to centralization and to a command-and-control corporate model are still operating in the "second (industrial) wave." Peter Senge, a leader in organizational learning, notes that "Almost everyone agrees that the command-and-control corporate model will not carry us into the 21st century. In a world of increasing interdependence and rapid change, it is no longer possible to figure it out from the top."[3] In the language of information technology, open-book management is not just an upgrade of management methods—it is a breakthrough in business operations.

2

This chapter synthesizes the lessons learned from the seven study companies and uses their experiences to develop a general framework for open-book management. However, it is not possible to give a cookbook recipe for implementing open-book management because each company did it its own way, which is, perhaps, the key lesson: There is no one best way to make the cultural shift to open-book management.

Open-Book Management Takes a Champion or Two

As already mentioned, SRC began to practice open-book management at the time of its establishment in a leveraged buyout, when it was in financial difficulty. The company's CEO, Jack Stack, developed The Great Game of Business as a means of getting employees to literally help the business to survive. The other six study companies, however, started practicing open-book management when they were not in financial difficulty.

In each of the seven companies, the CEO is a champion of open-book management: Without the CEO's vision and support, the shift to open-book management would not have been possible. Speaking for Plow & Hearth, CFO Dawn Mahoney Cottrell notes that open-book management could not have been implemented "without the total support of the president, Peter Rice, and his willingness to have the associates know the financial results and his support of the training necessary for them to understand the information."

What motivates a CEO to support open-book management? In the case of ComSonics, CEO Dennis Zimmerman believes that integrating an ESOP with open-book management and pay-for-performance gives the organization synergy. He says the employee on the workbench is going to have a significant impact on how successful the business is, and "if you don't share financial information with the fellow on the workbench, empower him to do a better job working for you, then you have missed the message."

Similarly, Bob Collins, CEO of GE Fanuc, says that when you get into one of those tough situations in business, "you turn to your 'go-to people.' Those are the people who can always handle the difficult problems; they represent about 20 to 30 percent of your workforce. So if you want to improve productivity, you have to work on getting that other 70 percent of the workforce performing at their maximum level of productivity." It was that idea that led GE Fanuc to create a "vision-powered organization" in which open-book management became vital.

In three companies—Mid-States Technical Staffing Services, Physician Sales & Service, and North American Signs—the CEO's personal business philosophy was a stimulus for open-book management. The entrepreneurs who founded Mid-States Technical and Physician Sales & Service believed that open-book management was the way to operate their companies, and they developed their corporate culture around the concept, although the founder of Mid-States Technical freely admits his original approach to open-book management was flawed. At North American Signs, open-book management reflects the personal values of the two brothers who took the company over from their father.

The CEOs of the four other study companies championed open-book management, but the stimulus for and process of becoming an open book company varied. ComSonics began to implement open-book management in earnest when it became 100-percent employee owned, although some information was shared previously with employee-owners. GE Fanuc became open book through its Vision-Powered Management, Work Out, and High-Involvement Workforce (HIWF) initiatives. Plow & Hearth has a strong quality initiative, and open-book management is an extension of that effort. And as previously noted, Springfield ReManufacturing became open book when it was in financial distress. A summary of each company's open-book management stimulus is shown in table 2.1.

Regardless of the specific circumstances that prompt a company to adopt open-book management, the CEO must lead the effort. According to John Gardner, a renowned expert on leadership, "Leaders teach."[4] Certainly, the CEO should be the premier teacher in an open-book culture. Springfield ReManufacturing's Stack emphasizes that CEOs who teach send the message that things are constantly changing and that continuous improvement is essential. This does not mean that CEOs must literally teach courses but that they must "teach the teachers"—the people on their staff who will carry the message to the employees on the shop floor and in the warehouse. They must also support the training and education effort that will need to be sustained over the long term.

2.1
nulus for Open-Book Management at the Study Companies

Company	Open-Book Management Stimulus
ComSonics	Employee stock ownership plan
GE Fanuc	Vision-Powered Management, Work Out, and High-Involvement Workforce initiatives
Mid-States Technical	Employee mistrust/suspicion, flawed open-book management system, and CEO philosophy
North American Signs	Owners' beliefs and values
Physician Sales & Service	Employee stock ownership from inception and CEO philosophy
Plow & Hearth	Total quality management initiative
Springfield ReManufacturing	Leveraged buyout and financial distress

Implications for the CFO

Because sharing financial information is key to open-book management, the CFO must also champion the open-book management approach. However, this support may require a change in the traditional parameters of the CFO position.

In fact, a major finding of this study is that the role of the CFO in an open-book company differs markedly from the traditional CFO function. At the outset, the functioning of an open-book culture will obviously rely heavily on the financial talents and willing cooperation of the CFO. The CFO is the "gatekeeper"—the key financial expert in the company who maintains the store of information upon which open-book management largely draws. CFOs who try to preserve business as usual in an open-book culture will severely restrict the potential of the system in the following ways:

1. They will not be actively involved enough in explaining the implications of the open-book numbers.

2. They will consciously or unconsciously resist disclosing critical information.
3. They may believe that open-book management is detrimental to the company (fearing that information might be leaked outside the company, for example) and intentionally subvert its smooth functioning.

Table 2.2 presents a summary of these destructive CFO roles.

The CFO must follow the CEO's lead in championing open-book management, and there was a strong sense of that happening in the study companies. The CFO must be the financial coach or chief financial educator. At Physician Sales & Service, a public company, CFO David Smith is actively, though indirectly, involved in the effective and efficient use of open-book information by the company's operating units. He is committed to providing the needed back-office support from corporate headquarters. Recently, his staff designed and implemented a revolutionary new intranet-based system for each operating unit to download its detailed monthly general ledger in Microsoft Excel format, and supplied the macro tools necessary to manipulate the data in virtually any possible way.[5] This initiative is indicative of Smith's constant search to make open-book management at PSS even stronger and

Table 2.2
Destructive Roles a CFO Can Play in Open-Book Management

Destructive CFO Role	Description
The AWOL Expert	CFOs will not be as actively involved as needed in explaining the implications of the open-book numbers. They refuse to share expertise.
The Gate-Locking Gatekeeper	CFOs are the gatekeepers of the financial information storehouse. They consciously or unconsciously resist disclosing critical information.
The CFO Commando	CFOs believe open-book management is detrimental to the company and intentionally subvert its smooth functioning.

more effective. But Smith didn't have to reorient himself to the company's open-book culture—PSS was open book from the start, and Smith has spent most of his professional career there.

CFO Larry Pearson has been immersed in developing the open-book culture at GE Fanuc for almost 10 years. It speaks impressively for Pearson that he worked for 20 years with GE in non-open-book environments before assuming a very active and persuasive part in transforming GE Fanuc's culture. Pearson's ongoing performance evaluation criteria clearly show that he plays a value-added role in the company, especially in the areas of customer satisfaction, teamwork, growth, and quality. Open-book management is integral to the company's success in all of these areas.

Plow & Hearth has shared financial information for about 10 years and during that time has evolved into a real open-book company[6] with the dynamic participation and commitment of CFO Dawn Mahoney Cottrell. Before Cottrell joined the company in 1989, there was some information sharing, but according to CEO Peter Rice, it began to happen consistently under Cottrell's leadership. Cottrell views herself as "chief financial educator" and explains, "I see the financial person's role as being really good with financial information but being even better at managing and coaching people and understanding things other than just the structured financial data." As the chief financial educator, Cottrell designed and taught two courses on open-book management that were offered to all employees.

Bill McIntyre, CFO of ComSonics, has been an open-book champion and chief financial educator for more than 10 years. CEO Dennis Zimmerman gives McIntyre credit for being the architect of the company's open-book system. In fact, Zimmerman says McIntyre "took a lot of heat early on because of the time and energy it took to put the information together." McIntyre was clearly committed to making the system work and ensuring that employees understood the information. On the education front, McIntyre answers the financial questions employees drop in the company's question-and-answer boxes (e.g., "What is our break-even point?") and is available for one-on-one discussions on financial matters. He also wrote a series of articles for the company ESOP newsletter on such topics as financial ratios and profit vs. cash.

But perhaps most important is McIntyre's overall contribution to the openness that is pervasive in all aspects of ComSonics' business—

and this openness is especially critical because ComSonics is 100-percent employee owned. One employee says, "I've talked to Bill [McIntyre]. Frankly, I don't think there is a question that can't be asked, even if it is uncomfortable.... We don't always like the answer, but that's what having information available is all about."

Operations Manager Brenda Wiese performs many CFO duties at Mid-States Technical Staffing Services. Mid-States Technical has never had an official CFO because of its relatively simple finances. Wiese was promoted to operations manager when her predecessor (and boss) left the company. Company founder Steve Wilson was CEO when the former operations manager left, and he believes she resigned because of open-book management. Wilson says, "In her mind, her power was based on her control of the information, and she was not comfortable with the fact that the power really *didn't* have to do with controlling the information." Wiese, on the other hand, is a strong open-book advocate who is enthusiastic about the part she plays in making the system successful. She is actively involved in training and day-to-day operational issues connected with information sharing.

Controller Michael Major of North American Signs has played a strong leadership role in the company's open-book management initiative, which began in 1996.[7] Major had been encouraging the company's owners to open the books for some time, and he feels the open-book culture dovetails nicely with the owners' personal values. Once the implementation began, Major conducted training programs and lately has spearheaded the effort to get employees more actively involved as trainers, game designers, and presenters at periodic open-book meetings.

We have noted that CFOs of the command-and-control ilk will not do well in an open-book culture unless they are willing to change—and change quickly. There is simply not a place for Theory X in real open-book management because it clashes almost head-on with the fundamental premises of opening the books. Managers at our case-study companies made the point again and again that traditionalist CFOs must leave if they cannot adapt, because they will be out of sync with everyone else. A CFO who is not "with" the system will be against it and will naturally sink into the role of the AWOL (absent without leave) expert, gate-locking gatekeeper, or CFO commando. No open-book culture can live up to its potential with a CFO who plays any of these destructive roles.

Wilson of Mid-States Technical is especially vocal about the difficulties encountered with a traditionalist CFO: "It's a control issue, because what we've got to do with open-book management is to convince every employee that business literacy and business finance are not that difficult. And yet, when I've got a guy with an MBA, he has a vested interest in proving to everybody that it *is* that difficult."

Stack of SRC echoes this concern with his observation that some financial people are inordinately fearful that employees will misuse the information, for example, by leaking it outside the company and thereby causing difficulties with customers and competitors. Stack observes further that financial people may believe they are the only ones with financial skills in the company and may fear that sharing financial information will only produce chaos. And sharing this information certainly *could* cause chaos if the company fails to give employees the financial literacy skills they need to understand and use the information effectively; hence, the importance of training.

There is strong support for the notion that CFOs must possess the following skills or attributes if they are to have a positive impact on the implementation and maintenance of an open-book culture:

- The ability to motivate others (Stack calls it "cheerleading")—to enable a "buy-in" on open-book management throughout the company and to ensure the continued commitment of all to sustain it into the future.

- The ability to coach others on how the business makes money and on what the financial information means.

- The ability to adapt—to understand their new role in the open-book culture and to execute it professionally and enthusiastically.

- The ability to communicate effectively—to communicate in everyday language and avoid unnecessary jargon or technical lingo, and to enunciate clearly the goals of the company in its open-book investment.

- The ability to set aside prejudices and irrational fears—to avoid a traditionalist mentality and ensure that open-book management will be given the chance to succeed.

There is no doubt a CFO must be up to the task of champio..ing open-book management. The CFOs at the study companies have found the work fulfilling and exhilarating. To a large degree, open-book management is flourishing at their companies because of their efforts and commitment.

A Commitment to Training

Sharing information—financial and otherwise—is at the heart of open-book management. Knowing where one stands in relation to a target is essential, especially when monthly, quarterly, or annual bonuses are based on hitting critical numbers. In companies that require threshold profit, cash flow, or return on assets to be reached before bonuses are triggered, employees must understand how these numbers are determined if their actions on the job are to be aligned with the bonus criteria. Financial executives might be surprised at the misconceptions that surround accounting and finance. For one, employees may confuse revenues and profits and think a "$100-million company" means the company had $100 million in profits. For another, employees continually overestimate profit margins. When Steve Wilson was CEO at Mid-States Technical Staffing Services, he surveyed his employees, asking them to estimate the company's percentage of net income to sales. The responses ranged as high as 75 percent, when the true figure was closer to 7 percent.[8] Training in these and other basic financial topics helps dispel myths that are prevalent in the workplace.

Training employees to understand business operations and financial information is basic to open-book management. But how is that training best accomplished? Some companies find that formal training courses work best; others prefer to incorporate training informally into the daily activities of an open-book management environment. An overview of the training approaches used by the seven case-study companies is presented in table 2.3.

When a company decides to launch open-book management, it might offer short, formal courses to educate employees, as GE Fanuc, Mid-States Technical, North American Signs, and Plow & Hearth did. GE Fanuc offers a course developed by the controller's office called Understanding the Numbers. When Mid-States Technical launched

Table 2.3
Summary of Training

Company	Training Program
ComSonics	■ Early training focused on understanding capitalism. ■ Does not rely on formal training courses about financial information. Instead, it employs the following: — Series of nine articles written by CFO, "Finance—The Basics," arranged in question-and-answer style. — Responses to questions submitted in Q&A boxes in lunchrooms. — An open environment receptive to questions from employees. — Seminars offered as part of annual ESOP week (employees given paid time off to attend). ■ Supervisory training courses are offered.
GE Fanuc	■ Training workshops (100 hours)—for all associates. Focus is on meeting-facilitation skills, goal setting, problem solving, conflict management, and negotiation. ■ Understanding the Numbers (one day)—focuses on basic financial statements, ratios, variances, and productivity measures.
Mid-States Technical	■ Initial one-day program led by individuals from Springfield ReManufacturing. ■ Series of four 1-1/2 hour sessions based on business simulation with simplistic terms/numbers.
North American Signs	■ One-time company-wide day of training when open-book management was launched.
Physician Sales & Service	■ Challenge meetings (12 times a year)—employees play a board game like "Family Feud." At branch level, employees split into two groups and focus each month on a different topic (e.g., one month, questions might be on understanding account receivables and the next on inventory control). ■ On the Spot—branch meetings during which employees are asked questions about the business.

Table 2.3
Summary of Training (Continued)

Company	Training Program
Plow & Hearth	■ Open-Book Management I (3 hours)—focuses on revenues, gross margins, cost of goods sold, marketing margins, and overall understanding of the income statement. Takes a product (Limelite) from the Plow & Hearth catalog and traces it through the income statement; associates from different departments work in groups of two on the case. Course written and taught by CFO. Required of all associates.
	■ Open-Book Management II (4 hours)—focuses on understanding concepts of fixed expenses, variable expenses, and earnings before interest and taxes (EBIT). Uses same case study as Open Book I, and associates from different departments work in groups of two on the case. Course written and taught by CFO. Required of all associates.
	■ Profit and Cash Game: Developing Business Literacy (3 hours)—played in teams of five, with two teams to a course. Teams compete to see who comes closest to meeting financial goals set at outset of game. Objective is for employees to see big picture. Course taught by CFO. Required of all associates.
	■ Leadership Institute (40 hours)—focuses on team-building skills and a variety of leadership issues. Required of all associates.
Springfield ReManufacturing Corp.	■ Orientation session at factory level when employees are hired.
	■ Corporate orientation two to three months after start date for half-day to expose employees to open-book management; the other half-day is dedicated to the *Yo-Yo workbook*,* which introduces them to basic accounting terms and business concepts.
	■ Attendance at portions of the Two-Day Great Game Overview Seminar for employees who have been at the firm for at least one year.

* Denise Bredfeldt, *The Yo-Yo Company (the Beginning)*, (Springfield, MO: The Great Game of Business, Inc.,® 1993).

open-book management, Wilson developed his own training material because at the time, no good material was available. He went to each division and taught employees, using a simple but highly relevant example of starting and operating a design business. By doing the training himself, he gained the employees' trust.

CFO Cottrell of Plow & Hearth has written and taught two open-book management courses to associates. She now offers a third course, which is a business simulation.

Springfield ReManufacturing puts great emphasis on orienting new hires to open-book management. The company conducts a series of formal open-book management activities for new employees.

ComSonics has a series of ongoing informal training activities, such as CFO McIntyre's articles on basic accounting and finance, which appeared in the company's ESOP newsletter, and the open access employees have to management, which encourages employee questions. Also, during the company's annual ESOP week, employees can attend a seminar on understanding financial information.

Physician Sales & Service has never relied on formal courses. However, the company has developed some very creative mechanisms for training. In monthly "challenge meetings," branch employees, who are divided into two teams, play a version of the game "Family Feud," answering questions asked on a given subject. The questions one month might focus on inventory and the next month on accounts receivable. Also, PSS uses branch meetings called "On the Spot," during which corporate executives ask employees questions about the company.

One very effective informal activity is the time spent in meetings sharing financial information with employees. Whether it is a weekly "huddle meeting," as SRC calls staff meetings at which financial information is shared, or a monthly meeting at GE Fanuc, these are valuable ongoing training sessions. Several companies (GE Fanuc, Mid-States Technical, North American Signs, and Plow & Hearth) have employees present the financial information at such meetings. At GE Fanuc, an associate who is not in accounting or finance makes the presentation of the monthly report card in a company-wide meeting. At Plow & Hearth, an associate might explain a specific item on the income statement. The companies believe that having associates make presentations is very effective because employees like to have a peer explain the information rather than someone from the accounting department.

An important aspect of training is how the information is presented. Using pictures, stories, and graphs has been an effective approach in the study companies. For example, McIntyre at ComSonics makes great use of graphs to display financial information. The graphs are posted on lunchroom bulletin boards. During the early stages of open-book management at Plow & Hearth, Cottrell would take one of the company's products and explain how items on the income statement related to that product. GE Fanuc uses the term "report card" in the monthly presentation of financial and nonfinancial information because the company believes associates can identify with a report card from their school experiences. At ComSonics, CEO Zimmerman has used the analogy of the northbound train to tell the story of the company's long-term plan. In order to move a train, he notes, "you have to plan ahead—lay track, build bridges, do the right kind of grading." In similar fashion, a business has to plan if it is to compete successfully.

When teaching adult learners, it is important to make the training as experiential as possible. Rather than just having employees listen to a lecture on how the business makes money and on the meaning of financial statements, companies often find it more effective, for example, if employees play a game, as they do at Plow & Hearth. In that company, all employees take a formal course, playing the "Profit and Cash" game to learn basic business concepts. At GE Fanuc, the basic course begins with a discussion of a personal balance sheet, income statement, and cash-flow statement. With an understanding of what their personal financial statements would look like, employees are better prepared to consider a company's financial statements.

In thinking about training employees, it is important to recognize that many employees may fear numbers and have limited experience with basic mathematics and financial information. It may be necessary to review what a percentage is and how it is calculated. Also, many employees will not be familiar with the fundamentals of corporate finance. So using games, experiential exercises, pictures, stories, graphs, and nontechnical language will be necessary. Training is a challenge in an open-book company, but the benefit of having employees who think and act like owners makes the effort worthwhile.

2

Incentive Programs

We have emphasized that the effective practice of open-book management goes far beyond mere information sharing. Employees may have a general interest in or curiosity about the company's fortunes, perhaps as they search for assurance that their jobs are not in jeopardy because of rumored financial problems, for instance. Or they may simply be interested in how much the boss makes. But curiosity alone does not justify the enormous commitment required to launch and maintain a real open-book culture. Patrick Kelly, founder and chairman of PSS, explains it this way: "I don't believe [the employees] care if they see the financials and know if you're making money or not. They only care relative to what it means to them."

It is no coincidence that each of the seven case-study companies has in place an effective incentive program tied directly to the open-book management numbers. Open-book management is doomed to immediate and decisive failure without serious incentives—employees will have no real stake in the outcome, and open-book management will die from lack of interest. But the incentive plans these companies have established vary widely in key characteristics. Some companies call their incentives "bonuses"; one calls it "gain-share"; another "pay-for-performance." They distribute incentives to employees at vastly different intervals, ranging from every month to once a year. Most divide the incentive compensation pool in proportion to regular pay, but one company divides it evenly. In all cases, however, virtually all employees in

Table 2.4
Comparison of Study Company Incentive Plans[1]

Company	Incentive Pay Trigger	Amount Based On[2]	Interval of Payment[3]	How Pool Is Divided Among Employees[4]
ComSonics	Production: labor margins vs. hurdles[5]	Savings	Quarterly + 25% holdback	Performance evaluation
	Management: measurable objectives vs. hurdles	Lump sum increments	Monthly/ biweekly and year-end	Specific to manager

Table 2.4
Comparison of Study Company Incentive Plans[1] (Continued)

Company	Incentive Pay Trigger	Amount Based On[2]	Interval of Payment[3]	How Pool Is Divided Among Employees[4]
GE Fanuc	Pretax operating income, cash flow, and promises kept vs. hurdles	Percentage of pretax operating income adjusted for actual performance vs. hurdles	Annually	Proportional to annual pay (expressed as number of days' pay)
Mid-States Technical	Pretax profit vs. bucket[6]	Percentage of pretax profit equal to bucket	When bucket filled (approximately 6 times/year)	Proportional to annual pay
North American Signs	Pretax profit vs. hurdle	Percentage of excess pretax profit	Monthly + 20% holdback	Proportional to number of hours worked
Physician Sales & Service	Pretax profit, sales, and asset days vs. hurdles	Percentage of excess pretax profit	Semiannually	Equal amount per employee in branch
Plow & Hearth	Earnings before interest and taxes (EBIT) vs. hurdle	Percentage of excess EBIT	Annually	Proportional to annual pay
Springfield ReManufacturing	Currently, return on assets vs. hurdle, but changes regularly	Flat percent of annualized pay (different rates for hourly vs. management if hurdle met)	Quarterly	Proportional to annual pay (hourly and management separated)

Notes:
1. Most employees at all seven study companies earned incentive pay under these plans during the most recent fiscal year. Physician Sales & Service applies its incentive plan within each branch, so employees at underperforming branches did not receive bonuses.
2. With the exception of ComSonics and Springfield ReManufacturing, all companies based the incentive pool on a pretax profit measure, even though the hurdles might be in terms of other measures, such as sales or asset days.
3. The frequency of the incentive pay distribution for rank-and-file employees varies from monthly (North American Signs) to annually (GE Fanuc).
4. Physician Sales & Service is the only study company to split the incentive pool equally among employees of an operating unit. North American Signs bases the split on hours worked, with overtime hours weighted proportionally higher. GE Fanuc, Mid-States Technical, Plow & Hearth, and Springfield ReManufacturing split the incentive pool proportional to regular pay.
5. Income hurdles are expressed as a percentage of sales (North American Signs, Physician Sales & Service, Plow & Hearth) or as an absolute dollar amount (GE Fanuc, Mid-States Technical). For example, Plow & Hearth's hurdle is an EBIT to net sales of 5 percent. For Physician Sales & Service, the first sales hurdle is the minimum acceptable forecast; the asset-days hurdle is 90. GE Fanuc's hurdle for promises kept (on-time delivery) is 95 percent.
6. Mid-States Technical's bucket is a certain dollar amount of pretax profit (say, $150,000). When a bucket is filled, a bonus is triggered. The next bonus is triggered when another bucket is filled.

the company (1) can earn significant additional compensation if the company meets certain financial or operating targets; (2) learn at least monthly of their progress toward earning the compensation; (3) understand what they can do to affect their earning of the compensation; and (4) receive the compensation quickly after it is measured. Table 2.4 details the key attributes of the incentive compensation plans in effect at each of the study companies.

None of the case-study companies relies significantly on discretionary bonuses that are determined after the fact by management whims.[9] All the plans incorporate set criteria that identify the compensation trigger and direct the calculation of the bonus dollar amount. These compensation formulas are well publicized and generally understood by employees for a very simple reason—their own personal stake in them is so high. The complexity of the compensation formulas varies drastically. At one end of the spectrum, Springfield ReManufacturing's plan is simple. If the company meets its overall return-on-assets target, each hourly employee receives a quarterly bonus of 13 percent of total pay.

At the other end of the spectrum, PSS has a rather complex arrangement built around a baseball metaphor. Each of the company's 60-plus branches has the opportunity to create a bonus pool that can vary in size from 5 percent of net profit in excess of a 5-percent-of-sales hurdle rate (a "single") to 20 percent of excess net profit (a "home run"). Roughly one-fourth of PSS's branches hit home runs and earn the maximum bonus. The largest bonus payout in PSS's history was $9,300 per employee at one branch. For a PSS truck driver making $18,000 per year, this payout represented a 52-percent bonus—a powerful incentive for employees at all branches to focus on their own open-book numbers.

Most of the companies have used the same bonus triggers for some time, adjusting them incrementally to the specific hurdle numbers. SRC and, more recently, GE Fanuc have altered their compensation formulas to use different triggers. Stack of SRC has long believed that bonus plans should be easy to understand but the targets somewhat difficult to obtain (a "stretch"); uniform across the company; and focused on one or two critical numbers at a time. In fact, SRC has used 21 different triggers in the past 14 years. Currently, SRC bases its quarterly bonus on return on assets, but it has used the debt-to-equity ratio, inventory accuracy, and the current ratio in previous years. Stack also believes that the bonus program should be an effective, ongoing training tool, which partially explains why SRC's triggers are constantly changing. As employees try to achieve their bonus, they learn what it takes to improve the critical numbers and, in turn, enhance their basic business skills.

GE Fanuc, on the other hand, had used only two bonus triggers: pretax operating income and cash flow. But Bob Collins, GE Fanuc's president and CEO, was concerned about the company's inability to improve its promises-kept performance. Promises kept is a measure, in percent, of how often customers receive orders by the promised delivery date. This is significant for GE Fanuc, which produces programmable and computer numerical controllers used in highly automated, just-in-time manufacturing environments. Missed delivery dates are a serious matter. Yet GE Fanuc had been unable to raise its promises-kept statistic above 75 to 80 percent. Therefore, in its current fiscal year, GE Fanuc began experimenting with a third trigger—promises-kept performance—which is weighted equally with profit and cash flow. Collins decided to carve out one-third of the bonus arrangement and devote it to promises kept: to put one-third of the bonus at risk. If promises-kept performance for the year is below 95 percent, one-third of the bonus disappears. After the change was implemented, the promises-kept metric improved dramatically—from 78 percent in February 1997 to above the 95-percent hurdle in June and beyond. Because of this success, Collins expects to substitute other third triggers in place of promises kept in future years.

One of the more inventive triggers is the bucket system devised by Wilson of Mid-States Technical Staffing Services. When he implemented full open-book management in 1993, he was reluctant to base bonuses on profits earned during a month or a quarter because these time periods were, in his view, an arbitrary "accounting thing." In his very labor-intensive business, a large percentage of operating costs consisted of payroll taxes and workers' compensation premiums that are "capped" per employee per year. For example, after the company reaches the yearly social security maximum for an employee, it pays no more social security taxes on that employee until the next year. So profits early in the year are unrealistically low, while profits near the end of the year are unrealistically high.

Wilson's ingenious solution was to use a "profit bucket" as the bonus trigger. The company pays the first bonus for the year when the first profit bucket is filled, usually a few months into the year. As time passes and capped expense items disappear, buckets fill faster and faster, until they are being filled every few weeks near year-end. Wilson's bucket plan has been widely publicized in open-book management literature and has contributed to his status as something of a folk hero in open-book management circles.

Despite considerable variations in compensation triggers, five of the seven case-study companies base the size of their incentive pools on pretax profits. (One of the five uses profit before *taxes* and *interest*.) ComSonics rewards its production employees (who make up most of its workforce) on the basis of labor savings and its managers on various levels of pay-for-performance. SRC, as noted, pays a flat percentage of total pay if the bonus is triggered.

The frequency of bonus payments is one of the most interesting variations among the seven companies. Each company has a payment frequency that it is most comfortable with and each steadfastly defends the choice. Wilson calculated the Mid-States Technical bucket size on the notion that the bonus should be paid "every two months on the average." Wilson thinks "monthly is too often" and "quarterly is not often enough." GE Fanuc's Collins believes bonuses should be paid annually to minimize the risk of poor performance late in the year offsetting good performance early on, which might force the company to take back a quarterly or semiannual bonus. To reduce the possibility of "take-backs," ComSonics and North American Signs pay bonuses more frequently than annually but hold back a portion of the bonus until the final results are tallied at year-end. PSS's plan is probably too complicated to be applied more often than twice a year.

Five of the seven companies in this study divided the incentive pool proportionally. Four of these five companies used proportion of total pay—higher-paid employees receive a higher share of the pool than do lower-paid employees. GE Fanuc has found it helpful to equate this proportional bonus with a certain number of days' pay. For example, when management announces the final bonus number, it is in the form of X days' pay rather than Y percent of pay. North American Signs divides the incentive pool in proportion to hours worked, ignoring variations in pay scale. The other two companies use different methodologies. ComSonics splits its incentive pool for production workers according to performance evaluations. PSS uses the most revolutionary approach of all: Each employee within a branch receives the same bonus regardless of annual pay. So a truck driver earning $18,000 per year makes the same bonus as a salesperson earning $60,000 per year. PSS feels this approach is consistent with its strong emphasis on teamwork and its desire to recognize each person's contribution to branch—and company—success in a significant way.

Employee ownership is widespread at five of the seven companies, either through direct ownership of stock, through a company ESOP, or through a combination of direct ownership and ESOP. These five are ComSonics, GE Fanuc, Mid-States Technical, PSS, and SRC.[10] At North American Signs and Plow & Hearth, stock ownership is concentrated among a few individuals. It is interesting that even in companies with broad levels of employee ownership, open-book management has dictated that strong incentive plans coexist with the incentives inherent in ownership. This situation is something of a paradox: We expect owners to be naturally concerned with profit, so why do they need any further encouragement? The most likely explanation lies in the concept of *linkage*[11]—a term that describes the effort to provide a direct connection between profits and employee actions.

Business owners are by nature concerned about profits because higher profits can lead to higher dividends and a higher stock value, among other things. But the emphasis in open-book management is on what individual employees can do, often as members of a team, to drive profits (and other financial measures such as cash flow) higher. In other words, open-book management helps link the actions of the employee and the resulting impact on profits. An effective open-book culture will give employees a strong sense of this linkage and will cultivate it through training, frequent feedback, and, ultimately, the reward itself. Without the linkage, open-book management runs the risk of becoming just another fad, destined to be pushed aside when the results don't live up to the promise.

2

How Open Is Open-Book Management?

Open-book management implies that the books are literally *open*—that nothing is hidden or withheld from employees. While this may be true in theory, it is decidedly not true in the seven study companies. Not surprisingly, the information most frequently withheld is individual salary information for rank-and-file employees. Occasionally, compensation for senior management is available either directly (which is rare) or indirectly as a separate line item on an income statement or trial balance (e.g., under the Executive Compensation caption).[12]

Physician Sales & Service reveals the most detailed information within a given operating unit. PSS branch employees, for example, have access to virtually all of their own operating data, including individual compensation. But as a public company governed by Securities and Exchange Commission (SEC) rules, branch employees have little access to information for other branches or the consolidated company. In fact, PSS tightened up this area in late 1996 because a stock analyst speculated—erroneously—that PSS would not meet its sales target for that quarter. For a high-growth, high-earnings-multiple company like PSS, such a speculation is very serious: PSS's stock price promptly dropped some 35 percent as a result of the analyst's claim and was a long time recovering.

All seven study companies regularly disclose detailed operating data to employees and place particular emphasis on numbers that affect incentive compensation. Frequently, companies will display charts or graphs to help employees understand the numbers or to indicate trends. But disclosure does not mean that employees receive their own printed copies of reports or have continuous access to information. Some companies (notably, GE Fanuc) will review detailed company-wide performance data with employees (using slides projected on a screen, for example) but will not distribute any corresponding printed material or even post the information outside the meeting. Table 2.5 shows the type of information shared routinely with employees at ComSonics and GE Fanuc.

The specific choice of information revealed is not particularly important. This information will vary markedly from company to company and be unique to a company's individual circumstances. Real open-

Table 2.5
Examples of Information Shared

ComSonics shares the following information:

- Monthly financial statement for each product, each strategic business unit (SBU), and the total company.
- Graphs of year-to-date revenue, profit, and cash flow.
- Graphs of value added per employee labor dollar for each product, each SBU, and the total company.
- Quarterly financial statements.
- Daily report; daily and month-to-date actual results against budget for sales orders and shipments; customer satisfaction indices; cash flow; capital expenditures.
- Graphs of internal customer satisfaction indices.
- The company's five-year plan (each employee receives a copy).

GE Fanuc shares the following monthly reports:

- Cash flow and profitability.
- Product leadership (quality).
- Customer satisfaction.
- Growth and market share in orders.

book management obviously requires broad—but not total—information sharing. PSS's Kelly puts it this way: "You don't have to expose everything, but enough where the employees feel they've got a stake in the organization, they've got a share in the organization." In general, a successful system of open-book management should have the following characteristics.

1. Trust. Open-book management is largely about trust. Employees might have access to only part of the company's information storehouse but still *trust* that management has provided information that is correct and truthful. Employees believe that management *trusts them* to use the information wisely and discreetly.
2. Understanding. When certain information is withheld, employees should understand *why*. An open-book culture is expected to

be generally open; employees usually understand that they can't be privy to all company information. But management cannot appear to be arbitrary, capricious, or secretive. For instance, PSS prides itself on responding to any employee query unless the answer would violate a confidentiality agreement (a pending merger, for example) or violate SEC rules. Employees understand that, excepting these circumstances, their questions will be answered.

3. The sharing piece. Incentive compensation is a major element of open-book management. Management must disclose detailed information that employees can and will use—either individually or as a team—to achieve their incentive compensation. We call this information the "sharing piece" (a term introduced by Pat Kelly in this study). If a company is not willing to disclose the entire sharing piece, it should change its compensation plan accordingly. The study companies were unanimous in their adherence to this principle.

Kelly of PSS and Wilson of Mid-States Technical firmly believe that CEOs adopting open-book management should be prepared to reveal their own salaries at the outset. Clearly, this information is not the kind needed on the job. However, Kelly and Wilson think it is a reflection of trust.[13] Every company that adopts open-book management will have skeptical employees who don't believe the books will really be open. Some employees might pose the following challenge: "If the books are really open, Mr. CEO, then how much do you make?" (Kelly experienced this in PSS's early years.) If handled poorly, this question could very well undo the open-book management initiative. The CEO should be prepared to deal with it. Wilson believes that a CEO-owner drawing too much in salary should restructure things—take more dividends and less salary, for example—before implementing open-book management. Kelly and Wilson are in the minority on this issue of revealing CEO compensation; such disclosure was not normally made in the study companies.

At a minimum, an open-book company must disclose its sharing piece regularly, truthfully, and completely. The sharing piece (a basis for incentive compensation) can be anything the company wants it to be. But it should be broad enough and important enough to warrant the status of the term open-book. A trivial or narrow sharing piece is business as usual, not an example of open-book management.

Empowerment Accounting

How do companies empower employees? Empowerment is more than giving employees the power to make decisions. In most organizations, management expects that employees will "make intelligent decisions to help the company operate more effectively."[14] Empowerment in an open-book company is *"recognizing and releasing into the organization the power that people already have in their wealth of useful knowledge and internal motivation."*[15]

Empowerment begins when employees are entrusted with information. Information must be shared with them, and they must be trusted to use that information appropriately.[16] Empowerment accounting is a benefit that flows from open-book management;[17] if financial information is not shared, empowerment lacks substance. The thought of disclosing sensitive financial information can be quite disturbing to management, but it is necessary in order to make informed decisions. If management expects employees to help the company perform well, employees must know as much about the company as possible. To be empowered, employees need to know how their daily job performance affects the organization's bottom line. When management shares information, it sends an important message to employees: that it has nothing to hide from them; that management and employees are in this together.[18]

Employees in the study companies had taken ownership of their specific job as well as of the product or service that their company sold—in other words, they felt empowered to share their knowledge whenever it might make a difference to the company. At GE Fanuc, for example, a factory associate related how open-book management had changed his attitude: He no longer focused only on his workstation; he now took ownership of the product, the line, and the business.

Employees in the study companies felt empowered to suggest ways to reduce costs, improve operations, or save money on the purchase of equipment that they might need to do their job. During a downturn in sales at Plow & Hearth, employees made a number of suggestions on how to reduce costs and save money. At ComSonics, employees were sensitive to cost when requesting a new piece of equipment for their workstation. At both Mid-States Technical and Plow & Hearth, employees are responsible for line items in the budget; they are empowered to oversee a specific line item for their work unit. At North American Signs, employees understand that if their job has nothing to do with the profits of the company, the job should be eliminated. PSS managers know that if they perform poorly, the company will not fire them, but their employees will. By sharing financial and other information with employees, the case-study companies have achieved a level of empowerment that would not have been possible otherwise.

All businesses face a downturn in fortunes at some point in their history. It is interesting to note how open-book management has enabled companies to cope with adverse circumstances. When Plow & Hearth faced a softening market for catalog sales and rising costs for catalog production in 1995, employees made many suggestions to save money. Kelly of Physician Sales & Service says that open-book management saved his company twice: When banks required greater profitability than the company had in order to continue loans, employees understood the requisite pay cuts. When ComSonics faced a downturn in revenues and shared the information, employees were prepared for the layoffs that eventually followed. As already noted, Springfield ReManufacturing credits its very survival with using open-book management to combat severe financial problems.

Impact of Open-Book Management on Employees

According to SRC's Stack, the work experience should teach people "how to build strong lives." Open-book management facilitates that goal. In addition to empowering employees, open-book management impacts employees' attitudes and their view of work. A factory associate at GE Fanuc indicated that he felt he was a better person because he could use at home many of the things he was learning on the job about dealing with people. Another employee noted that she commuted a long distance just to work in an environment like GE Fanuc rather than at a sweatshop factory much closer to her home.

People spend some of their best waking hours at work, so the workplace should be more than just a place to get a paycheck. In an open-book culture, employees feel engaged; they see the big picture of how the company makes money, and they share in the company's successes. Thus, their work becomes more enjoyable. And, as the saying goes, "If you enjoy what you do, you never have to go to work." Open-book management promotes an environment in which work becomes more meaningful and fulfilling.

Open-book management can also enhance employees' job security because they learn new skills and improve old skills. Employees who understand financial information are therefore more valuable in the job market.

Concluding Comments

Becoming open-book requires more than a few adjustments in the way a company operates. It requires nothing short of a paradigm shift—a fundamental change in the relationship between a company and its employees. Each of the seven case-study companies successfully implemented open-book management, and their open-book management systems share some similar characteristics.

In each company, the CEO was a committed champion of open-book management and took a leading role in creating the requisite open culture. The CFO also championed open-book management and typically assumed the role of coach and chief financial educator. Each CFO was a strong and enthusiastic player in the open-book culture. (All agreed that a "business as usual" CFO wouldn't last in an open-book management environment.) Training took a variety of forms at the study companies. Some had formal training programs; others accomplished training informally, usually in conjunction with an incentive plan. But in all cases, continuous training was very much in evidence.

Lucrative incentive programs tied to profits and other open-book numbers were an important part of each company's culture. The plans varied in complexity, but employees across the companies generally understood the plans and knew what it took to achieve the incentive compensation. Regular reports were made to employees on their progress toward earning the compensation. And because incentive plans wouldn't be very meaningful if employees couldn't affect the results, empowerment was an integral part of each company's culture. Often empowerment was done in teams.

The companies differed in the amount and types of information shared, but always the information was extensive and meaningful. All companies disclosed the sharing piece (the numbers that constituted the basis for the incentive plans) in detail. Finally, there was solid evidence that open-book management has made a positive change in the life of the average employee. Employees are more business literate and seem to appreciate the culture of trust and openness characteristic of open-book management, as compared with the other, more closed cultures they had worked in before. Some said they would find it very difficult to return to the "old way" if they ever left their current jobs.

Endnotes

1. Alvin Toffler, *The Third Wave* (New York: Bantam Books, 1980) 226. The First Wave was the agricultural phase and the second was industrial. The latter phase continues to overlap with the information wave.
2. John Naisbitt, *Megatrends* (New York: Warner Books, 1982) 7.
3. Peter M. Senge, "Communities of Leaders and Learners," in "Looking Ahead: Implications of the Present," *Harvard Business Review* (September-October 1997): 30.
4. John Gardner, *On Leadership* (New York: The Free Press, 1990) 18.
5. This system, called the A-Team Net, was the subject of a popular presentation at The National Gathering of the Games V held in September 1997 in St. Louis.
6. As the term is used in this study, a "real open-book company" fulfills the four requirements of open-book management discussed in Chapter 1: Share information; train and empower employees; and reward them for success. A company that shares information only is not open book in the widely accepted sense of the term.

7. North American Signs began its gain-sharing program in 1989 and began sharing sales information in 1994. The first company-wide training session was held in early 1996, and monthly company-wide meetings were broken down into separate meetings of four smaller cross-functional groups in late 1996.

8. This response is not unusual. Anthony Rucci, Chief Administrative Officer of Sears Roebuck, reported recently that when he asked hourly associates and managers a similar question in visits to 40 to 50 stores, the median response was 45 cents after tax, when Sears was actually earning 1.7 cents on the sales dollar. See Stratford Sherman, "Bringing Sears Into the New World," in "From the Front" *Fortune* (October 13, 1997): 183.

9. For example, it is common for companies to have profit-sharing plans. Often, the amounts contributed to the plans are at the total discretion of management: Employees do not find out their compensation until well after the fiscal year has ended. At that point, there is obviously nothing an individual employee can do to affect that year's compensation, so the plan is not a motivator. And there may or may not be any "incentive" compensation for them to affect next year: The plan is simply too vague.

10. GE Fanuc is a joint venture 50-percent owned by GE Corporation, a public company. Mid-States Technical is a wholly owned subsidiary of AccuStaff Incorporated, also a public company. Obviously, employees of GE Fanuc and Mid-States Technical will hold the stock of the respective parent companies, not of the subsidiaries.

11. "Linkage" refers to tying an incentive to an outcome in a direct way. Strong linkage will presumably result in the alignment of employee and company goals.

12. This indirect disclosure might only serve to show that senior managers don't make outlandish salaries. It probably will not reveal the exact amount of the salary, because the total could include two or more managers.

13. Wilson also did much of his own open-book management training. As discussed elsewhere in this study, his employees didn't

believe the information he had been revealing, and thought that he kept one real and one fictitious set of books.

14. W. Alan Randolph, "Navigating the Journey to Empowerment," *Organizational Dynamics* (Spring 1995): 20.
15. *Ibid.*
16. *Ibid.*, 22.
17. Gerald F. Morris, "Owning the Numbers," *CFO* (March 1995): 72. The term "empowerment accounting" was used in this article, although not in the context of open-book management.
18. Randolph, "Navigating the Journey to Empowerment," 22.

3

ComSonics, Inc.

It has always been my firm belief that employees contribute to the growth of a company as much as capital; and employees should, therefore, participate in that growth.[1]

Warren L. Braun
Founder and Chairman of ComSonics

Warren was pretty open with the communications, which probably had a lot to do with his idea of ownership. It is awfully hard to talk about giving people ownership without communications. And so he spent a lot of time trying to communicate the ideas of ownership and what it meant to be an owner. I think that influenced our sharing of financial information with our employees. We share more information today than Warren ever did, and we have continued to grow open-book management.

Dennis A. Zimmerman
President and CEO

Company Background

ComSonics was founded by Warren Braun, an engineer, in 1972. It grew out of an existing part-time consulting and engineering business that Braun had started in 1965. The consulting firm provided services to the cable television (CATV) industry and operated out of the basement of Braun's home in Harrisonburg, Virginia. The business grew to the point that about 22 people were working out of Braun's basement. One of the "boys from the basement," as they were called, was Dennis Zimmerman, the company's current President and CEO.

As the story goes, a Harrisonburg zoning administrator eventually sent Braun a letter indicating that operating the business out of his basement with all the employees' cars parked around his house was clearly out of character for the residential neighborhood. Braun found a new location, and the consulting business was incorporated in 1972 as ComSonics. The company also shifted its thrust from consulting services to product development and production. From this beginning, ComSonics has grown into a 100 percent employee-owned company engaged in manufacturing and repairing CATV equipment for cable system operators.

Current annual revenue is approximately $11 million. The company employs 149 people at its corporate headquarters in Harrisonburg and has 6 sales representatives located throughout the country. About 45 percent of the company's business is repairing headend, distribution, and test equipment produced by any manufacturer. At last count, ComSonics held 18 patents in the communications field. ComSonics remains at the forefront of cable technology with such products as Video Window (a video signal measurer), GeoSniffer (a global leakage detector), Sniffer Sleuth (the most complete self-contained leakage control package available), the WindowLite Installer (a revolutionary new meter for cable installers), and the Path Finder II (an underground cable locator). In addition to manufacturing and marketing its own products, the company is the largest independent CATV repair facility in the United States. The company has never lost sight of its original commitment to its customers and to research and development.

In 1982 *Inc.* recognized ComSonics as one of the 500 fastest growing privately owned firms in the United States, with a 310 percent growth rate over the five years from 1978–1982. ComSonics received the U.S. Senate Productivity and Quality Award (USSPQA) for the Commonwealth of Virginia in 1984. This award, similar to the Malcolm Baldrige National Award, was established in December 1982 by the U.S. Senate to recognize organizations on the state level that are exemplary for productivity and quality improvement. In 1990 ComSonics won the U.S. Senate Productivity Award for Continuing Excellence for Virginia. This award is available only to organizations that have previously won the U.S. Senate Productivity Award. To win the Continuing Excellence Award, a company must demonstrate continued improvement in the areas of employee involvement and participation, top management commitment to quality and productivity, and consumer and supplier involvement. A company has to show that these efforts were translated into successful operating results.

Employee Stock Ownership Plan (ESOP)

Although the development of the ESOP concept in the United States goes back to the 1950s, it was not until 1974 that the U.S. Congress recognized ESOPs as qualified, defined contribution employee-benefit plans and gave them tax advantages. Braun believed that there was no better way to express appreciation to those who have helped start and build a company than to make them owners. So in 1975, he established an employee trust that bought ComSonic's shares. At the time, it was the first ESOP in Virginia and one of only about 50 in the United States.

The trust initially bought 29 percent of the company's shares with funding provided by ComSonics. In 1983 the trust purchased more shares, increasing ownership to 39 percent; in 1984 the trust increased ownership to 49 percent; and in 1985 ComSonics became 100 percent employee-owned, reportedly making it one of 12 such wholly employee-owned companies operating in the United States at that time. For the last purchase, Braun acted as guarantor for the leveraged buyout of his remaining 51 percent of company shares. In 1990 Braun retired from the company when the loan was refinanced, and he was no longer the guarantor. The company makes annual tax-deductible contributions to the trust so that it can pay off the loan. The trust, which holds the shares, releases them as the loan is paid off. The shares are allocated to eligible employees. To participate in the ComSonics ESOP plan, employees must be over 21 years of age and have 1 year of service with at least 1,000 hours worked. Employees have individual trust accounts and receive allocations based on their compensation. The shares received gradually vest over a period of 7 years. The value of the ComSonic shares is established annually by an independent business appraiser. A 100 percent ESOP may be viewed as a somewhat risky investment because, unlike a public company in which stock is owned by the general public, risk in an ESOP company is shared only by people inside the company.

3

Open-Book Management

An employee-owned organization seems a natural one for the implementation of open-book management. After all, the employees own the business, and as owners, they should have access to the company's financial information. However, as Zimmerman noted, it does not necessarily follow that employee-owned companies practice open-book management. He related his favorite open-book management story:

> I go to ESOP conferences and talk with CEOs who have controlling ownership of their companies. When I tell them about the extent of the information we share with our employee-owners, they are pretty appalled. They question it and comment on what could happen if the information were disclosed outside the company and how people outside the company might use that information.
>
> My best rebuttal is that most people I know in the management world share financial information with their golfing buddies, with their attorney at the country club, or even when they are talking with their doctor or dentist. These people know if the guy is having a good year or bad one. If it is a good one, he brags about it, and if it is a bad one, he doesn't. Or, if Dun & Bradstreet calls, he shares the financial information with them. Yet the employee on the workbench building the product is going to have a lot more impact on how successful the business is than the golfing buddy, attorney, doctor, or Dun & Bradstreet. If you don't share financial information with the fellow on the workbench, empower him to do a better job working for you, then you have missed the message. It all goes back to the old problem that has always been there between the boss and the employees. I mean who is running what and who is doing what? The guys on the workbench are making our money.

According to Bill McIntyre, Director of Finance and CFO, open-book management was not practiced prior to ComSonic's becoming 100 percent employee-owned in 1985. Soon afterward, ComSonics began to practice open-book management, although it is only recently that the company has begun using the term to describe what it is doing. As John Dickie, Director of Human Resources, said, "We did what we did without knowing anything about it."

Information Shared

In sharing financial information, ComSonics "is very open internally and very closed externally," according to McIntyre. Except for specific salary information, considerable financial information is shared internally, but no financial information is shared externally. The company has gradually expanded the amount of information shared with employee-owners to include the following:

1. Monthly financial statements for each product, strategic business unit (SBU), and for the total company. This information is distributed to all management personnel, with a copy available for any employee to review in the company's library, which also contains considerable historical financial information that is available to all employees.

2. Graphs of year-to-date (YTD) revenue, profit, and cash flow. This information is posted in each lunchroom and updated monthly.

3. Graphs of internal customer satisfaction indices. This information is posted in each lunchroom and updated monthly. Customer satisfaction is measured by the specific indices of warranty units, manufacturing backlog of orders for current shipment, returns, and repair days' turnaround.

4. Graphs of value added per employee labor dollar for each product, SBU, and for the total company. This information is posted in each lunchroom and updated monthly. Value added is equal to revenue minus the cost of material. The company uses value added per employee labor dollar as the primary measure of managerial efficiency.

5. Graphs of incoming phone calls. This information is posted in each lunchroom and updated monthly. An increase in phone calls generally means more revenue.

6. Quarterly financial statements. A summary current quarter and year-to-date income statement and summary balance sheet is distributed to all employees. A written discussion of the results is included.

7. Daily report. On a daily basis, the company distributes to about 30 employees a report showing daily and month-to-date actual results versus budget for sales orders, shipments, customer satisfaction indices, cash flow, capital expenditures, and any other item warranting special emphasis that month. Performance relative to customer satisfaction indices is assigned a grade from A through F.

In addition, each employee-owner receives a copy of the "Northbound Train" (the company's five-year plan) and measurements against that plan.

The story behind using the northbound train as a symbol for the company's long-term plan is an excellent example of the company's effort to communicate with its employee-owners. Since Zimmerman became President and CEO in 1990, he has had two annual major management meetings with the five operating directors (see figure 3.1), in addition to his many other operational meetings with them. At the spring meeting, the focus is short-term planning and preparation for the coming year's operating budget. The focus at the fall meeting is long-term planning. Zimmerman stated the following:

> At the fall meeting we focus on what is happening in the industry long-term and what ComSonics is going to be involved in long-term.
>
> It was evident that the information from the fall meeting was staying inside the heads of the operating directors and wasn't getting to the employee-owners. We were getting some complaints and questions from employees about where ComSonics was going to be in the year 2000 and that type of thing.

He had read a book titled *The Northbound Train* by Karl Albrecht, which focused on strategic planning, and it inspired a new idea:

> I adopted the idea of a train to tell the story of our long-term planning. If you are going to move a train, which has a lot of power, you have to plan ahead—lay track, build bridges, do the right kind of grading. So to me it was a way of starting a story that I could tell on the factory floor. At the annual meeting, I talk about the northbound train, where it's going and what's happening. Everyone gets

Figure 3.1
Executive Management Organization Chart

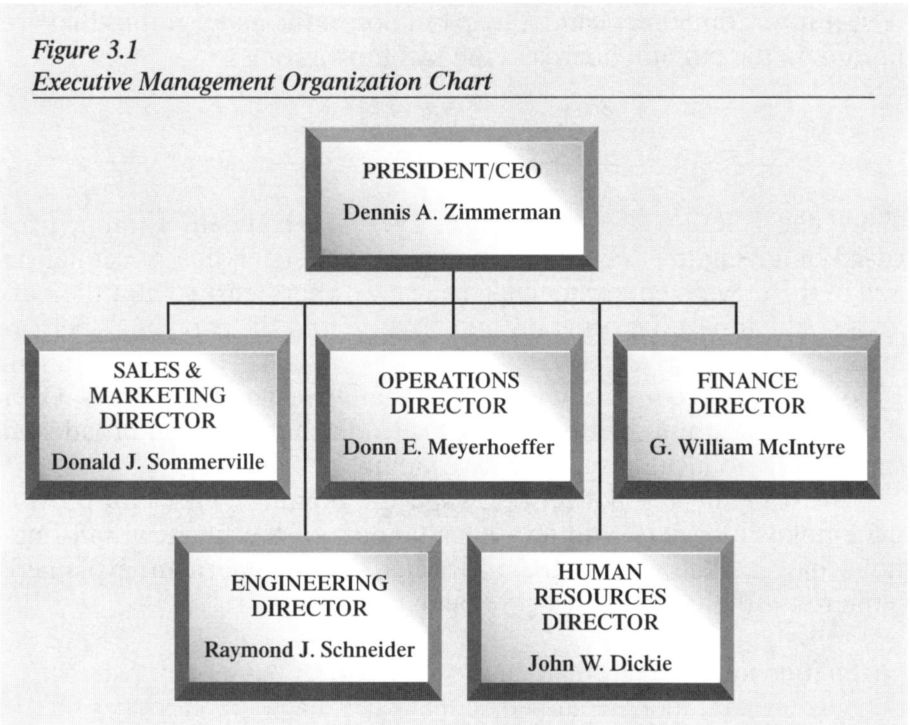

> a copy of *The Northbound Train* book. People give me trains and whistles, and I get all kinds of train memorabilia from the employees.

When the company had a downturn in revenue two years ago, Zimmerman stated, "There was a lot of talk around here that the train must be stalled, it's not moving, it is on the wrong track, and it is not going north. But trains take time to get up to speed, and last year was a much better year."

In sharing information with employee-owners, Zimmerman observed the following:

> I am a believer in pictures, stories, and graphs. Our guys are not invested heavily in the stock market and this operation is their only investment. And so you have quite a challenge to communicate. You've got to use pictures, stories, and graphs to communicate.

A visitor to ComSonics cannot help but notice the many graphs that are posted on the bulletin boards in the two lunchrooms.

Training

When the ESOP was established in 1975, the company's training focused on giving the "new owners" a basic understanding of capitalism and of the meaning of ownership. The new owners learned how their efforts could impact the company and, in turn, how the company's performance affects the stock's value. Dickie, the Director of Human Resources, was a consultant when the training began in the 1970s. Over the years, the training effort under his leadership has been broadened significantly to include supervisory training.

The company has not relied on specific training courses for providing employee-owners with an understanding of the financial information that it shares with them. Rather, as Zimmerman explained, numerous other approaches have been used:

> Sharing financial information is such a part of our culture and the ongoing education of our people that when a new graph goes up on the wall, we say, "Here is the measure," and ask, "What does it mean?" And in the monthly meetings of the departments or sections, it is explained. Most of our training has been to provide the information and then to educate people on what the information means, how to improve it, and what we are looking for.

Zimmerman stressed that getting employees to understand what it takes for the company to be profitable is not something you can do as a "quick fix where you do a spurt of education in a year or so." Rather, his opinion is as follows:

> You continue to push the information down and train your people and build a cultural base where a handful of your employees think like owners. If you can get 15 to 20 percent of your people who have been with the company for a while to think like owners, it is a powerful tool, and I think one that will really stand the test of time.

Employee-owners at ComSonics have learned to interpret financial information with the help of the following:

- A series of nine articles written by CFO McIntyre, entitled "Finance—The Basics," which were published in *SHARE* (ComSonics' ESOP news bulletin).
- Responses to employee questions submitted in the "question and answer (Q&A)" boxes in the company's two lunchrooms.
- An open environment where employee-owners feel comfortable bringing their questions to one of the directors or to their immediate supervisor.
- Seminars offered as part of the company's annual ESOP Week.

Articles in *SHARE*

The nine articles written by McIntyre and published in *SHARE* over a three-year period covered these subjects:

- The balance sheet.
- Income statement (general).
- Income statement (ComSonics).
- Financial ratios (part 1).
- Financial ratios (part 2).
- Profit versus cash (one transaction).
- Profit versus cash (multiple transactions).
- Capital expenditures and depreciation.
- ComSonics' criteria for approving capital expenditures.

Each article was written in a question-and-answer format. In the first article, for example, questions included "What is a balance sheet?" "What are assets, liabilities, and equity?" and "What are examples of typical assets?" Taken as a group, the articles provide an excellent overview of basic accounting and finance.

Q&A Boxes

Of the Q&A boxes in the two lunchrooms, Zimmerman said, "We'll answer any question as long as it is not slanderous." Questions submitted by employees are assigned to one of the company's directors, who develops a response, usually within two weeks. Questions of a financial nature are handled by McIntyre. The following are examples of financially related questions that have been submitted in the Q&A boxes:

1. Through May we have achieved 95 percent of sales revenue according to the graphs in the cafeteria. Why then is our profit before tax less than 30 percent? It seems sales is doing its job. Who isn't?
2. What is our break-even sales point and how do we arrive at that?
3. Since July 1989, line repair's "value added per employee labor dollar" or productivity has fallen 27 percent. There has been a steady decline unlike all the other departments' ups and downs. When considering that prices for repair have been raised, it makes the decline in value added per labor dollar even worse than 27 percent. What is being done to fix it?

Open Environment

ComSonics' open environment has also done much to teach employee-owners about the financial affairs of the company. ComSonics has developed a culture where employee-owners feel comfortable asking directors or supervisors any question about the company's financial affairs. Tony Dean, a line repair technician, stated the following:

> There is not a circumstance where even the newest employee doesn't at some time or another consult the charts that are on the lunchroom bulletin boards. They're a good snapshot, and they're a good introduction for newer employees to get comfortable and familiar with actually seeing the information, because in a lot of places you are not privileged to know anything about the financial affairs of the company.

> So then a person would normally get up the courage to ask a question. They may ask me. They may ask one of the senior technicians. They may go to my supervisor Jerry, who is well versed on the financial information. Or, if I really need a question answered, I'll go talk to the CFO, and I've done that. I've talked to Bill [McIntyre]. Frankly, I don't think there is a question that can't be asked, even if it is uncomfortable, within this building. And I've personally asked some very uncomfortable ones. We don't always like the answer, but that's what having information available is all about.

In commenting on the ComSonics environment, Dean also observed the following:

> ComSonics is a relaxed environment, and I mean that in all aspects; everything is that way. The information is available and it's like you lead a horse to water and let him drink if he wants to. There is always someone who knows the answer to your question and someone who can direct you to the answer. And if you want an answer, ask any question.

Gerald Bohus, product test technician, provided this view:

> An ESOP's not a perfect world, but for me personally it gives me more of a satisfaction of knowing that I can take part in this company, and I can understand and know just what Dennis [Zimmerman] knows. If I have a question I can go right to him and he'll point-blank tell me. I may not like his response, but he's always said, "I'll give you an answer but I may not necessarily give you what you want to hear, but you'll get an answer." For me personally that has made me think that I do have an effect in this company.

The directors and Zimmerman are very visible among the employee-owners and thus in a position to respond to a variety of questions from many different people. Zimmerman has lunch every month with a group of employee-owners, and he holds a monthly meeting with all employee-owners. In a general discussion, Zimmerman and four of the six directors of ComSonics made the following observations:

- By disseminating financial information, you're also creating an opportunity for people to misunderstand, but the good news is that we have an environment where people can ask questions and then we use that as a way to educate them.

- Education on open-book management is really a day-in-and-day-out activity. It's not something for which you can just take a course. To be successful, you've got to adopt it as part of the culture. And when it is part of the culture, you don't have little blips on the radar scope where you held a seminar or you invited in a speaker.
- We encourage people to ask why. If there is something that is different about ComSonics than other places where I've worked, it is that, from top to bottom in this organization, people are much less reluctant to ask a question. And when somebody asks you why you are doing something, you respond, "I'm glad you asked that question and let me tell you..."

As an example of the kind of question that someone might ask, McIntyre related the following: "One of my favorite stories relates to an accounts payable clerk who became concerned because one of the regional sales managers played golf at a sales meeting and submitted the green and cart fees on his expense voucher." As McIntyre noted, "In an employee-owner culture, people, in general, care about how money is being spent." In this case, the accounts payable clerk thought it was a waste of company money to pay for the golf. However, McIntyre used the question of the reimbursement to explain how spending four or five hours with customers, and riding in a golf cart with one, might lead to additional business and actually save the company money compared with how much it could cost to travel to visit customers and spend a few minutes with them. After McIntyre finished, the clerk said, "You are right" and thanked him for the explanation. If McIntyre had not taken the time to explain the reasoning behind the reimbursement, he said, "Within two days, the entire company would have known that we spent $50 to reimburse a regional sales manager for a round of golf."

McIntyre also gave the example of a technician who came to him and said, "I was looking at the company's balance sheet, and I noticed that the total assets were the same dollar amount as the total liabilities and equity. Is that just a coincidence?" This question provided the opportunity to do some basic instruction in accounting. McIntyre concluded, "In many companies, people would be afraid to ask such questions, but here they ask the question, and they get a response."

Seminars

A final way ComSonics educates employee-owners about financial information is through seminars offered during the company's annual ESOP Week, which is organized each year by the ESOP Employee Advisory Committee. This seven-person committee is elected by employee-owners, and the chairperson is a member of the ComSonics Board of Directors. The purpose and goals of the advisory committee are presented in figure 3.2.

Figure 3.2
ESOP Employee Advisory Committee

Roles and Missions

The ComSonics ESOP Employee Advisory Committee, authorized by ComSonics Employee Stock Ownership Plan, and elected yearly by currently employed ESOP Plan Participants, in accordance with Advisory Committee election rules, hereby presents its Roles and Missions to:

- Research and communicate the corporate issues on which Plan Participants are empowered with vested voting rights as lawful owners, and to organize such a vote in accordance with Advisory Committee voting rules and the Employee Stock Ownership Plan;
- Serve the ESOP Participants in an advisory manner with regard to ESOP issues;
- Elevate the understanding of our ESOP and its purpose through timely and organized communications;
- Communicate the meaning of Corporate Ownership, and the benefits, rights, and privileges thereof to all participants;
- Enhance the interest and involvement in our ESOP on a Corporate level;
- Maintain and foster ComSonics' role as a model ESOP Corporation on a local, state, and national level; and
- Organize and facilitate any educational programs and special events in keeping with these Roles and Missions.

During the 1996 ESOP Week, held during October, seminars included the following:

- Sales and marketing.
- New ComSonics products.
- Sleuth demonstrations.
- How to read your quarterly financial report and what it means.

Employee-owners were given paid time off to attend these seminars. In addition, the week included numerous social events. An essay contest was held, and the winning essay by Jerry C. Cummings—"If I Were on the Outside Looking in, How Could I Tell That ComSonics Is an Employee Owned Company?"—was published in an issue of *SHARE*.

ComSonics has received a number of awards from the ESOP Association for Communications Excellence. In giving the award to ComSonics in 1996, the panel of judges cited the many specific events and programs sponsored by the ComSonics ESOP Employee Advisory Committee. The judges also commented, "The company was organized from the beginning, from the top down, to be ownership oriented."

In 1997, the ComSonics ESOP Employee Advisory Committee presented a half-day conference on the work of their committee to members of the ESOP Association's Western Virginia Region of the Mid-Atlantic Chapter. McIntyre, Vice President of this regional association, is also active at the national level in the ESOP Association. At the annual convention of the ESOP Association in May 1997, McIntyre led a session on open-book management, and his thought-provoking discussion questions about open-book management are presented in figure 3.3. These questions could serve as a guide for companies that are considering implementing open-book management.

Pay-for-Performance

At ComSonics, Zimmerman said, "We are all compensated in the long-term as owners for making good decisions and doing a good job." However, he continued, "It is difficult for everybody to come to work and think of themselves as long-term owners, so we have a pay-for-perfor-

Figure 3.3
Discussion Questions on Open-Book Management

These questions were developed by Bill McIntyre for a session he led on open-book management at the 20th Annual Convention of the ESOP Association, held in Washington, D.C., May 14–16, 1997.

Open-book management is the sharing of financial information with employees.

1. What do you believe is gained from sharing this information with employees?
2. What information are you currently most comfortable releasing?
3. What information would scare the heck out of you to think that the employees might know it?
4. How would you communicate the information to the employees? What frequency? What format? What media? Who should do the communication?
5. Who should receive the information?
6. What education is required in order for the sharing to be worthwhile? How would you accomplish that education (if any)?
7. Is there a competitive advantage to your company practicing open-book management?
8. Are there any competitive disadvantages to your company practicing open-book management?
9. Are there any dangers for your company practicing open-book management? Can you overcome those dangers? How do you overcome those dangers?
10. What if the news is bad? What if the bad news would reflect poorly on management? Should you do something different?
11. What behavior do you expect from people who have this information?
12. What benefits should employees expect to receive from using this information? Should the benefits be financial benefits? Or are nonfinancial benefits appropriate?

Figure 3.3
Discussion Questions on Open-Book Management (Continued)

13. What key information should be released? Revenue? Profit? Compensation? Operating statistics? Should all employees receive the same information?
14. For a privately held ESOP, should the independent appraiser's report of stock value be distributed to all employees?
15. What information re the ESOP Trust should be distributed? Note that the ESOP Trust and the company are two separate entities.
16. Do you make attendance at open-book management discussions/presentations mandatory for all employees? Should you "force" open-book management on the employees?
17. Your company has been practicing open-book management energetically for five years. Maybe 30 percent of the employees have bought into the idea totally and enthusiastically act like owners on a daily basis. Approximately 40 percent of the employees appreciate the information, understand a little of it, and try to do a good job but don't really see the connection between their job and the fortunes of the company. The final 30 percent of the employees have no interest in the financial information, view their job as "just a job," and couldn't care less about the success of the company as long as they can receive their paycheck. Is open-book management a failure? Should it be discontinued?

mance system." Zimmerman is quick to point out that ComSonics does not have a bonus system. He believes that an ESOP, open-book management, and pay-for-performance fit together very well at ComSonics.

Zimmerman instituted the pay-for-performance system in 1991, and over the years the system has been constantly reviewed and revised. As he described it, pay-for-performance starts at the beginning of the year when he makes a contract with each of the company's five directors. They, in turn, make contracts with their key personnel. The contract involves certain measurable objectives that personnel need to accomplish to receive their pay-for-performance compensation. As an example, measurable objectives for Donn Meyerhoeffer, Director of Operations, include such items as inventory turnover, manufacturing margin, and labor ratios.

For compensation purposes, the system operates with three levels of performance—a threshold, a target, and a cap (or maximum). Directors are paid on a monthly basis for performance, which is deemed to be at the level of threshold up to the target, while the managers below them are paid biweekly for similar performance. Compensation for performance from the target to the cap level is distributed at the end of the year. Zimmerman and the directors have at risk as much as 40 percent of what they might be paid in salary for a comparable position at another company. For example, if the salary for a comparable position at another organization was $100,000, attainment of the performance objectives at the threshold level might result in a salary of $80,000, while performance at the target level would give a $100,000 salary and meeting the cap objectives would lead to a $120,000 compensation. As Dickie observed, "That possible variation in salary would tend to get someone's attention rather quickly." The system functions by drilling down the performance objectives that Zimmerman contracts with the directors. As Don Sommerville, Director of Sales and Marketing, noted, "The higher you are in the organization, the more your target compensation is at risk."

For employee-owners on the production or repair line, the measurable objective is labor margins, and the pay-for-performance amount goes into a pool that is shared with the work unit. Seventy-five percent of the amount earned is distributed on a quarterly basis, and any remaining amount is distributed at year-end once the final results are determined. Payment of 25 percent of the amount is delayed because ComSonics' business is cyclical, and the measurable objective could deteriorate before year-end. The distribution among the work group is not divided evenly but is based on the supervisor's evaluation of individual employees' performance. The employees on the line do not have any pay at risk and can earn an annual compensation that is more than what their hourly rate might produce. In essence, for the hourly employee-owners, the pay-for-performance system tends to work like a bonus system, but, for the sake of continuity, it is called pay-for-performance.

Although some would like to have a straight pay check each month, Donn Meyerhoeffer, the director of operations, offered this justification for the pay-for-performance system:

> We are a small company, so the philosophy is if we do well, we are going to be paid well. If we don't do so well, we are not going to be paid as well. And if we do what is expected, we should be getting a total compensation that is equivalent to what you would get in another company our size and in this location.

Reflections on Implementation of Open-Book Management

As previously mentioned, in Zimmerman's view, an ESOP, open-book management, and pay-for-performance go together well at ComSonics. As an ESOP, the employees are the owners. With open-book management, much financial information is shared with employee-owners, and under the pay-for-performance system, if the owners use the information in their daily jobs to make the company profitable, they will benefit in two ways—their shares will increase in value and their pay will increase.

In reflecting on the sharing of financial information with employees, Zimmerman stated that McIntyre is the real architect of the system, and he offered these additional insights:

> Bill McIntyre puts the information together, and he took a lot of heat early on because of the time and energy it took to put the information together. The financial information system that we have today is a lot more complicated than what we were doing previously. And it took time, and it took a lot of patience to go down that road to put the system together; but today we have information that is digestible. And that's part of it, too. Providing the information is one thing, but people have to be able to understand it.

McIntyre joined ComSonics in January 1986, which was about six months after Braun had sold the remaining 51 percent of the company to employees. McIntyre has an MBA from Stanford Graduate School of Business, is a Certified Public Accountant, and had a number of years of corporate experience in accounting and finance positions before joining ComSonics. In reflecting on the position of CFO, he said:

> The job depends upon the size of the company. If you're in a smaller company, the chief financial officer needs to be more involved and knowledgeable about the operations of the company than if you were in a larger company. The CFO of a large company may spend most of his time talking to bankers. In a company our size, the CFO must get involved also in the accounting system.

When McIntyre joined ComSonics, the accounting information system had not changed to keep up with the growth of the business. He stated that his first focus after he joined the company was to set up an accounting system oriented to SBUs. He noted the following:

> It's really crucial to be able to push a couple of buttons and get the reports you need, which is what feeds the open-book management system. If you don't record the data at the detail level and set up a system so that you can summarize it accordingly or break it down as needed, you are lost from the word go.

With the accounting information system that McIntyre designed, ComSonics has been able to do more and more with open-book management during the past 11 years.

In reflecting on some of the benefits of open-book management, McIntyre related the following incident:

> From 1990–91, we took a huge drop in revenue. There were a whole bunch of reasons for it, not particularly internal. It was a bad market. While this was happening, we realized that we had too many people. We needed to have a layoff, and we were distributing the financial information that showed that the revenue was going down. We announced a layoff. It was the first time in the history of the company that we've ever had to lay off people. We actually had to have two layoffs. The reaction of the employees was, "We've seen this coming for months. What took you guys so long?"

McIntyre added, "One guy went so far as to say that the list of people who actually left differed from his list of whom he thought should be laid off by only one person." In reflecting on this situation, Zimmerman recalled, "The employees had seen the information and they did not find a shock in the layoff. Everybody knew when I called them together why the layoff was going to happen."

Sommerville, Director of Sales and Marketing, offered this observation:

> The more employees understand about how a business functions, the more they benefit. And I think that if they don't learn it somewhere else, they might as well learn it here. I do think that probably having that understanding is going to get more in the long run from the people than anything else.

Sommerville did raise an interesting question about whether open-book management "is good for all sizes of companies. Maybe there has to be a definition of what we are talking about when we say open-book. It may be different with a certain size company or certain type of company."

In the final analysis, open-book management must be drilled down to the individual work unit to be implemented effectively. As an example of how this works at ComSonics, Meyerhoeffer explained how the manager of repairs operates:

> Jerry has weekly departmental meetings with each of his groups for about 20 minutes, in the cafeteria usually. If it is the first week after the financials have come out, he'll go over them. He will say the company did such and such, this was our budget, and here is what we accomplished. He will go over the pay-for-performance and indicate what the group has in its pool.

Tony Dean, one of the technicians in this work group, stated that Jerry was very well versed on the financials, adding, "I make it a regular practice every day at lunch to look at the graphs and charts posted on the bulletin boards in each lunchroom." He said that he paid attention to the information for the whole company as well because the company is an ESOP.

Dean pointed out how having some knowledge about the financial status of the company influences the decisions employees make on the workbench, and he cited two situations as examples. The first one related to the purchase of a piece of equipment:

> I went through a process where my meter, the one the company had bought, was old, run down, and not operational. It was time to get a new meter, so I sat down with my technical coordinator and we looked at meters. And what we came up with was in the range of

> about $50 up to about $250. What I picked was about the $70 version. It was something that we hashed out between us rather than just him saying here is your $50 meter or here is your $250 meter.

A second incident related to inventory:

> If I take or check out of our stockroom a part and sit it on my desk, that financially affects our pay-for-performance plan and affects how the company and how the department is doing. I would be extremely less likely to buy that part and just have it sit on my desk because of the impact it would have on the end-of-the-month statements when it is charged to my department.
>
> We have a mobile bin that has stockroom parts, and when we check them out, we check them out to that bin. Having looked at the financials last year, we carried about $8,000 per month on that bin. We became more aware of what we were putting on there. We were just putting way too many parts on there and letting them sit. We've cut that in half. This year we have parts of between $3,000 and $4,000 on the cart instead of $8,000.

These situations indicate that employee-owners understand how decisions they make affect the profitability of ComSonics.

Case Summary

ComSonics integrates an ESOP, open-book management, and pay-for-performance, and Zimmerman, the President and CEO, believes that integrating the three approaches provides a syncrgy for the organization. CFO McIntyre is the architect of the accounting system and has played a key role in developing what information is shared with employee-owners. ComSonics has provided a variety of opportunities for its employee-owners to learn what the financial information means through the articles on basic accounting and finance written by McIntyre; the Q&A box in the lunchrooms; the openness of its culture, which encourages employee-owners to ask any question; and a variety of ESOP-related activities.

The ComSonics philosophy toward open-book management has been summarized by McIntyre as follows:

We encourage employees to participate in understanding the company's financial information. We make that financial information available to all employees. We provide all employees with the opportunity to learn about our company's financial information. We do not make it mandatory for all employees to participate in our open-book management. We believe that the more employees are aware of, and understand, the financial impact of their actions, the more they will behave like business owners and make decisions and take actions more beneficial to the company and, ultimately, to themselves.

People Interviewed

Dennis A. Zimmerman, President and CEO

G. William McIntyre, Director of Finance and CFO

John W. Dickie, Director of Human Resources

Donn E. Meyerhoeffer, Director of Operations

Donald J. Sommerville, Director of Sales and Marketing

Gerald Bohus, Product Test Technician

Tony Dean, Line Repair Technician

Meetings Attended

The ESOP Association Western Virginia Region of the Mid-Atlantic Chapter, Session on ESOP Employee Advisory Committees, January 16, 1997. Discussion leaders were members of the ComSonics ESOP Employee Advisory Committee.

References

Karl Albrecht, *The Northbound Train*, AMACOM, 1994.

William Seidman and Steven L. Skancke, *Competitiveness: The Executive's Guide to Success*, M.E. Sharpe, Inc., 1989: 103–104.

Joan C. Szabo, "Using ESOPs to sell your firm," *Nation's Business*, January 1991, 59–60.

Sam V. Volard and Tim Brennan, "More than an ESOP—ComSonics, Inc.," Unpublished paper, 1988.

Endnote

1. Senator Russell Long, "Another Successful ESOP Company," Proceedings and debates of the 98th Congress, 1st session, *Congressional Record*, 129, no. 52, April 21, 1983.

4

GE Fanuc Automation North America, Inc.

We have a very empowered organization. You can just walk through this place and you'll see that. We have, without any question, the most highly empowered associates of any business in this country. That's been a key part of our productivity, frankly. We've gotten tremendous productivity out of the factory in the past four to five years. The company has also attained a very healthy competitive position, not that we don't have work to do. We do, but if you stack us up on any measure—financial, customer satisfaction, quality—we are near the top of the pile. This company is very strong in that sense.

Robert P. Collins, President and Chief Executive Officer
GE Fanuc Automation North America, Inc.

Company Background

GE Fanuc Automation Corporation (the parent) was formed in 1987 as a 50/50 joint venture between General Electric (GE) and FANUC Ltd. of Japan. The parent organization and GE formed a subsidiary called GE Fanuc Automation North America, Inc., of which the parent owns 90 percent and GE owns 9.9 percent, while FANUC Ltd. owns 0.1 percent (see figure 4.1).

The joint venture brought together GE's automation operation in Charlottesville, Virginia, which was doing leading-edge work on programmable logic controllers (PLCs), with FANUC Ltd., which served the market with leading-edge computer numerical controllers (CNCs). Under the joint venture agreement, each company focused on what it

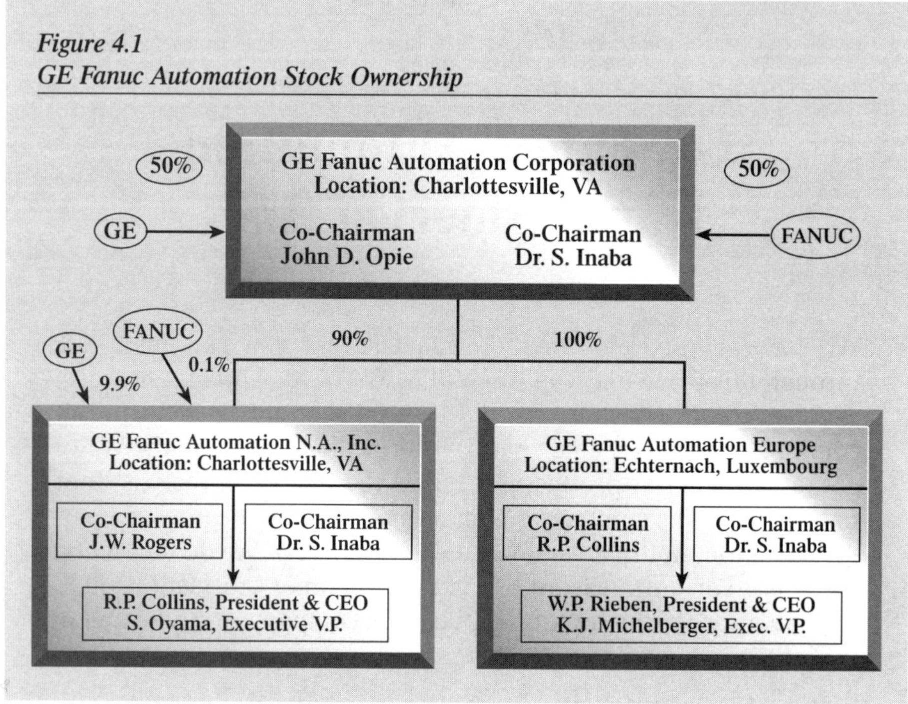

Figure 4.1
GE Fanuc Automation Stock Ownership

did best; FANUC Ltd. became the center of excellence for CNCs, GE became the center of excellence for PLCs and factory software systems.

PLCs and CNCs are the "brain and nervous system" of automated factory technology. PLC products are programmable controllers that direct the motions and sequencing of production equipment in a variety of industries. For example, PLC devices control the robots on an electronic welding assembly line in the automobile industry. CNC products control machine tools in the metal working industry. A CNC device, for example, is used to control the cutting head of a milling machine that turns a blank of steel into a gear.

The joint venture provided GE a market outside the United States for its PLCs and gave FANUC an entry into the North American market for its CNCs. Jack Welch, GE's chairman and CEO, and Dr. Seiuemon Inaba, FANUC's CEO, saw the merger as one that would benefit both sides.

Robert Collins, who has served as President and CEO of GE Fanuc Automation North America (hereafter referred to as GE Fanuc) since the joint venture was formed, led the GE team that formed the venture. Collins provided this overview of the 10-year joint venture: "Despite the fact that the cultures were vastly different, we found a lot of common underlying ingredients. Both companies were interested in technology. Both companies held quality of the product as a high priority." According to Collins, FANUC's motivation for entering the joint venture was similar to that of GE:

> They needed to reach the global market and they had tried to do it on their own and weren't too successful. We desperately needed the global market reach. We had tried some on our own in Europe and weren't very successful. You start looking at the economics and compare building the global infrastructure yourself to venturing with somebody who can provide synergy and leverage. The conclusion most often is to either acquire or venture.

Collins's assessment is, "In 10 years we've never faced a serious crisis in decision making in this business, and I'd have to say it's because we share mutual interest and synergy in thinking and stress constant communication with our parents." Robert Breihan, Senior Vice President, Sales and Marketing, gave this evaluation in the *GE Fanuc Times* in May 1997: "By all measures, you'd have to say that it's been one of the most remarkable joint ventures, not only in GE's history, but in the history of corporate America."

The joint venture had a 10-year term and was up for renewal this past year. Describing how Dr. Jack Welch and Dr. S. Inaba felt about the joint venture, Collins shared the following story on extension of the joint venture for another 10 years:

> I sent a letter to Welch and Inaba. Twenty-four hours later, I had a note back from Jack saying "I approve the extension for 10 years." Inaba sent back a note saying "I approve for 10 years and please advise Dr. Welch." In 24 hours, the leaders of both organizations said this is a no-brainer, just renew it.

With its headquarters in Charlottesville and 1,600 employees worldwide, GE Fanuc had sales of $515 million in 1996. It has extensive operations in the Asia/Pacific region, Europe, and in the Americas. The company has 15 major training centers and better than 250 distributors in more than 55 countries. The company serves every segment of the manufacturing and process industry, with customers ranging from the largest and most well-known companies in the world (e.g., General Motors) to companies serving small-niche markets.

GE Fanuc has received many awards, including recognition by *Industry Week* as one of the top 10 manufacturing companies in the United States; admiration from former Secretary of Labor, Robert Reich, as a best-practices company in his Model Workforce program; and kudos from President Bill Clinton as a best-practices company for his Workforce 2000 initiative. Also, in 1991, GE Fanuc achieved ISO 9000 certification under the European Community's International Standards Organization, which stipulates international standards of manufacturing quality. GE Fanuc was awarded the most comprehensive certification, which covers all aspects of the production cycle, from design through servicing.

Jack Welch and Work-Out

In 1981, Jack Welch became GE's chairman and CEO. His strategy was that GE would only be in businesses that were number one or two in their markets and that could compete successfully in the global economy. As a result, he led the divestiture of $11 billion in assets and spent $20 billion on new acquisitions. His disposals included GE's small-appliance division and among his purchases was the NBC television network. GE's workforce was trimmed from 400,000 in 1981 to about 220,000 today. He consolidated 150 business units into 12 basic businesses. Revenue was $26 billion in 1981, and in 1996 it was more than $79 billion. In the *Business Week* Global 1000 for 1996, GE was listed as the largest company in the world in market value capitalization at $198 billion.

Welch believes that the key to GE's survival will be its ability to continually boost productivity beyond levels achieved in the past. To that end, he has preached empowerment and cooperation. His vision for GE is that it would be "boundaryless," with no barriers between hourly workers and managers, between functions in the company, between domestic and international operations, and between the company and its customers.

Along with the boundaryless concept, Welch initiated in January 1989 a program called "Work-Out," which focused on eliminating useless and unnecessary work, and enabling people to do their jobs by working together. This initiative started with "town meetings" in which people from different functions in the organization would come together to express their ideas for improving processes and eliminating unnecessary work. In many instances in the Work-Out sessions, people were attending meetings and solving problems with people in the organization with whom they had had very little contact previously. The idea was to listen to people and to energize them to improve the company. GE's 1989 annual report articulated Welch's vision for Work-Out:

> The individual is the fountainhead of creativity and innovation, and we are struggling to get all our people to accept the countercultural way. Only by releasing the energy and fire of our employees can we achieve the decisive, continuous productivity advantages that will give us the freedom to compete and win in any business anywhere on the globe.
>
> We have seen, with the demolition of the control superstructure we once imposed on our business, and we are beginning to see even more clearly, as Work-Out starts to blossom, that controlling people doesn't motivate them. It stifles them. We've found that people perform better, even heroically, when they see that what they do every day makes a difference.

While Welch was launching Work-Out, in 1989 Collins took a slightly different tack initially, and launched at GE Fanuc what he called "vision-powered management." A critical issue that Collins had to address early on with GE Fanuc employees was to get them to believe that his initiative was not just the latest management fad that would run its course and leave the organization, its culture, and its operations essentially unchanged. Collins recalled:

> I remember standing in front of this whole workforce in 1989 and telling them if they would trust us to go down this path of this vision, the empowerment, the high-performance level, that we would not lay anybody off. I was convinced that, otherwise, people would

> tune me out because their view was going to be the typical reaction to management's initiative—this is just a way to reduce the number of employees. So, I felt to unblock their minds I had to basically get up and tell them that this was not going to wind up in a reduction of people. In fact, what it would do is lead to a growth of the business and improvement in productivity and ultimately a growth in jobs, and that is certainly what has happened.

Collins reflected on that period and admitted that he had taken a risk in saying that the company would have no workforce reduction if employees would trust him and go down the path he had envisioned:

> If Jack Welch had heard me say that we would not have any reduction of the workforce, he probably would have said, you head downtown and find the nearest psychiatrist and spend a few weeks with him because you need to have your head examined. You could end up putting yourself in a real box. But I was really convinced that we were going to be able to make something different happen without reducing the workforce.

Collins added, "The employees began to believe me after a year of really high-paced activity of setting up small meetings with people. The whole staff and I spent an awful lot of energy meeting with everybody in this company."

Vision-Powered Management, Work-Out, and High-Involvement Workforce

Collins conceptualized vision-powered management by reflecting on his more than 30 years' experience with GE:

> I can't tell you how many cases I've run into in the business environment where Pareto's Law seems to work. No matter what the situation is, it is the old 80/20, 70/30 kind of approach.
>
> One of my thoughts, in terms of employee productivity, was as you run your business, when you get into one of those really tough business situations that confront a business manager, you turn to your "go-to" people—the people that have the extraordinary energy, the

> extraordinary intellect that can always handle the tough problems. You turn back to these people time and time again. I do it as a business leader. And this goes on in every business.
>
> Management hasn't figured out a way to spread that 20 to 30 percent performance capability across the full workforce. I just think intuitively that Pareto's Law is at work as it relates to getting people to perform at the maximum level of their performance capability. So if that is true, then the conclusion is theoretically you can get three to four times more productivity by working on that 70 percent of the workforce. If that intuitive conclusion is correct, how do you unlock their productivity? That was the genesis of the idea that led me to say, "Let's create a vision-driven organization."

In Collins's view, the essence of vision-powered management is this: "A sense of purpose on the job is as fundamental to a person's existence as the need for food, shelter, and companionship." He felt that by creating a clearly understandable vision of the company and the values it sought to embody, the purpose of every employee's work would become clear to him or her, and a deeper, more focused commitment would follow. Collins was quick to point out that his effort to create vision-powered management "could only begin because Jack Welch had created an environment in GE that encouraged individuals and divisions to create their own personalities and seek their own methods of achieving high levels of employee involvement and business performance."

When Collins launched the process to state a vision for GE Fanuc in 1989, he was ably assisted by Helene Mawyer, Senior Vice President of Business Development. Together they enlisted the participation of Collins' staff and a handful of highly respected managers of the company. They embarked on a six-month process that resulted in a booklet of about six pages containing a statement of objectives, strategies, goals, action plans, and the like. The vision booklet was launched with an offsite meeting of all employees, during which Collins presented the comprehensive vision. The evening was capped off with a dinner. As Collins said, "It was a great night and everyone thoroughly enjoyed the meeting. I was very pleased with the feedback I received and felt we were off to a great start."

Following this unveiling of the vision booklet, the vision statement was emphasized at monthly operations review meetings held in the company's auditorium. During these meetings, employees may attend a session either in the morning or in the afternoon. The meetings are a major event in GE Fanuc's implementation of open-book management and feature a graded report card on the company's performance. The key measures on the report card are growth and market share, customer satisfaction, product leadership (quality), and cash and profitability. Further discussion of the report card is deferred to a later section.

Six months after distributing the vision booklet, Mawyer suggested that GE Fanuc determine how many employees had bought into the vision. The company conducted an audit of employee understanding. To its dismay, the audit found that the vision booklet had not been understood and accepted by the workforce. As Collins remarked, "Most disappointing was the knowledge that most people could not recall very much of what had been emphasized in the booklet."

Collins and his team went back to square one with some very important lessons learned. First, they needed participation by a much larger segment of the employee population. Second, the vision needed to be more simply stated. A team representing a broader group of employees drafted the next iteration. Drawing on some of the thoughts contained in the original booklet, the team condensed the vision into a single statement as follows:

> To improve our customers' productivity with the best industrial automation technology, reliability, and services worldwide.

The vision statement is focused externally on the customer; no mention is made of profits. GE Fanuc is in business to satisfy customers, and, if it does, profits will flow. The statement uses the term "reliability" instead of "quality" because a reliable product, over time, is a quality one.

The team working on the vision added a statement of values to serve as a guide for the conduct of the workforce. These values included being truthful, working quickly with quality and simplicity, and being profitable. The team also suggested that the statement be presented to employees without fanfare at a monthly operations review meeting and that the employees be asked to signify their support by signing the statement voluntarily. After the presentation, hundreds of employees voluntarily signed the statement. The vision came not from the top down but from the bottom up, and it was the employees' vision. Collins remarked, "It was perhaps their first real taste of empowerment."

In the next stage of changing the GE Fanuc culture, Collins borrowed from Welch and began holding a series of "town meetings" with groups of about 50 employees at off-site locations. The composition of the groups was purposefully mixed so as to begin to introduce the notion of work teams and horizontal work processes. The objective, at this stage, was to empower the workforce to remove junk work.

When Welch initiated Work-Out, GE Fanuc had some of the problems that he was trying to eradicate. At GE Fanuc, boundaries existed between management and workers and an atmosphere of mistrust and suspicion prevailed. The organization had layers of management, endless approval processes, and trails of paper that no one was using.

According to Collins, the numerous meetings with the workforce to remove junk work accomplished two things. First, it served to convince the workforce that he was serious about changing the way GE Fanuc would be managed. Second, by getting the employees involved, they began to practice empowerment. At the end of the Work-Out process at GE Fanuc, the workforce had identified more than 200 projects, which, when completed, would reduce junk work substantially. These reductions would, in words borrowed from Welch, contribute to the corporate goals of "speed, simplicity, and self-confidence." To Welch's list, GE Fanuc added the fourth goal—shared vision. According to Donald Borwhat, Senior Vice President of Human Resources and Public Relations, this fourth goal "may be the most important" of all because it's the "glue that ties the employee to the company's purpose and it is the driver of high-performance organizations."

Following Work-Out and completion of most of the related projects in 1991, Collins was concerned with how to sustain the momentum that had been achieved. The company launched a new initiative known as High-Involvement Workforce (HIWF), aimed at helping transform GE Fanuc from a functional-based organization to a team-based one. Several critical attributes of HIWF are as follows:

- It uses a horizontal management process instead of vertical functional management.
- It eliminates labels such as "hourly" and "salaried" and replaces them with the single term "associate."
- It changes managers' roles from traffic cops to coaches.

The premises of HIWF are that every employee is a potential contributor, that those closest to the work should influence the decisions, and that employees are empowered to influence results. A new workplace was emerging at GE Fanuc, and people were treated as professionals. As a symbol of this new vision, casual Friday dress was extended throughout the week by senior management.

Today, production associates are organized into 42 teams of 10 to 12 people. Training workshops for all employees—more than 100 hours, paid and held during work time—have included meeting facilitation skills, goal setting, problem solving, conflict management, and negotiation. Each HIWF team meets once a week for about an hour. A coach, who was formerly a supervisor, is assigned to each team to assist if needed. Also, various associates from the salaried ranks serve as external-support resources for all teams. On a tour through the factory, one notes HIWF teams having their meetings. Also, as part of open-book management, numerous graphs are posted near each factory cell giving information related to the GE Fanuc report card. Interestingly, each cell individualizes the information it posts in order to present the information in a manner that is meaningful to that HIWF team.

One associate offered the following comments about HIWF:

> What I like about the situation now is I get to give my input and see the ideas I have being done. A lot of times when you have more ideas, you get better results. If I get a chance to give my ideas, it is apt to make me want to do my job better. That's the part I really like about it. What you want is everyone's mind involved.

Before HIWF, another production associate said he approached his work in this manner:

> This is my chair, this is my workstation—I own this workstation—and this is all I do all day long. I am not worried about what you're doing. You need help. I am sorry, I can't help you. The supervisor comes up and tells you what you are going to do today.

Since HIWF, however, this associate stated that people's attitudes are different:

> Now you take ownership. This is my product. This is my line. This is my business. I have an impact. You have people who are more fo-

> cused—you not only have an idea, but you are not scared to share your idea. In fact, if things are not really going right here, you might say, let's check with one of the other lines. If they had a similar problem, let's call together a little subcommittee team if we have to. It may be a one-meeting deal. But let's improve the process, and you know that the ideas you come up with are going to have valid input to the process.

A third associate offered this opinion:

> I commute an hour and half each way, every day, just to come to work here. Basically, I have never worked in an environment like it. I came out of a pull-each-other's-hair, sweatshop environment. When I came to this business, I was overwhelmed by the amount of employee involvement and that was just at the very beginning of high involvement. And so, when I knew that I had an opportunity to help make some changes—this vision they had about empowering all employees—it sounded so good to me.

One of the three associates summed up the personal impact of HIWF this way:

> Since I have been here at GE Fanuc, going from the way that it was with the supervisors to the way that it is now, I feel like I am a better person. A lot of the things you learn here, you take them home with you, and you practice them everywhere. And when I wake up in the morning, I say, "Hey, I am going to work today."

In transitioning to HIWF, GE Fanuc was able to keep all its promises to employees, including the promise of no layoffs. Although productivity declined during the early stages of HIWF, it is now much higher and it has continued to grow.

The Bonus Program

> The real driver for the bonus program, I think, was the need to move away from a purely functional-based business into a team-based business. It was a real driver because we had to have some kind of reward for people operating as teams. I had done a lot of

> thinking about that and how an incentive bonus operates for top management.
>
> Top management, in virtually every company, just blows it out to maximize their bonus, and our people would be no different. We needed some scheme to create that extra level of contribution in this whole team environment and that is why we settled on a very simple bonus plan for them. It was based on cash flow and pretax income at the outset because we wanted to drive behavior to make the company more productive.
>
> In my view, to be profitable, you have to satisfy customers. Profits and cash are a result of satisfying customers, but you have to manage productivity, profits, and cash. You want people's minds tied to whatever work they do on a day-to-day basis. Are they maximizing cash and profit? Are they looking for ways to cut costs? Are they looking for ways to improve efficiencies? So we are trying to drive a mechanism that forces people's mind-sets there, but, more important, that encourages them to contribute as a team.
>
> Bob Collins

At about the same time GE Fanuc implemented its HIWF team program, Collins created the company's bonus plan. This plan was designed with two overarching objectives: It should direct team behavior to the company's two major success indicators, profits and cash flow; and it should be simple. GE, under Jack Welch, does not use traditional bonus plans widely. Incentive compensation tends to be in the form of "gain sharing" and stock options. As a unit of GE participating in many of GE's employee benefits, GE Fanuc grants GE stock options to a wide cross section of its employees. Although parent company stock options can be of benefit in driving overall behavior and creating a mechanism for retention of key employees, they were not far-reaching enough—particularly in light of the need to direct both office and factory associate-based teams toward the desired behavior. And Collins rejected gain sharing as too complex for his purposes. A bonus program, on the other hand, can be structured simply if it can be related to high-level business objectives.

Collins considered his bonus program as absolutely necessary for accomplishing the goals of vision-based management at GE Fanuc, but he had two major concerns: the riskiness of the program and the potential wariness of the GE Fanuc Board of Directors. Collins gives the following account:

> When we considered the bonus plan, that was a big-risk decision because we had absolutely no guarantee that we were going to be able to afford to pay a bonus even if we made the numbers. And so we had to find a way to budget the payout and build it on top of our financial commitment to the Board, in other words—to finesse it through the Board. By that I mean, we still had to deliver very strong earnings improvement, but at the same time [CFO] Larry Pearson and I had to dig out enough extra net income to fund the bonus payout.
>
> I told Jack Welch a one-liner once that we had profit sharing—a bonus. He didn't really blink. He understands the value of performance-based incentives. I think we are such a small part of GE that we are kind of an experiment to him.

Don Borwhat, Senior Vice President of Human Resources and Public Relations, recalls the meeting with GE in which the bonus plan came up:

> Some of the compensation experts said, "You can't put in a bonus program like that." We said, "Why? We've been doing it now for a year and it works." Jack Welch said, "I think it's great—go for it." Others were saying, "How are you going to figure it out? People are going to be upset if you don't do it right"—which is absolutely true. GE had some horror stories.
>
> But our profit sharing is based on the business measurements. It is not cost avoidance; it is not on any fluffy stuff; it is hard measurements. And if we make our numbers, or if we exceed those numbers, everyone's bonus is going to go up once we hit that threshold. If we commit to give $50 million net income to our Board and we make $55 million, why not share a portion of that with all of the employees who have focused on these objectives throughout the year?

The GE Fanuc bonus plan weighs profits and cash flows equally in arriving at the bonus payout amounts. Profits are defined as sales less variable and fixed (base) operating expenses, plus interest income and minus interest expense. It is the line labeled "pretax operating income" in the company's income statement. Cash flow is the same as cash flow from operations reported in the traditional statement of cash flows required under generally accepted accounting principles.

Profits are an obvious component of the bonus plan, but one might wonder why a company 50-percent-owned by deep-pocketed GE would be particularly concerned about cash flow. Collins explains it this way:

> Because we are an independent company, we cannot depend on our Parent Companies for cash. As a result, we have a different level of independence than we would have if we were a member of FANUC, or a full member of GE. And you can never abuse that independence. You have to always continue to earn that independence by delivering results. I remember when we first formed this company, the first thing we had to do was go out and get money. We were in a state of shock. We didn't have to worry about money before. We reported on cash as a member of GE, but you never felt cash before. All of a sudden that insulation we had was gone. But cash is a simple philosophy. Cash comes from profits.

In GE Fanuc's open-book management approach, pretax profits and cash flow are reported to employees monthly during the operations review. This meeting occurs about halfway through a month and includes a progress report on how the company is doing at attaining its profit and cash-flow objectives for the year. Accordingly, employees receive an inkling of the level of bonus they might expect for the year. The financial statistics are measured through the end of the previous month. The operations review is held twice on the same day and is videotaped to send to associates in the field. At the end of the formal presentations, a question-and-answer session is held, with Collins or one of the senior executives fielding questions from associates.

The presentation on profits and cash flow, part of a segment called the "report card," is made by associates selected for each meeting by the company's human resources department. The presentation consists of several PowerPoint slides projected to the audience that show a highly condensed income statement, actual to plan, and several graphic representations of the progress toward meeting bonus plan objectives. This presentation is employees' only exposure to the actual results because the numbers are not available in any other form, such as bulletin board posting. The company does not distribute printed copies of the income statement and the graphic slides. Figure 4.2 shows a sample of these slides without dollar amounts and percentages.

Note that in the upper right corner of the income statement slide is a letter grade, which can range from A+ to F. A letter grade from this scale is assigned each month to profitability and cash-flow performance. There are other key measures reported in an open-book manner, and letter grades are assigned to them. These measures are as follows (see page 90):

Figure 4.2
GE Fanuc Report Card

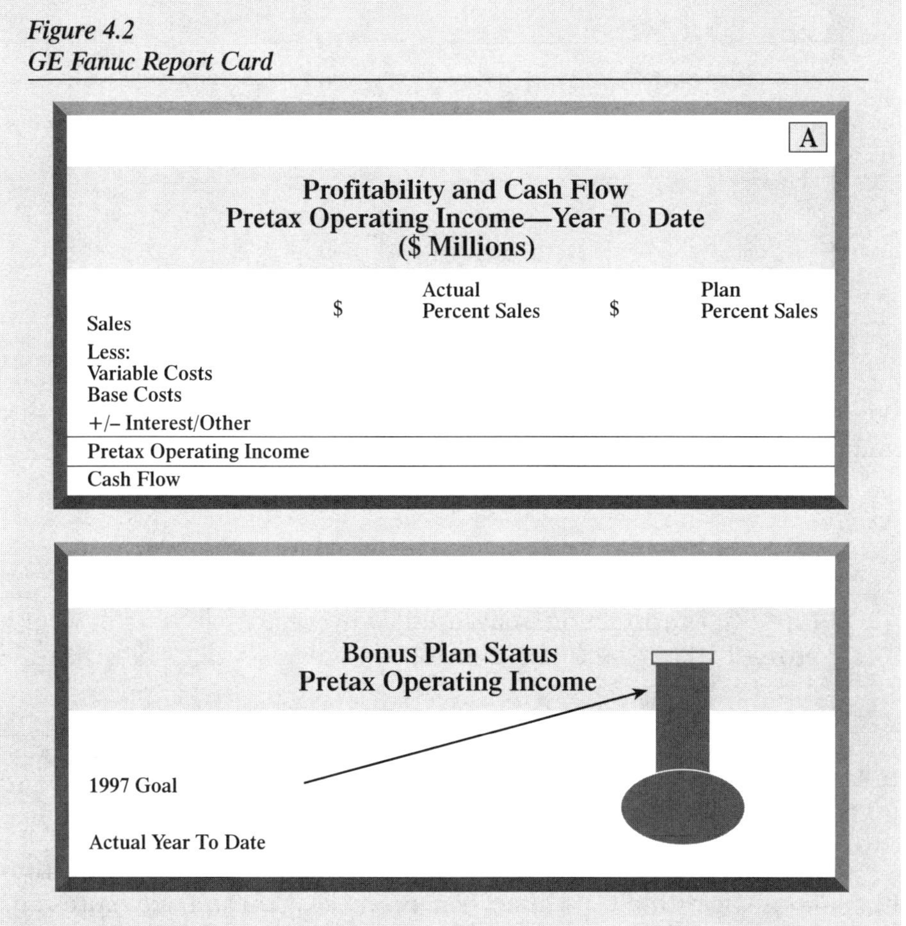

Figure 4.2
GE Fanuc Report Card (Continued)

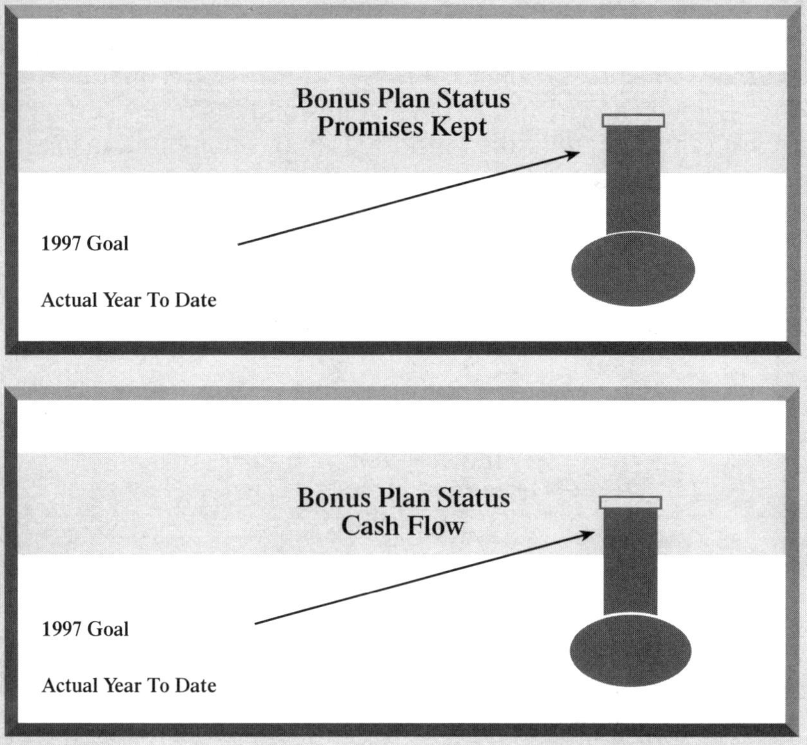

Bonus Plan Status
Promises Kept

1997 Goal

Actual Year To Date

Bonus Plan Status
Cash Flow

1997 Goal

Actual Year To Date

- Growth and market share, measured in overall orders trend.
- Customer satisfaction, measured by average cycle time in weeks, promises kept as a percentage of total promises, and overdue items in weeks.
- Product leadership (quality), measured by test defect rate, customer survey scores, cost of quality as a percentage of sales, and product return rate as a percentage of the goal.

Historically, promises kept had been an important—and troubling—statistic within GE Fanuc. The promises-kept statistic represents the percentage of the time GE Fanuc delivers product by the promised delivery date. Unhappiness with promises-kept performance led to the only major change in the bonus plan since its inception. This change is discussed in detail in the next section.

The report card part of the operations review ends with a slide recapping the grade in each category and showing an overall grade of operating performance to date (figure 4.3). Only the grade for cash and profitability on this slide is a direct indicator of bonus progress for the current fiscal year, although the other grades may be viewed as leading indicators of cash flow and profits (and bonuses) in the future.

GE Fanuc's bonus plan can be very lucrative. If goals are met or exceeded, employees are paid a significant bonus stated in number of days' pay two weeks after the close of the fiscal year. For 1996, the bonus payout was 7 days' pay. For instance, a worker drawing $25,000 a year earns about $100 a day; that worker would receive a bonus check in mid-January 1997 for $700 (7 days × $100) less taxes. Over the eight years the plan has been in effect, bonuses have ranged from 0.9 days' pay to 16 days' pay.

The calculation of the bonus payout in days' pay is straightforward and based on the company's actual performance in profits and cash flow versus the plan. A detailed presentation of the bonus calculation

Figure 4.3
Overall Report Card

Report Card—April 1997	
Growth and market share orders	A–
Customer satisfaction	
PLC	B
CNC	B+
Product leadership	
quality	A
Cash and profitability	
Pretax operating income	A
Overall	**B+**

appears in figure 4.4. It should be emphasized that when the ambitious profit and cash-flow targets are exceeded, a substantial boost in the bonus payout is triggered, but healthy bonus payments still result when performance meets the targets.

By using days' pay to state an employee's bonus amount, GE Fanuc has elected to make the bonus proportional to each employee's regular pay level. Obviously, higher paid employees will receive a higher dollar bonus but the same number of additional days' pay. Collins steadfastly defends this choice (see page 93):

Figure 4.4
Example of Bonus Pool Calculation

For years 1996 and earlier, the bonus pool was calculated using GE Fanuc's performance in profits and cash flow in equal parts. Performance is measured by the percentage of actual to plan. For example, if actual profit is \$40 against a plan of \$50, the performance percentage for profit is 80 percent (40/50). The actual calculation of the bonus pool depends on whether profit and cash objectives are both met:

- If profit and cash-flow objectives are *both* met (percentages of 100 percent or higher), the bonus pool for the year is 3 percent times pretax operating profit for the plan plus 15 percent times pretax operating profit above the plan. For instance, if actual pretax operating profit is \$60, the bonus pool is \$3 (3 percent × 50 + 15 percent × 10).
- If profit and cash-flow objectives are *not* met, the bonus pool is calculated as follows:

  Profit side—Profit performance percentage × 3 percent × net operating profit × 50 percent.

  Cash-flow side—Cash performance percentage × 3 percent × net operating profit × 50 percent.

Suppose the profit percentage is 90 percent and the cash-flow percentage is 85 percent. Based on an actual pretax operating profit of \$40, the bonus pool would be \$1.05. This is calculated in the following manner:

Profit side:	90 percent × 3 percent × \$40 × 50 percent =	\$0.54
Cash-flow side:	85 percent × 3 percent × \$40 × 50 percent =	\$0.51
Total bonus pool:		\$1.05

In these examples, attaining *both* profit and cash-flow objectives raised the bonus as a percentage of pretax operating income from 2.63 percent to 5 percent.

> In the beginning, we struggled with how we would actually pay the bonus out and a lot of people argued that they wanted to have it differentiated. But some people said, "Take the amount of money and divide it by the number of people and give everybody the same amount," which we were totally against. Let's say for example that we had $1 million to pay out, and let's say we had a thousand employees; some people wanted to give everyone a $1,000 bonus.
>
> We had the delicate job of dealing with that question because everybody says, "Well gee, I work hard, I contribute even though my job is different. I work just as hard as Larry does so I should get the same amount that he got." So we brainstormed how the hell we would answer that question. I remember standing in front of an operations review dealing with that matter, and I basically said to everyone, "How would you feel if you wound up getting four days of extra pay, and somebody over there got 20 days of extra pay? How would you feel about that if you were in the bonus plan and you worked hard and you felt that you contributed just as much as that person? Like me, you would say, that's not right!
>
> So when we led them down the path of talking about this, not in terms of dollars or percentages but purely in terms of days of extra pay, bingo, that sold it. We got everybody off that other kick. But we had to handle it delicately.

Discussions with factory associates revealed a high level of employee awareness of the bonus plan and a strong linkage between the open-book information presented at the operations review and the annual bonus payout.

Employees receive the final bonus results reported on a slide in January. Figure 4.5 illustrates the bonus calculation. The slide works from actual profit and cash flow to the bonus payout in days' pay. Employees can then multiply the number of days by their daily pay rate to obtain their bonus amount. Collins notes that employee interest in the operations review meetings increases as it gets closer to the bonus payout:

> They usually know in the fall I'm going to give them a pre-announcement of what the bonus is going to be. So you'll see the attendance starting to build up. At the December meeting they're expecting to get a pretty good handle on what it's going to be and

Figure 4.5
19XX Bonus Plan

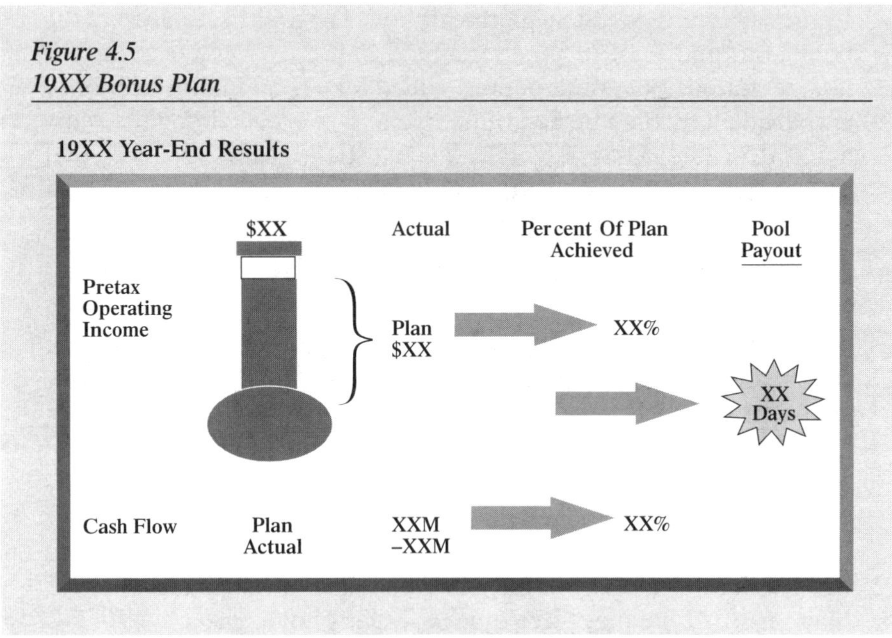

> the attendance will be much higher at that meeting. Because of Christmas bills, we tell them ahead of time, so they can start planning on that.

The company made a conscious decision to pay bonuses annually instead of quarterly or semiannually. Collins is adamant in his defense of this decision, which was based on the risk that more frequent bonus payments based on good profits and cash-flow performance early in the year could be erased by poorer performance later in the year. Collins says, "I never want to take it back. When you give a bonus, you can never take it back."

Overall, GE Fanuc is happy with the way the bonus plan motivates profitable individual and team behavior. But Collins goes further in his praise of the bonus arrangement:

> It's not just a motivator; it's a bonding methodology. You create a lot more commitment of people to a business with the concept of profit sharing. You'll see this in small businesses all around this country. They get a lot of leverage out of profit sharing.

Promises Kept and the Bonus

Customer satisfaction is at the root of business success, and promises kept is one of three components of GE Fanuc's customer satisfaction metric; it refers to the company's ability to fulfill its delivery date commitment on an order. Timing is especially critical for the company's customers because its products are typically used in highly sophisticated equipment manufactured in automated, just-in-time environments. Missed delivery dates can be quite costly for customers and will obviously have an impact on GE Fanuc's perceived reliability as a supplier.

Collins viewed the situation as follows:

> If we don't make the delivery date, it is a problem. We openly track our problems on the report card. We knew that we were not doing very well in this. We were batting around 75 to 80 percent or between a D and C+ grade. That means we are ticking off one out of every four customers. We had been struggling for several years to get this metric improved. We implemented fundamental foundation work in the factory in terms of process improvement, capacity improvement, cycle time improvement, all that sort of thing.
>
> Bob Collins

Because customer satisfaction may be viewed as a leading indicator of profits and cash flow, declines in customer satisfaction should show up in reduced profits and cash flow, other things being equal. Theoretically, a bonus program predicated on profits and cash flow will motivate team behavior in a way that improves promises kept and thus increases bonus amounts. But that is theory, not fact. GE Fanuc's bonus program seemed to be doing nothing at all to motivate teams to better manage promises kept. There was simply insufficient linkage between the promises-kept metric and the bonus plan itself.

This reality was especially troubling to Bob Collins. He was unhappy with the promises-kept percentage and looking for a way to solve the problem:

> I was not only unhappy about *our* performance—I was totally unhappy with *my own* inability to get the problem solved. You get to a point in your life when you say, screw it. It is easy to get mad, and I

> figured that would really get people's attention. That would really create the crisis.
>
> We hadn't created a crisis, that was the problem. We had a lot of people worried, we had a lot of people working on it and it was very highlighted. Everybody knew we were doing poorly because report cards for two years showed Ds and Fs [for promises kept]. It hadn't improved enough. You hear this constantly, "You've got to create a crisis sometimes to get a final resolution to a problem."

GE Fanuc's substantial factory investments should have had a positive impact on promises kept. These initiatives included rearranging the factory into manufacturing cells and increasing capacity. Still, success for promises kept eluded the company. Collins's frustration with GE Fanuc's inability to improve promises kept significantly erupted into swift and decisive action in 1997. His solution was deceptively simple. He merely put one-third of the very lucrative bonus pool "at risk." Previously, the bonus was based 50/50 on profits and cash flow. Now the bonus calculation includes a third variable, the promises-kept percentage. If the overall promises-kept percentage meets or exceeds 95 percent for the year, the third piece of the bonus pie stays intact; if the promises-kept percentage is less than 95 percent, the third piece for that year disappears forever. A worker who might expect a bonus of $1,000 just as Christmas and holiday bills are coming due would see the bonus shrink to $667 if promises-kept goals were not met.

In addition, the grading scale applied to promises kept in the monthly report card was tightened to reflect the higher expectations. The old performance level for promises kept of 70 percent used to merit a C– grade. Now 70 percent is an F. Under the old scale, an 80 percent corresponded to a grade of B–. Now an 80 percent is also an F. A promises-kept result of 90 percent used to be an A–; now it's a C. This is clearly a no-nonsense approach to the dilemma of the weak promises-kept performance.

At first glance, it might appear that Collins' target of 95 percent promises kept was unduly optimistic, especially since the percentage had been hovering around 70 to 75 percent (or lower) for two years. But this view ignores the substantial impact of the HIWF teams and the fact that the infrastructure was in place to support a large positive shift in promises kept under the right conditions. Even with these factors in mind, the results have been surprisingly quick and impressive. Promises kept moved from 78 percent in February 1997, to 86 percent in March, to 93 percent in April, to above 95 percent in May and June.

As one tours the GE Fanuc factory floor, graphs of local promises-kept performance over time are prominently posted in every manufacturing cell. It is easy to discern in these graphs a large and seemingly permanent shift in the promises-kept metrics. It is clear that teams have risen to the occasion and placed promises kept at the top of their priorities. In fact, from discussions with factory associates, promises not kept are treated as rare and disturbing events, dealt with quickly and decisively. It is hard to imagine promises kept drifting back into the danger zone even without Collins' bonus "stick."

Now that the promises-kept problem has been managed so convincingly through the bonus plan, Collins sees other possibilities:

> Every business in our industry has to get better at introducing new products. Our track record there is spotty. Some things we do really well; some things we don't do very well. And the area that has been more elusive than others is software products. We've got to come up with some way to drive those developments better.
>
> I think this promises-kept thing will wear off in about year: a year from now it will be running like a finely oiled machine. So that will come off and we'll probably toss on something about new software product development because that is an area we have a really strategic business issue with.

The promises-kept situation demonstrates the power of the GE Fanuc bonus plan to stimulate rapid, dramatic improvements in operating results when combined with a vision-powered work environment built on a bedrock of HIWF teams and open-book management. GE Fanuc is emerging as a laboratory for testing the types of business practices most likely to bear fruit for American manufacturing long into the 21st century.

Business Measurement Framework and Performance Screens

GE Fanuc had a vision statement, a leadership team that understood the vision, employees who were committed to the HIWF, an open-book management process built around the report card and monthly operations review, and a bonus plan. According to Collins, "What GE Fanuc further needed was a way to make the vision statement a reality for every employee of the business, not just the leaders. The measurement framework accomplishes this task."

The measurement framework (figure 4.6) was developed not for one-time use, but rather as a process that will need continuous feedback and refinement as the organization continues to learn. This framework enables employees to visualize and measure their individual contributions to the company's success.

The framework provides a process to drill down the vision statement and make it operational. It boils down the vision statement to a single definitive concern: "to satisfy customers profitably." Each of the strategic objectives relates to the metrics on the report card, and the metrics are communicated at the monthly operations review meetings. Also, each objective, along with hard measurements, is on the "performance screen" of one of the CEO staff members (i.e., the vice presidents). The performance screens begin with Collins, and he shares his with his staff. They, in turn, develop their performance screens and share them with one another and with the next tier, and so it goes throughout the entire company. The performance screens are signed by the person preparing the screen and by that person's designated coach. The performance screens are continually reviewed during the year both to track progress and to make adjustments to operations, if necessary. Factory associates have three objectives—quality, cost reduction, and cycle time—these are the focus of their respective team.

The CFO's Role

CFO Larry Pearson began his career at GE 30 years ago, when he was hired as a finance major right out of college to join the company's financial management training program. He held finance positions in

Figure 4.6
Business Measurement Framework

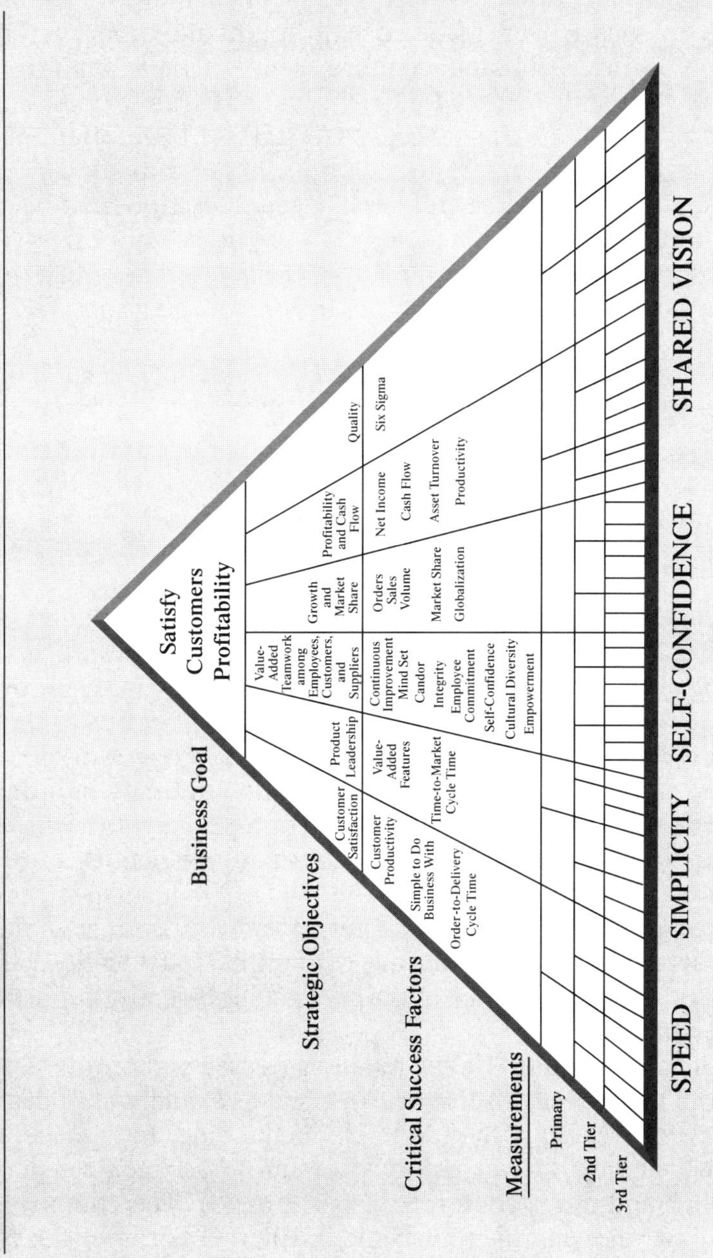

several GE units before transferring to GE Fanuc in 1987. Almost immediately, he was actively involved with Collins and others in the transformation of the GE Fanuc culture. Since arriving at GE Fanuc, Pearson has worked closely with Collins and GE Fanuc operating management to help craft the vision-based, HIWF team-oriented, open-book management structure now pervasive in the company.

Pearson's performance screen is a concise description of his current role in the GE Fanuc organization. It is obvious from this document that Pearson's is a value-added role. The objectives for Pearson's performance in 1997 are in the following five major categories:

- Customer satisfaction.
- Value-added teamwork.
- Growth and market share.
- Profitability and cash flow.
- Quality.

Customer satisfaction targets include a goal of "continued simplification of customer transaction processes," which will be measured by improving accuracy of billing transactions by one Sigma, improving rebate processing time to 30 days, and improving processes to reduce inventory on credit hold by 20 percent. Value-added teamwork focuses on objectives such as valuing integrity, promoting diversity in hiring practices, developing process and scorecards for Six Sigma[1] projects, and analyzing factory overhead rates for process improvements. Profitability and cash flow include objectives related to cash management; improvements in receivables, payables, and inventory turns; and the initiation of one new action per month to reduce working capital. Quality centers on support for GE's Six Sigma initiative and high-quality reporting and controllership.

To educate associates on the meaning of cash and profitability—key metrics in the company's report card—Pearson and his staff designed a course several years ago entitled "Understanding the Numbers." The course, which runs in two half-day sessions, had been taught by the comptroller and other volunteers from Finance. The comptroller left GE this past year, and his replacement, Ellen Greer, sees the resumption of this course as one of her priorities. Reflecting on this course,

Human Resources Vice President Don Borwhat said that all associates had to be brought up to speed, even veterans:

> We found out that even with our managers when we said, "Inventory turns, working capital, ROS, ROI, and all of that, you guys all know what that means, right?"—everybody shook their head and no one knew what it meant but a very select few. We forced every manager in the business to go through that [training].
>
> What would happen is, they'd say, "I've been a manager for 20 years. I'll go through that if you force me to go through it." Afterwards, the guys around us would say that that was the best thing we ever had. And I would say, "How could you work here and not know what inventory turns mean?" Well, that is the problem. I think everybody else in the room knows. Well, we found out no one else in the room knew, so we put everybody through it.

GE Fanuc believes the key to training associates in financial information is to relate the training to their everyday lives. One slide in the formal presentation, for instance, shows a personal balance sheet with assets of cash, savings accounts, real estate, and cars, among others. Liabilities include outstanding bills, credit cards, and mortgages. Net worth is shown to be the difference between assets and liabilities. The next slide then relates a personal balance sheet to GE Fanuc's balance sheet. The same analogy is drawn between a personal operating statement and GE Fanuc's operating statement, and personal cash flow and GE Fanuc's cash flow. Other concepts discussed are working capital, return on sales, variances, and productivity measures.

Formal training in accounting and finance is augmented on a day-to-day basis by having team members address the many problems and issues facing their team. Most of these issues relate in some fashion to financial concepts and metrics, and so financial information is part of the associates' everyday working lives at GE Fanuc.

Case Summary

During its 10-year existence, GE Fanuc has moved very quickly to become a high-performance, open-book, team-based organization. The initial impetus for these revolutionary changes was the Work-Out program introduced by Jack Welch in the late 1980s. Bob Collins took Welch's directive and synthesized it with his own vision-powered management paradigm to create a culture that is unique within the GE umbrella.

Don Borwhat and Larry Pearson observe that GE Fanuc is like a beta test site within GE for new and innovative management practices. HIWF teams and open-book management were practiced at GE Fanuc before they were instituted at any other GE unit. All-employee bonus plans are not widespread within GE, yet the plan at GE Fanuc has promoted extraordinary performance and productivity. The combination of the bonus plan with the other innovative aspects of the GE Fanuc culture pushes operational performance to impressive heights. This combination demonstrates organizational synergy at its strongest.

The corporate culture that Bob Collins and his associates have created at GE Fanuc represents the best that American management insight and ingenuity have to offer on the manufacturing front. GE Fanuc points the way for the factory of the future: highly automated, yet leveraging its human capital to the fullest through empowerment and an open-book culture.

People Interviewed

Robert P. Collins, President and CEO

Larry E. Pearson, Senior Vice President, Finance

Donald C. Borwhat, Jr., Senior Vice President, Human Resources and Public Relations

Michelle M. Clatterbuck, Manager, Organization and Staffing

Donald S. Splaun, Jr., Manager, Advanced Manufacturing Technology

Ellen Greer, Comptroller

Factory Associates: Barbara Bishop, Flow-line Operator; Cindy Houston, HIWF Process Assistant; and Mark Lynch, Technician Trainee Program

References

Ted Forbes and Lynn A. Isabella, *GE Fanuc North America A, B, C.* Charlottesville: University of Virginia Darden School Foundation, 1993.

GE Fanuc Times, May 1997.

Gillian Flynn, "Workforce 2000 Begins Here," *Workforce*, May 1997, 78–84.

Endnote

1. Six Sigma refers to a defect reduction program that translates into no more than 3.4 defective parts per million.

5

Mid-States Technical Staffing Services, Inc.

We were sued by two employees who were stockholders. I'm on the witness stand testifying and the employees' attorney says to me, "Mr. Wilson, isn't it true that your company kept two sets of books?" And I said, "Yes, that is absolutely true, *technically*—we have always run cash basis statements and accrual basis statements because I run the company somewhere in between." And my employees believed that I was stealing money from the company because we had two sets of books, cash and accrual.

Fortunately, we had a judge who was a former businessperson and who knew those were two good sets of books and that everything was there. So when that was all done, I was pretty discouraged about being sued over information that had been misconstrued.

And as a result of that, I was really just ready to throw in the towel. The hell with the employees. I want nothing to do with this. I never needed to be this big in the first place. I can run a small company and make good money without all the headaches. I have always been a believer in open-book management, and I always ran the company that way from the day it was founded. But I met Jack Stack [CEO of SRC] and went down and spent some time with him.

What I learned was that my philosophy was fine, it was my methodology that was incorrect. And so that's when I kind of re-did it with the new methodology, and it restored my faith. The results were tremendous and after probably four years of being the chief executive of a high-stress, highly emotional organization, I became the chief executive of a place that was fun to work in and made more money than it did when it was chaos.

Steven D. Wilson, Founder and Former CEO,
Mid-States Technical Staffing Services, Inc.

5

Company Background

Mid-States Technical Staffing Services, Inc., was started by Steve Wilson in 1986 in Bettendorf, Iowa, to provide specialized engineering and drafting "temps" to local businesses. A company would contact Mid-States Technical to arrange for a temporary engineering or drafting specialist to work on its premises for a period of time. As with most temporary agencies, these contract positions could turn into full-time jobs. In the early years, Mid-States Technical was a franchisee of a national temporary agency but later broke off this affiliation.

In the late 1980s, Wilson saw a need to establish a separate operation to provide contract engineering and design services to clients off-site, in Mid-States Technical's own facility, using Mid-States Technical's employees and equipment. Previously, Mid-States Technical had as many as 58 of its temps, or contractors, working at the offices of John Deere, its largest client. The logistics of this had become unwieldy, so Wilson worked out an arrangement with John Deere for the work to be done at a Mid-States Technical design center to be set up nearby. A description of the services offered in the design centers appears in figure 5.1.

The company grew rapidly and was quite profitable. In 1991, Mid-States Technical was ranked 212th on *Inc.* 500's list of fastest growing private companies in the United States. But ironically, Wilson's greatest crisis occurred around this time also. As described earlier, Mid-States Technical was sued by two former employee-stockholders. The attorney's questioning of Wilson about two sets of books reflected a fairly common belief at Mid-States Technical that the company was considerably more profitable than Wilson had been telling his employees, and that Wilson was taking home an income several times higher than he professed—that he was "raiding the coffers," so to speak. Wilson did a survey of his employees in which he asked what they believed to be the company's percentage of net income to sales, among other things. Some employees responded with answers as high as 75 percent, when in actuality the percentage was closer to 7 percent.

Wilson eventually won the lawsuit, but he was hit hard by the realization that the employees simply did not believe the financial information he had been disseminating. Demoralized and discouraged, Wilson

Figure 5.1
Design Center Services

Design Center Services

Mid-States Technical Design Center is proud to offer a wide variety of design services. Our ongoing goal is to expand upon our capabilities and adapt to the changing needs of our customers.

Architectural Design and Drafting
Electrical Design and Drafting
Mechanical Design and Drafting
Tool Design
Technical Writing and Illustrating
Translation
(Paper to CAD, CAD to CAD, IGES, DXF)
3-D Wire Frame and Solid Modeling
Parametric Feature-Based Modeling and Design
Database Storage Facilities

Mid-States Technical operates with the latest revisions of Computervision's CADDS 4X and 5, Pro/ENGINEER, AutoCAD release 12, and Manual Board Design and Drafting, among others. Through our strategic alliances, we also offer a flexible workforce in any other engineering discipline you require.

Commitment

Utilizing the latest in computer software, our fully trained expert staff is committed to quality work in a timely fashion. Our staff offers

Fresh Design Perspectives
Efficient Budget Expenditures
Flexibility to meet your specific needs
Expertise and Professionalism

All employees at Mid-States Technical receive paid holidays; vacations; medical, dental, and life insurance; and pension benefits. These benefits help ensure long-term commitments to your projects and programs.

Maximize Manpower Flexibility Without High Costs

Our services will help you cut costs by *eliminating:* Overloads and Backlog, Recruiting Expenses, Continuous Retraining, Payroll Taxes, Unemployment Costs, Vacations, Holidays, Fringe Benefits, Pension Costs, Administrative Complications, Computer Utilization Expenses, and Computer Obsolescence.

Source: Company marketing literature

finally found his solution in what he called "real" open-book management as opposed to the flawed version he had been practicing.

Open-book management was formally implemented at Mid-States Technical during 1993. In late 1993, Mid-States Technical was acquired by AccuStaff Incorporated, a large temporary staffing company based in Florida. In a fairly standard earn-out arrangement, Wilson continued as CEO of Mid-States Technical for three years, stepping down in January 1997. During the earn-out period, Wilson continued the day-to-day management of Mid-States Technical and was able to earn substantial sums if the company's growth exceeded certain targets, which it did. Since January 1997, Wilson has provided consulting services to Mid-States Technical and to AccuStaff, and has pursued other business interests. Between 1993 and the present, Wilson has become something of an open-book management guru, lecturing frequently about his successful experience with open-book management. In fact, Wilson and Mid-States Technical were the subject of an entire chapter in John Case's seminal 1995 book, *Open-Book Management: The Coming Business Revolution.*

AccuStaff is a high-growth New York Stock Exchange company, with sales of $2 billion, a price-earnings ratio of about 35, and a total market capitalization of some $3 billion. But AccuStaff was a private company at the time of the Mid-States Technical acquisition in 1993. AccuStaff went public in an initial offering in August 1994, at a price of $2 per share, adjusted for two subsequent stock splits. Since then, the stock price has increased to a current level of about $25 per share, reflecting a compound annual growth rate of 132 percent. The AccuStaff Internet site contains a description of the company and its activities (figure 5.2).

Mid-States Technical has seven offices located in Iowa, Indiana, and Kentucky. Four of these are stand-alone design centers, performing drafting and other services for clients and employing engineers and draftsmen. The locations in Davenport, Indianapolis, and Louisville house design centers and provide staffing services (placement of temporary professional workers). Company revenues are split about 50-50 between contract engineering/design work and staffing services. Until just recently, Mid-States Technical was the only open-book subsidiary of AccuStaff. A recent AccuStaff acquisition also uses open-book management but apparently not to the extent that Mid-States Technical does.

Figure 5.2
AccuStaff (parent) Company Description, Internet Home Page

Services
AccuStaff Incorporated, headquartered in Jacksonville, Florida, is an international provider of business services, including consulting, outsourcing, training, and strategic staffing services, to leading businesses. The Company is organized into four divisions: *Professional Services,* which provides personnel for technical/engineering, scientific staffing, legal, and accounting functions; *Information Technology,* which provides project management, consulting services and skilled IT personnel; *Commercial,* which provides clerical, office automation and light industrial services; and *Teleservices,* which provides international customers with trained customer care and telemarketing personnel. What sets AccuStaff apart from the rest of the staffing industry is our unique company culture and our customized services to our clients. AccuStaff is a company of specialists, rather than a specialist company. Our industry-focused professional managers are resident in dedicated specialty service offices. Our decentralized and entrepreneurial culture drives quality service delivery in each market we serve.

History
AccuStaff Incorporated was formed through the merger of four regional staffing companies, each with a solid history of staffing expertise in their local and regional markets. The company has grown internally through strategic acquisitions and through opening of branch offices to expand client partnerships. On November 15, 1996, a merger with Career Horizons, Inc., was completed, making AccuStaff the fourth largest U.S. provider of strategic staffing, consulting, and outsourcing services. AccuStaff now has more than 950 branch, franchise, and associated offices in 45 states, the District of Columbia, Canada, and the United Kingdom, and combined annual estimated revenues in excess of $2 billion in 1997. One of the fastest growing providers of strategic staffing solutions, AccuStaff became a public company on August 16, 1994. Its common stock trades on the New York Stock Exchange under the symbol ASI.

Vision 2000
Our growth strategy is to become an international premier strategic staffing organization.

AccuStaff Companies
AccuStaff has grown tremendously over the past several years through strategic acquisitions in all areas of business, and as a result, operates today under many names. Although the Commercial Division has begun transitioning to the AccuStaff name, the Professional Services areas will keep separate operating names because it is critical to their professional image and reputation. This strategy is consistent with the concept of AccuStaff as a "company of specialists" rather than a generalist or a singular specialist company.

5

Wilson and Mid-States Technical's senior management attribute much of the company's financial success and its favorable work climate to open-book management.

Wilson did very well in the AccuStaff buyout. In a February 1997 article in *Inc.,* he was quoted as saying, "If this had been a straight cash transaction, my company would have gone for 3 to 5 times earnings, but since it's part of a roll-up, Wall Street places the value at 10 to 12 times earnings."[1] The article also noted that with the buyout Wilson had achieved his objective of wanting "work to be optional by age 44." Although it's probably impossible to quantify this in dollar terms, Wilson and others believe that much of the attractiveness of Mid-States Technical as a merger candidate in late 1993 was due to the company's successful implementation of a formal open-book management system. AccuStaff founder and then-President and CEO Delores Kesler confirmed this:

> Steve is very much an engineer in his approach to management and to his business. He has that plan-full, methodical process that he brings to almost everything he does that we saw in relationship to developing his company and to running Mid-States Technical. And we felt his embracing the open-book management process was a true advantage in the acquisition of Mid-States Technical by AccuStaff because all his employees and key managers were inside the loop.
>
> They were very aware of what was going on in the company. There were no secrets. They were a part of its success, and they felt that what they were doing was an integral part of the company's development. They also knew that going forward they would be a part of the success after the acquisition as a part of AccuStaff. There were no surprises in the process as sometimes can be the case if the employees are brought some information. So the open-book management concept, I think, was a big part of his success prior to the acquisition by AccuStaff as well as afterwards.

Imagine such a view a year earlier when Wilson was still reeling from the effects of the lawsuit and the accompanying internal strife and mistrust.

The Origins of Open-Book Management at Mid-States Technical

Jack [Stack] and Norm Brodsky [CEO of CitiStorage] were speakers at the *Inc.* 500 conference, and they were doing a presentation on whether or not to give your employees equity. Jack is a big believer in giving equity; Norm Brodsky is totally opposed to giving equity. And of course Jack and Norm are on opposite points on many issues. Both very successful, just different styles. And in that presentation it was getting to be somewhat of a dog fight. And I made the comment that really what you're telling us is, if you give your people equity, it will not cause them to think like owners. But if you can get them to think like owners, then it's acceptable to give them equity.

And that statement put Norm and Jack on the same wavelength. So that was really the issue. And afterwards Jack came up to me and just told me how much he appreciated my comment to calm things down, and he said, "You obviously think the way I do." And I'm sitting here being sued by my stockholders who don't think like owners, and yet I'm still wanting to give equity. And so that's what really started that relationship with Jack. And I told Jack, "Quite honestly, right now I'm on Norm's side but I understand where you're coming from. I made the mistake of giving people equity *before they thought like owners.*"

Steve Wilson

The early 1990s were prosperous times for Mid-States Technical, yet the company in many ways was in utter chaos. The following three problems were at the root of the company's difficulties:

- **Problem No. 1—The Lawsuit.** Two of Mid-States Technical's key salespeople left the company in 1991. At the time, Mid-States Technical had six stockholders including these employees. When they were originally given their shares, they each signed a noncompete agreement. According to Wilson, one of his competitors financed the lawsuit, which had as its goal the nullification of the noncompete agreements. Wilson ultimately prevailed but not without heavy dollar cost, loss of focus, many sleepless nights, and considerable soul-searching about the "two sets of books" issue. Wilson estimates that the lawsuit caused a 30 percent loss in volume and a greater than 50 percent drop in profits.

- **Problem No. 2—Internal Turmoil.** Again according to Wilson, the two departing employees had intentionally generated considerable strife during their last six months with the company, apparently in anticipation of leaving.
- **Problem No. 3—The Persian Gulf War.** This conflict upended Mid-States Technical's growth forecasts.

Wilson was ready to do things differently, and so he turned to Jack Stack and open-book management for help. Chief Operating Officer (COO) Jim Kieffer, who was manager of the Dubuque design center at the time, recalls the following:

> Four of us got in our van and we drove down there [to Springfield, Missouri] and went through the [open-book management] conference. To be honest, I was really excited about it because I was not financially literate myself. I had been reading a lot of income statements. Steve was starting to share income statements with me before we went there and was starting to talk about sales and whatnot. I needed to know. Dan Rather was doing a show there at the same time—very exciting!
>
> Steve scheduled training for the four of us to go through a strategic planning process after we got back. We hired a local accounting firm and took advantage of strategic planning methods. Steve had made the decision even before going to Springfield that he knew to succeed and to continue to grow that other people had to be capable of making decisions, understanding why we did what we did, knowing the critical numbers of the business. He said, "Don't be afraid of open-book management. If anything, it's going to benefit you as a manager."

Wilson, Kieffer, and their colleagues returned from Springfield highly motivated and ready to reap the benefits of open-book management for Mid-States Technical.

Wilson said earlier that his pre-1993 open-book philosophy was fine but his methodology was flawed. By this, he meant that he had shared financial information with his employees, but the process was an empty one because (1) most employees really didn't believe the information, and (2) those who did had little power to influence the numbers and had no stake in the outcome. This situation prompted his conclusion that he had given equity to selected employees before they "thought like owners." To correct these problems and implement open-book management so that it would work, Wilson and his managers focused their efforts on training, incentives, and empowerment.

Training: Building Financial Literacy

> How can you put together a team if the players don't get to see the playbook? If the players don't know all the rules of the game, and the coach is trying to educate them move by move: "No, don't do that, you'll be out of bounds." And the player's saying, "Where the hell is out of bounds?" "Don't worry about it. I'll tell you when you get close." Or the coach has to walk out on the field between every play and give each individual player his instructions for the next play.
>
> You can't build a team without an effective communication process, and I don't believe you can have an effective communication process if people don't have *business literacy.* We communicate so much more effectively now [at Mid-States Technical] because they can speak financially. It doesn't take good instinct and caring and people out of it; it just puts it in the context of the fact that we're a business. We're a social organization second, and a business organization first. So we teach you the business language and then we can have a social conversation.
>
> Steve Wilson

By necessity, building financial literacy was the first step in Wilson's implementation of open-book management. And he began the process in an interesting and cryptic way:

> We posted all the financial information for almost three months before we ever launched: put it on the bulletin boards. [Employees] were beginning to wonder what all this stuff was. And the managers paid attention to who was asking questions, who was looking at it. And people looked at it and didn't really understand it and were wondering what it was all about. And we let them try to figure it out.
>
> And then we did our one-day launch and said, "That's why the numbers have been up there. We're going to teach you what they mean: that's your job security. We're going to teach you to walk up to that board and know exactly what's going on around here and get you involved in running this company."

At the outset, Wilson handled much of the training himself. After an initial one-day program for all employees led by people from Springfield ReManufacturing, Wilson traveled to each of the locations with a supply of facsimile "Mid-States Technical Money," and in a series of four hour-and-a-half sessions took the employees through a game simulation of how a real business works, but in somewhat simplified terms. Wilson explains his purpose as follows:

> I built the training because there wasn't any really good training material available. And what I actually did was I built a simplified model of running your own little design operation. We took them through it, showed them how it ran for the year, and then we put up their division's year-end financial statement and that was it. They had just run their division for the prior year, so it was very relevant to them because it wasn't a fictitious deal. It was at the end their own deal . . . with simplified numbers. We didn't get into a lot of little details.

The memory of Wilson's training sessions is still fresh in COO Kieffer's mind:

> Steve came around to every division, and he bought everybody pizza, and he asked them to sit down and have lunch with him. And he trained them. He set up different buckets where you put your money. He borrowed a hundred grand from "Granny" to set up a business. He went through and showed them how you can run out

> of cash in a hurry without reviewing accounts receivable issues. He went through the whole cash flow. And that caught everybody's interest right out of the chute. It really educated them: yeah, it takes money to be able to go out and take a risk like this and make something successful.
>
> This is what a computer costs, this is what the software costs, this is the maintenance to use that software. Here's what the plotter did. Then he went through and really detailed and explained monthly expenses, the full set-up of operations. After that he started following up with explaining about sales, how we break out our dollars, how we price our stuff, explaining about labor pricing versus facility pricing, and then how, after we take out our employee cost [of sales], we get our gross margin.

Kieffer believes that Wilson was correct in doing the training himself, especially since there had been so much suspicion and mistrust on the part of employees regarding the numbers Wilson had been sharing with them previously. Says Kieffer:

> Coming from the man who ran the business, the man who started the business, our employees truly believe that he wanted to do this. I think hearing it from someone else may have made them wonder, does Steve still have his own books and are they showing us separate books? They found out right away that these *are* the books.

By all accounts, these initial sessions were very productive and encouraging. Employees could now read and interpret those financial statements that had mysteriously appeared one day in a prominent place on the company bulletin boards.

Follow-up training with existing employees has been much more informal and spontaneous. Wilson thinks that is fine:

> A lot of this is financial literacy and not classroom training. It's just every week, working with the numbers. It's getting them to ask questions and get curious and get involved. And then, when they ask the question, giving them a reasonable, simple answer and encouraging them to work the numbers themselves, getting the salespeople to compute their own margins. And if you're going to give a guy overtime, or you're discounting a price, what does that do?

> And we give them worksheets to go through that. We walk them through every number. It's repeat. It's every day. We train all the time, but we don't do a lot of formal training anymore.

The company holds monthly meetings in each division to review the previous month's numbers, and this process reinforces the employees' financial knowledge. Operations Manager Brenda Wiese explains the process:

> We take the division's financial statements and put them on a transparency, and then one person a month has to present the information. We try to get them to volunteer: "Who wants to do it next month?" Last month, Lorie [in Administrative Services] did it [for the Davenport office]. She was responsible for standing up there and going over the financial statements. How the sales were and how direct costs were—if there's a problem with one line item, she might go through that.

Wiese says attendance is good at these monthly meetings; they're held during the lunch hour and the food is free. But beyond that, employees covered by the bonus plan want to know the latest information about the next bonus payment. And employees who are not included in the bonus plan still demonstrate a strong interest in how their division is doing. New hires do not go through any special training, so the monthly meetings are an important source of on-the-job training for them.

Incentives: Team Building and the "Bucket"

> How well would a football team work if the linemen are paid straight salary, and the backfield gets paid by the yards gained, and the ends are on a different pay plan? Everybody gets back into the huddle and wants the play called according to their best earning capacity. So if the ends get paid per catch, they don't really care whether it's a 2-yard pass or a 40-yard pass. And they start thinking, "Well jeez, I get paid the same if I take two steps and catch the ball as if I run my butt all the way down the field." And the backs are saying, "Well don't pass the ball because we don't make any money

> unless we run the ball." And the linemen are saying, "I wish you people would shut up and let's play the game."
>
> So that's why I felt I really had to do away with individual incentives. I later came to believe that probably a group incentive is acceptable. But you have to have a very, very careful balance; individual, group versus total company. And you have to ensure that nobody's individual incentive motivates them more than their teamwork incentive.
>
> [In 1993] we were in decline because of internal strife and competition, interdivisional strife and competition, prima donnas—just a tremendous lack of team spirit and cooperation in the organization.
>
> Steve Wilson

In 1993, Steve Wilson believed strongly that a single, uniform incentive plan was needed at Mid-States Technical to encourage all employees to work toward the common goal of overall company profitability. He was already dedicated to a full implementation of a formal open-book management program. So he devised an incentive plan that would provide a healthy bonus to all employees based on total company pretax income. He would pay the bonus periodically to the employees, and the open-book management information would advise the employees of the company's progress toward the bonus payouts. He didn't need cash flow to be incorporated directly into the plan because, as a service company with no inventory and stable, quality receivables, cash flow tended to parallel profits.

Wilson was unhappy with the idea of using the conventional accounting periods of month or quarter to calculate the bonus. For one thing, he considered them an arbitrary "accounting thing." And perhaps more important, they did not provide a realistic view of profitability because of one fundamental truth about the economics of Mid-States Technical's business: owing to its heavily labor-intensive cost structure, there were extra expenses early in the fiscal year for taxes and other payroll items that are "capped." That is, once a maximum for a given employee is reached during the year, no further cost is incurred for that particular expense for that employee. Examples of this are the employer's share of social security taxes, and federal and state unemployment taxes. Obviously, the company must price its services based on the average wage across the entire year; clients could not very well pay a higher price early in the year and a lower price later in the year. So Mid-States Technical naturally expects profits to be proportionately lower early in the year and higher later when these payroll items max out. A bonus plan based on profits during an accounting period would not be satisfactory because bonuses would start out too low and end up too high.

Instead, Wilson came up with a novel approach that has been discussed often in the open-book management literature since then: the bucket. The concept of the bucket is very—almost deceptively—simple. A bucket is defined as an earnings amount, say $150,000. When total pretax earnings for the year reach $150,000, the bucket is full, a bonus is paid, and a new bucket is begun. The bonus percentage has varied, but it is currently 7.5 percent for the first bucket and increases by 2.5 percentage points for each subsequent bucket to a maximum of 20 percent. If a certain sales growth target is met at the same time the bucket is filled, then the bonus payout is doubled. The bucket size started at $75,000. It remained at that level for two years, and then was doubled to $150,000 for two years.

When asked how he came up with the bucket size, Wilson candidly explains his methodology:

> I determined what the company should post as net income to be competitive in the marketplace. What is our desired result? Then I take that number and I multiply it by 1.35, which is the inflator for taxes on the bonus and all that kind of stuff. And then I make the assumption that ideally bonuses should go out every two months on the average. I like two months. Monthly is too often. Quarterly is not often enough. So my desired number times 1.35 divided by 6 is my bucket size, and then rounded to a reasonable number. And what that should do is allow us to pay out six bonuses during the year, pay the taxes on those bonuses, and come in with slightly more than my target amount.

When asked, Design and Drafting Specialist John Hentges in the Dubuque design center knew without prompting exactly how the bucket size was determined and explained it in a way similar to that of Wilson. Clearly, employees understand this incentive plan and what it can do for them.

Given the front-loaded payroll expenses, it takes about four months for the first bucket to be filled. But near the end of the year, a bucket is filled "every three or four weeks." The divisions post a picture of the bucket prominently on the employee bulletin board. Each week, the bucket is colored to the point where it is filled. Once the bucket is full, employees are paid the bonus the next week, and it is split among employees in proportion to each employee's pay. A description of a bonus calculation appears in figure 5.3.

When he implemented the bucket plan, Wilson eliminated the commissions that had been paid to the sales force manning the staffing side of the business. These salespeople were paid a commission on the income derived from their placement of temps. Mid-States Technical had been experiencing a problem referred to in the company as "hoarding résumés." An attractive résumé might be sent to the company from a prospective temp worker. A salesperson could come across the résumé (seeing it first early in the morning, for instance) and put it out of sight, and then later personally solicit the placement for this temp. Other salespeople wouldn't know about the résumé and thus have no opportunity to place the temp and earn a commission. Clearly, this was an

Figure 5.3
Employee Bonus Plan Calculation

The Mid-States Technical bucket plan currently applies only to design center and administrative employees. It has been eliminated for the staffing services employees.

Mid-States Technical distributes bonuses to employees as soon as a bucket is filled. Assume the bucket size is $150,000 and the initial bonus percentage is 7.5 percent. When pretax profit hits $150,000 (historically about four months into the fiscal year), the total bonus pool is $11,250 (7.5 percent × 150,000). This amount is divided according to each employee's regular income. For example, suppose an employee makes $30,000 per year, out of a total hypothetical payroll of $2 million. Then that employee would receive a bonus check of about $170 ($30,000 ÷ $2 million × $11,250). In addition, if a pre-established sales growth target is hit at the same time a bucket is filled, then the bucket is doubled and the hypothetical employee would receive $340 instead of $170.

The bonus percentage increases to 10 percent for bucket 2, 12.5 percent for bucket 3, and so on, to a maximum of 20 percent. In a recent year, the total bonus was about $3,700 per employee.

unhealthy situation. Such counterproductive developments soured Wilson on the notion of individual incentives, a distaste that he maintains to this day.

Removing the commission plan for salespeople and replacing it with a bucket plan covering all employees, salespeople and engineers alike, was bound to be controversial. When asked how he "sold" it to his salespeople, Wilson gave the following response:

> Great piece of advice a guy gave me one time—one of my accountants. If you can afford to buy your way out of a problem, do you really have a problem? So I brought all the sales guys in and said, "What would it cost me to take you off commission?" And we set up a salary program and I grandfathered them in.
>
> They had already given me their sales plan. I computed what their commissions would be on their sales plan and what they made in the current year. We arrived at a number that I guaranteed them for two years while we set up a salary structure. Then they would know where they were in the salary structure; that they would be able to do whatever necessary to adjust their performance to the salary structure; and that they would never be paid less than the guaranteed amount.

Only recently (as Wilson's earn-out contract was expiring) did Mid-States Technical return to the commission plan for salespeople. COO Kieffer explained that the new division manager of the staffing operation felt that he could show greater profitability with the more traditional and direct incentive of commissions. And recent results have borne this out. Mid-States Technical has instituted controls to reduce the possibility of résumé hoarding, lessening the danger of using commissions. Kieffer and Operations Manager Wiese, both strong open-book advocates, are somewhat skeptical of the long-term effects of the change, but for now, the benefits of the commission plan seem to outweigh the potential costs of diluting the effect of open-book management in the staffing side of the business.

Empowerment: Owning a Line Item

> Communication is vastly improved [with open-book management]. And to me the greatest thing is I used to be so frustrated, scared, upset—sleepless nights—because I had to make every decision here. And through open-book management, I was able to effectively delegate over two years probably 85 percent of my responsibilities. And previously when I tried to do it, it didn't work. And then I would get into a scuffle with them and they'd hand it back to me because they really didn't understand.
>
> That'd be like the coach telling the quarterback to call the plays but I've never given him the playbook. So he's out there trying to make up plays and I'm bitching at him from the sidelines, and when he does a bad play, I haul him over to the sideline and do a Woody Hayes on him and beat him up with the cooler because "that was a stupid play." "Well coach, what am I supposed to do? You just told me to go out and call plays."
>
> I really think one of the smartest things we did was to set up decision-making authorities. We created three levels of authority in the organization and assigned at what level decisions are to be made. And as well as granting authority to that level, we specifically *prohibited* any other level from making those decisions.
>
> Steve Wilson

Empowerment is observed most readily at Mid-States Technical in the notion of "ownership" of a budget line item. Most full-time employees who have been with the company for at least a year are responsible for budgeting and spending a particular line item of expense. (Some administrative employees own two or more line items.) Design Specialist Hentges, who owns the supplies line item for his division, explains as follows:

> Every November I have to put together a budget, a list of items that I am going to purchase throughout the year and when I'm going to

> purchase them. This is what I submit [to management], and they go over everybody's line items, and they kind of critique them; they take some things out to trim the fat off, so to speak.
>
> I have items budgeted for each month and I just purchase them. Every month we look at what's called a "trial balance" and everybody who has a line item goes down through their line item—they look to see what money was spent. I check mine.
>
> Because our bonus is kind of based on our performance, if I say I'm going to spend this much money [on supplies] and I spend a lot more than that, this could affect the payout of my bonus.

And everybody in the division would know that Hentges' line item was off as well, and that it would affect their bonuses. Hentges says the others always give him "a hard time about it" when that happens.

Responsibility for the line items is rotated among employees every year or so. Employees train their successors on the line items and make them experts on that particular item of expense. A sample budget worksheet (for administrative employee benefits) appears in figure 5.4.

This worksheet is the standard format used by Mid-States Technical for all budgeted expense line items throughout the company. Key characteristics of the worksheet include the following:

- The name of the preparer-owner (e.g., Lorie) is identified.
- The expense is budgeted for each month of the fiscal year.
- The expense is further broken down by component. For instance, component 2 for Employee Benefits is insurance.
- Supporting detail and/or computations are shown in the section called Notes. For example, the monthly expense of $240 for insurance is made up of $80 for the employee with initials BW, $80 for WM, and so on.
- Actual results are entered on the worksheet as they become available, and a percentage of actual to budget is calculated.

Lorie Reem, Senior Administrative Specialist in the Davenport home office, started with Mid-States Technical after the initial implementation of open-book management. We asked her how she adapted

Figure 5.4
Sample Budget Worksheet

MID-STATES TECHNICAL

Division: ADMIN		BUDGET WORKSHEET										Date:		8/12/97
Account #: 3420-0500		Description: EMPLOYEE BENEFITS										By: LORIE		
#	Budget item	Jan	Feb	Mar	Apr	May	Jun	Jul	Aug	Sep	Oct	Nov	Dec	TOTAL
1	AAA	$138				$46	$46							$230
2	insurance	$240	$240	$240	$240	$240	$240	$240	$240	$240	$240	$240	$240	$2,880
3	xmas party & activity & books	$4,000										$1,250		$5,250
4	joint emp trust	$10	$10	$10	$10	$10	$10	$10	$10	$10	$10	$10	$10	$120
5	games/cards/ candy/misc	$85	$85	$85	$85	$85	$85	$85	$85	$85	$85	$85	$85	$1,020
6	sams						$65							$65
7	tuition/wellness		$400			$400			$400			$400		$1,600
8	401k fee							$4,000					$1,500	$5,500
9	shirts for employees				$150							$2,500		$2,650
10	golf chamber function meals						$100		$100					$200
	TOTAL	$4,473	$735	$335	$485	$781	$546	$4,335	$835	$335	$335	$4,485	$1,835	$19,515
	ACTUAL													
	% ACTUAL/BUDGET													

#	NOTES
1	BW JK SM 1/YR LR 5/YR SI 6/Y 138 46 46 46 TO RENEW IOWA 56 NEW IOWA
2	BW 80 WM 80 JK 25 SI 55 240 240 240 240 240 240 240 240 240 240 240 240
3	XMAS PARTY 1/98 FEST OF TREES 11/98 $1000 BOOKS 11/98 $50 EACH * 5 1250
4	$10 / MO FEE
5	APPROX $25 GAMES, $20 CANDY, $40 CARDS
6	6/YR $10 RENEW*4+OWNER$25 65
7	WELLNESS $400 / EMP - 1 / QUARTER GUESS TUITION JPK 12/98
8	GUESS
9	APPROX $25 EACH - EMP PICKS UP BALANCE 150 ADM ONLY ALL MST 2500
10	

to the open-book management environment at Mid-States Technical. She answered, "It is just such a routine part of the business, and nothing is questioned. This is part of your job, and you will be in charge of line items. It is nothing that you would even question whether you want to be a part of it. And I think that has a lot to do with Steve Wilson having been so active in it."

Life as an Open-Book Subsidiary of a Public Company

The only inside information that Mid-States Technical employees have access to is for their own company. No AccuStaff inside information is ever distributed. So there are no concerns about adhering to Securities and Exchange Commission (SEC) rules regarding the practice of open-book management at Mid-States Technical. However, if, after the 1993 acquisition of Mid-States Technical, AccuStaff had imposed corporate policies and procedures, the "true" open-book management that Wilson and Kieffer had worked so hard to put in place could have been weakened or even eliminated. Fortunately, AccuStaff operates in a relatively decentralized fashion and rarely interferes in the internal operations of a subsidiary that is performing up to par. Remember also that AccuStaff founder and then-CEO Kesler had been particularly impressed with the success of Mid-States Technical's open-book management culture and labeled it an advantage in the acquisition. In addition, Wilson is quick to point out that AccuStaff could do nothing during the three-year earn-out period to negatively affect his ability to earn the incentive dollars built into his contract. Had AccuStaff attempted to dismantle Mid-States Technical's open-book management structure and had this move impacted sales and profits, Wilson might have had a cause of action against AccuStaff under his contract.

Philosophy aside, Wilson is pragmatic when he comments on AccuStaff's approach to Mid-States Technical:

> We're too busy making money and growing. Another one of my great expressions is "You never stop the parade to pick up a dime." And that's kind of the way AccuStaff is. We're marching on. We don't bicker about a lot of stuff. And so they [AccuStaff manage-

> ment] have always been supportive [of us]. Their attitude is, "Hey, the way you run your company is obviously successful. We're not going to tell you how to run it; just keep doing it."

These words take on additional significance when one considers how important Mid-States Technical was at one point in AccuStaff's growth curve. Says Wilson:

> The employees would get the published quarterly and annual AccuStaff reports and—it was kind of fascinating—they would come back to me the first year and say, "Damn, Steve, this year we produced 6 percent of the corporate revenues, but 26 percent of their net income."

Kieffer concurs with Wilson in his observation of AccuStaff's relationship with Mid-States Technical:

> One of the things that AccuStaff was very good about doing is they allowed us to continue our entrepreneurial spirit and they let us alone. For three years, AccuStaff never did a thing to us. Because we were so good at budgeting and producing our numbers, they believed in us. We always told them we'll do what we say and we did. So we always exceeded the goals and they had no reason to do anything. [AccuStaff President and CEO] Derek Dewan told me several times, "You guys are the best at budgeting in the organization."

It is interesting that Mid-States Technical does not have an official chief financial officer (CFO). Operations Manager Wiese (who has an accounting degree) performs many of the standard functions of a CFO but without the title. Mid-States Technical has *never* had a CFO since its founding in 1986; the establishment of open-book management at Mid-States Technical has not changed that fact. When asked if open-book management eliminated the need for a CFO, Wilson responded as follows:

> You need a CFO who's willing to play a different role. I would tell you, and if we continue to use the game analysis, as CEO, I'm the head coach and general manager, my COO is my offense coordinator and my CFO is my defensive coordinator. And I need them both.

Mid-States Technical, he noted, can do without a CFO because of the company's relatively simple finances—no inventory and relatively clean receivables.

His prior comments notwithstanding, Wilson feels that many accounting and finance-oriented people will have a real problem with open-book management because of a perceived loss of control. He believes that Wiese's predecessor left the company after open-book management was implemented for that very reason: "In her mind, her power was based on her control of the information, and she was not comfortable with the fact that the power really *didn't* have to do with controlling the information." Wilson is somewhat stinging and unequivocal in his criticism:

> Accountants are not strong supporters of real open-book management. It's the control issue because what we have to do for open-book management to work is to convince every employee that business literacy and business finance are not that difficult. And yet, when I've got a guy with an MBA, he has a vested interest in proving to everybody that it *is* that difficult. And to me that's kind of like the difference between being my defensive coordinator [in football] and an ESPN commentator. I need a defensive coordinator, not somebody on the sidelines critiquing the way we're playing the game. And accountants tend not to get down in the trenches.
>
> And it's unfortunate because if they could learn our way and help me bridge between the fundamentals of business and the high-level techniques that they're so good at, it would be an enhancement—instead of a conflict.

There is little doubt that open-book management has had a strong and lasting positive impact on the culture of Mid-States Technical. COO Kieffer is not one to make dramatic statements, but his view of what open-book management has done for him personally is unequivocal: "I owe a lot of my career and my success to open-book management. If Steve Wilson had never let me have the ability to truly make decisions, truly to run my numbers, I never would have been assertive enough to get where I am today."

Case Summary

From the formation of Mid-States Technical Staffing Services in 1986, founder Steve Wilson had always thought he was an "open-book" manager. A grueling lawsuit and trial in the early 1990s convinced him otherwise. Many Mid-States Technical employees thought he kept two sets of books; that he showed them the pessimistic numbers; and that he based his own take-home pay on the actual, much higher numbers.

A shaken Wilson vowed to fix things or turn Mid-States Technical over to someone else. He ultimately found the solution in "real" open-book management. Taking his cues from Jack Stack at SRC, Wilson focused on teaching business literacy, and did most of the training himself; providing incentives to his employees to work as a team for the common good by setting up his now-legendary bucket plan; and empowering his employees by making them individually responsible for the budgeting and control of expense line items.

Success came quickly and dramatically. A year after the open-book management launch, Wilson sold his company to AccuStaff in a very lucrative transaction. AccuStaff's founder attributes much of Mid-States Technical's attractiveness as a buyout candidate to the open-book management culture that was flourishing there. In his final three years at the helm of Mid-States Technical, Wilson was finally a happy businessman: stress was low, profits were high, and peace reigned.

People Interviewed

Delores Kesler, Founder and Former President and CEO, AccuStaff Incorporated

Steve Wilson, Founder and Former President and CEO, Mid-States Technical Staffing Services, Inc.

From Mid-States Technical Staffing Services, Inc.:

- Jim Kieffer, Vice President and Chief Operating Officer
- Brenda Wiese, Operations Manager
- Lorie Reem, Senior Administrative Specialist
- John Hentges, Design/Drafting Specialist

5

Reference

John Case, *Open-Book Management: The Coming Business Revolution*, New York: HarperBusiness, 1995.

Endnote

1. Hal Plotkin, "Jig may be up on fantastic stock multiples from roll-up acquisitions," *Inc.*, Feb. 1997:22.

North American Signs

Introduction

North American Signs (NAS), founded in 1934 by the late Maurice P. Yarger as South Bend Neon, was a venture into neon—a new discovery in business identification. The company's slogan was "Business goes where neon glows!"

The company has greatly expanded since then, from a South Bend firm serving the local area to a national organization with accounts such as The Limited, OfficeMax, Barnes & Noble, and Red Roof Inns. To reflect this shift in business, the company's name was changed to North American Signs in 1974. NAS also has a different slogan: "Our goal is helping you reach yours." The goal in the slogan has a double meaning: to help customers increase their profits by supplying them with well-designed and well-built signs, and to help associates reach their goals of security, self-development, and financial stability.

Now one of the top 100 sign companies in the nation, NAS had just under 100 employees and sales of more than $11 million in 1996. It is run by the founder's two sons, Noel Yarger, president, and Tom Yarger, vice president. The company is owned by Noel, Tom, and their mother, Carolyn Blake.

NAS's experience with open-book management has been a gradual, ongoing evolution. The company did not make a one-time, decisive conversion to open-book management, nor did it do so in response to any specific crisis or challenge. Instead, open-book management has evolved naturally from NAS's long-standing tradition of treating its employees inclusively and as a potent resource. NAS's success with open-book management has reconfirmed its deep commitment to open-book ideals; however, the company also realizes some of open-book management's potential problems and continues to fine-tune certain features in response to such problems.

Two factors have made NAS's experience with open-book management particularly challenging and instructive: The company is privately held and unionized. Both factors have presented special difficulties with regard to disclosing financial information, which the company has had to overcome to continue its commitment to the open-book philosophy.

Evolution of Open-Book Management

NAS has always considered itself a company with a deep respect for its employees, and thus has long provided them with opportunities to improve personally as well as professionally. This respect is rooted in the owners' personal values on family, church, and community involvement. Sharing information about the company is a natural outgrowth of their inclusive view of employees as members of the NAS family or community. As a result, NAS had been practicing elements of open-book management long before the company had ever heard the term.

When the Yargers did learn about the concept of open-book management, their response was enthusiastic. Tom Yarger heard what Jack Stack was doing at SRC and asked a number of staff to read Stack's book, *The Great Game of Business.* Since then, key NAS personnel have visited SRC and attended the Gathering of the Games conference. According to company Controller Mike Major, the decision to commit NAS more solidly to open-book management came from the Yargers themselves, while "the rest of us have augmented and kind of preached the gospel."

Although the company's implementation of open-book management has been gradual, several key events and decisions have marked the transition. In 1989 NAS created two internal teams to develop ideas for improving productivity and for helping the company grow and become more profitable. Out of the teams' work came the decision to implement a gain-sharing program for NAS employees. To keep employees apprised of the company's financial performance and the status of the gain-sharing bonus, Major began conducting monthly, half-hour meetings to share financial information. He also made himself available regularly to answer employees' questions on a more informal basis.

In 1994 the company started to share sales information with its employees. But once it did so, NAS leadership realized the need to provide more formal training so employees could interpret the data and understand more thoroughly what the numbers meant. This commitment to more formal training was implemented in 1996, coinciding with a major overhaul of the company's gain-sharing program.

From 1989 through 1996, NAS's gain-sharing program was based on keeping controllable costs below a level determined by cross-functional teams that went through the chart of accounts and identified expenses employees could control. As long as company expenses were below 82 percent of controllable expenses, a bonus was paid, subject to a work-in-process (WIP) adjustment.

One of the problems with the original format was that it did not tie directly to profits. For example, NAS might produce many signs in August but might have to wait until September to bill for 80 percent of them. However, the company was trying to measure and pay bonuses based on its actual productivity during August. NAS used a complicated WIP adjustment that was difficult even for financial people to understand.

To solve these problems, the company changed its gain-sharing plan in 1996, tying it directly to profits. In the current formula, NAS starts with a 3-percent profit baseline, which means that on both a monthly and cumulative year-to-date basis, the company has to generate a 3-percent profit on sales before paying any bonus. Once the 3-percent goal is reached, the company shares profits equally with its employees, although it holds back a 20-percent reserve until the end of the year in case of losses.

The bonus is based entirely on the number of hours worked, and employees working overtime get one-and-a-half times or twice the hours for overtime work. To establish a bonus rate per hour, NAS divides the total bonus dollars by all the hours worked by the entire company. Everybody receives the same bonus rate. (See table 6.1.)

Management changed its gain-sharing formula so people could understand more clearly how the company's performance affected the bonus. Under the old plan, it was difficult for people to see how changing a particular number or doing things a little better would affect the bonus. Perhaps the major problem with the old plan was the complicated WIP adjustment. Theoretically, gross margins of particular jobs

Table 6.1
Monthly Gain-Sharing Calculation

Monthly	JAN	FEB	MAR	APR. . . . . .DEC
Sales				
Margin $				
Margin percentage				
Building				
Art				
Selling				
Expediting				
Office				
Administrative				
Interest				
Step payout				
Total Overhead				
Other Income (Loss)				
Net Income Before Taxes				
Percentage of profit				
3-percent profit baseline				
Percentage of profit over 3 percent				
1. Bonus pool				
2. Prior month (loss) recovery				
3. Net bonus pool (#1 – #2)				
4. 20 percent bonus reserve (#3 × 20 percent)				
5. 10 percent (loss) reserve (#3 × 10 percent)				
6. Bonus (#3 – #4)				
7. 50 percent employee share (#6 × 50 percent)				
8. Step hours				
9. Bonus rate per hour				
Bonus Reserve				
Bonus reserve				
(loss) reserve				
Cumulative reserve (50 percent employee)				

could be terrific, but if WIP went way down during the month, there was no chance for a bonus. Now NAS can identify where its billing levels must be to provide a bonus. For example, if the company can reach $900,000 in monthly billings, there is the possibility of making serious bonus dollars, assuming that margins stay at or above the budget.

Since the change, people can recognize what bonuses to expect if the company reaches all of its targets. In early 1997 the monthly presentation included the new calculations, which use real numbers. The company shared its year-long budget for sales, margins, and overhead, by line item. This allowed everyone present to immediately track down to the bonus line.

In addition to changing its bonus plan, NAS also held its first company-wide day of training in 1996 to help employees understand the financial information more clearly. The program, led by the company controller and one of the owners, included exercises drawn from the Yo-Yo Company workbook created by SRC's subsidiary, The Great Game of Business.

Special Challenges

As NAS has implemented open-book techniques more formally, it has faced unique challenges because of its status as a privately owned, unionized company.

Because NAS is a union shop and negotiates contracts every three years, it was concerned that union officials might use selective information against the company during negotiations. On the other hand, some NAS executives believe that the environment of open disclosure and trust engendered by open-book management counterbalances the union's influence among company employees.

Tim Bragg, union steward at North American Signs, believes the open-book program is a good learning experience for employees because it enables them to see how the company is performing financially. According to Bragg, the program provides an incentive for people to work a little harder and helps them understand why their bonuses can't be larger. Bragg and the vast majority of union members don't think management is hiding anything or playing games with the bonus. Numbers are posted every month, and employees can ask for more information about how the numbers were computed. Bragg wishes that the numbers were calculated more quickly so that people could know the size of their bonus sooner. Beyond that, he has no complaints with open-book management. Mike Major similarly notes that the bonus is an add-on to an employee's contractually determined salary and doesn't cause a problem for the union.

NAS was also concerned about financial information being passed on externally and perhaps being misused or publicized in ways detrimental to the company. Because NAS is privately held, sells no stock, and thus publishes no informational reports, no one outside the company can obtain NAS financial information unless it is passed on by someone within the company. NAS struggled at length with how much information to disclose internally. For example, there was a specific concern that competitors or customers would learn that NAS made 40 percent or more in gross profits on certain jobs.

Several considerations finally persuaded company leadership that such concerns were worth the risk. For one thing, according to Major, the knowledge that other companies were opening their books internally gave NAS a sense of "safety in numbers." The company also concluded that even if competitors did obtain information about NAS's profit margins, it would be of little practical value to them. Finally, according to Noel Yarger, employees realize the need to keep such information guarded to (1) return the company's trust and loyalty and (2) avoid jeopardizing the possibility or size of their own bonus.

Adapting Open-Book Methods

NAS leadership does not think there is one best way to implement open-book management. Although SRC is considered the leader in the field, NAS did not follow the SRC model exactly. NAS executives do pay attention to what other companies are doing and determine whether new programs or approaches would work for them. However, they are also aware that each company, its employees, and its environment are unique, and that each company is typically at a different starting point in the process.

Accordingly, as NAS has implemented open-book management more formally, it has adopted certain open-book methods and adapted and modified others to meet problems as they arise. The company sees its use of open-book techniques as evolving, with future goals already formulated to meet current challenges.

At present, NAS communicates financial information to its employees in a number of ways. It shares company-wide information monthly and department information weekly (table 6.2). Production numbers are generated from payroll on a weekly basis. The data are graphed on a spreadsheet and posted for everyone to see. The only thing NAS does not intentionally reveal is individual pay scales, although employees can see pay ranges. NAS does not distribute the balance sheet, although it plans to do so in the future.

NAS differs from other companies in the amount and kind of training it has given employees to help them understand the information they receive. As noted earlier, the first formal training the company offered was a day-long, company-wide session held in 1996. NAS is not

Table 6.2
Weekly Department Production Report
(negative numbers are below the bid and are good)

Week Ending>>		01/11/97	01/18/97	02/08/97>>>	YTD Total	YTD $ DIFF
Dept	BID	13.7	16.8	17.4	365.69	
Team 1	ACT	12.86	30.06	14.97	314.84	
	DIFF	–0.84	13.26	–2.43	–50.85	
	percentDIFF	–6.1 percent	78.9 percent	–14.0 percent	13.9 percent	
($1,563)						
Dept	BID	153.09	66.5	331.77	1,800.36	
Team 2	ACT	95.8	64.25	245.08	1,394.82	
	DIFF	–57.29	–2.25	–86.69	–406.04	
	percentDIFF	–37.4 percent	–37.4 percent	–26.1 percent	–22.5 percent	
($12,478)						
Dept	BID	2.9	41.7	18.5	128.13	
Team 3	ACT	2.5	10.25	14.16	71.54	
	DIFF	–0.4	–31.45	–4.34	–56.59	
	percentDIFF	–37.4 percent	–75.4 percent	–23.5 percent	–44.2 percent	
($1,739)						
Dept	BID	87.41	112.66	164.37	1,499.29	
Team 4	ACT	75.51	117.37	185.80	1,500.92	
	DIFF	–11.9	4.71	21.43	1.63	
	percentDIFF	–13.6 percent	4.2 percent	13.0 percent	0.1 percent	$50

large enough to send employees off-site for extended periods of additional training. Instead, employees learn the techniques of open-book management as they participate in the system.

The primary learning ground is the monthly meetings at which financial information is shared and discussed. The company has restructured these meetings to make them more effective. For example, in November 1996, NAS began sharing monthly financial information with smaller, cross-functional groups of 20 to 25 people instead of with one large group of employees. Major believes the smaller groups generate more questions, livelier discussion, and more substantive comments because people feel more comfortable in these settings.

The company also began using employees to present the numbers at the meetings. Over the years, Major had become concerned that open-book management was being perceived as a management plan rather than a company plan, because he was always the presenter. Whenever a question arose, he (i.e., management) provided the answer. "After one meeting," he says, "I just threw the idea to the group that I was tired of doing this and it was somebody else's turn. I asked for a volunteer to do this next month and someone raised his hand." However, depending on volunteer presenters soon proved unworkable—as many thought it would—because few people are comfortable standing in front of 90 to 100 people.

Major then decided to approach people individually to see if they would agree to present the numbers. He now meets with the current and previous month's presenters several days before the meeting, walks them through the numbers, and identifies the highlights—the profit-and-loss statement and the sales report, which includes overtime and margin analysis by customers. There are several other reports related to company profitability Major brings to the meeting that he could share if particular questions arose, but the main concern for the workforce is the size of the bonus.

According to Major, "It's pretty neat when you have a sign painter, as opposed to your financial person, getting up and explaining profit before and after taxes, what overhead is, that the margin is 3 percent higher from last month, and what it is compared to budget." Major believes that having rank-and-file employees make monthly presentations about financial results presents a much better image to the rest of the company. In addition, people understand things much better when they teach them to someone else. Presenters take their jobs seriously because they don't want to be embarrassed in front of their peers.

As a result of these changes, the monthly meetings have become more informal and, according to Major, more effective. Now meetings can be conducted without one of the owners present, and employees consistently ask good, meaningful questions.

NAS hopes to get more rank-and-file employees involved in presenting. The company's goal is to have different people trained to become presenters at regular meetings and to get more people involved in monthly activities. Ideally, Major would like two-thirds of the company to have the experience of presenting the numbers at least one time, although realistically he believes that between 10 and 15 people will present the numbers on a rotation basis. Further, NAS hopes in future years to develop an in-house training group for presenters. Ideally, training would be once or twice a year, depending on the training group's turnover and effectiveness.

Despite its success at implementing open-book management to date, NAS still must overcome some hurdles to achieve its long-term goals for the program. One is the length of time it takes to get information to employees. There is currently a two- to three-month delay in getting certain numbers publicized. This delay is of particular interest to John Yarger, the president's son and heir-apparent, who has served NAS as a supervisor and management consultant. According to John, month-to-month comparisons are very difficult for employees to understand and interpret. He believes open-book management is just good feedback, and that it is essentially irrelevant to tell employees two to three months after the fact that their margins on a job were not high enough.

Accordingly, John is encouraging management to show employees more hourly and daily numbers; that is, to shorten the time frame so that everyone can see and react to financial statements sooner. Major says he would like to do what SRC does: generate a weekly profit-and-loss statement, as well as six-week and six-month projections.

A second stumbling block to NAS's implementation of open-book management has been employee resistance to the program. Larry Bigsby, an estimator at NAS, worked 12 years on the shop floor before joining the office staff; he has seen open-book management in action from both the management and labor sides. He notes that a small group of people in the shop do not trust the company or the information it discloses. Some employees naturally question the company's motives and wonder why it is disclosing financial information now. Some suspect the company is fabricating the numbers it presents to employees. For example, if a month's bonus is reported to be $15,000, they wonder how much it was before the company played with the numbers to get it down to something affordable.

Resistance to open-book management seems most evident in the attitude some employees have toward the informational meetings. According to Bigsby, a number of employees simply do not like attending the meetings. Those unwilling to participate in open-book management see the meetings as a waste of time. Major notes that some employees attend the meetings just to provoke trouble, or to gossip or sleep.

Major adds that such problems have diminished with the introduction of smaller groups. He feels that bringing people up to speed in interpreting the information will further diminish resistance. For most people, dealing with financial information on a regular basis is a new experience, notes Major. Sharing certain information with them before they have been trained to interpret it will only waste their time and may actually cause some resentment.

Despite some resistance and skepticism, NAS leadership feels most employees are committed to open-book management. Bigsby thinks most people realize the company is "wide open with what we are telling them," adding there are no secrets at NAS and employees know they can ask for any information they'd like, except for individual pay scales. As a result, the company is sharing more financial information than ever before.

Major hopes the company's commitment to complete disclosure will eliminate any remaining skepticism employees may have about management's intent. Like Bigsby, Major knows some will always suspect the company of incomplete or inaccurate disclosure, but he feels the majority of people believe the company is honest. As he puts it, "Why else would you have a program like this if you weren't trying to be honest with people?"

Major believes that employees' commitment to open-book management is an outgrowth of their interest in what is going on in the company. They want to hear what the company is doing, what plans it has for the coming year, what problems are occurring, and how those problems can be solved and avoided in the future. Bigsby concurs with this observation, saying that despite some resistance to the formal meetings, many employees approach him informally with questions about the company's financial picture. With this information they are better prepared and more willing to come up with new ideas, to work together across departments, and to try to reach the company's goals collectively.

One clear indication of employees' support of open-book management is their satisfaction with the gain-sharing program, open-book management's cornerstone. Employees have decided year after year that they want to continue the gain-sharing program. According to Noel Yarger, the company tried to motivate people to support gain sharing by enabling them to participate in the decision-making process and to have a stake in its outcome. Showing employees the books opened further possibilities for increasing their commitment and their understanding of how their actions could affect their monthly gain-share bonuses.

NAS introduces all new employees to open-book management during their orientation. In fact, Major expects that an explicit commitment to open-book management will become a condition of employment in the near future. He tells new employees that NAS is an open-book company, which means they will need to participate in groups; if they are going to be in management, they will have to be supportive of this open, group-centered organizational style.

Major says that when hiring, he looks for people who have worked in an open-book environment or who are open to it. He believes it is easy to develop people who are willing to accept new ideas but difficult to turn around people who have negative attitudes.

Success and Its Requirements

None of the interviewees were able to pinpoint specifically how open-book management has affected NAS's performance, and, as Major notes, the results of open-book management will probably never be quantified enough to fully satisfy a financially minded, analytical person. However, NAS leadership feels open-book management definitely has had a positive impact on the company. Opening the books challenges people to acquire an understanding of the company and of their work in it that they may not have achieved otherwise. By sharing so much information, the company gives all its employees a look into the company's vision of what the future holds. With the inclusion of a bonus plan, open-book management gives employees a stake in that future. Not only do employees see where ownership and management plan to take the company, but they also see how they fit into the plan, how they can affect it, and how much they will be rewarded for their effort. NAS leadership feels that employees need to know their role in the company's progress so that they can work together with the same end in mind.

Several NAS executives noted that open-book management should not be thought of simply as a tool to increase employee productivity. Instead, it must come from a sincere desire to see employees learn, really understand, and become involved in the business. Tom Yarger is convinced open-book management has helped his company's financial performance, especially in the past two years, citing NAS's ability during that period to make several good bonus payouts. He is more concerned, however, with open-book management's impact on employees and on the work environment.

He is convinced open-book management accomplishes the following:

1. It gives employees the resources they need to develop their capacities and interests beyond their baseline job function.
2. It makes people feel they can stretch their capacities and make a real contribution, a real difference in their jobs.
3. It meets the human need to understand and be involved in the larger context of one's work.

When people feel involved, utilized, and meaningful, they make sincere efforts and decisions along the way, instead of simply doing what their supervisor tells them to do. Thus, Tom does not feel open-book management is a passing fad; it represents a long-term trend toward developing employees' larger human potential.

As NAS has adopted and modified certain features of open-book management, and has experienced and responded to certain problems, its leadership has gained significant insight into the requirements that make success with open-book management possible. Noel Yarger feels the benefits of open-book management clearly outweigh the risks, although he acknowledges that because the risks are great, a company must consider the program very carefully before implementing it. He emphasizes the absolute need for top management and ownership to be committed to open-book management; otherwise it will not work well. Noel believes most companies in America do not have a management team that is prepared to take the risks. Open-book management "is definitely not appropriate where the top ownership or management is uncommitted and does not feel that the possible benefits will outweigh the risks," he says.

Major concurs with the view that commitment to open-book management must come from the top, saying management and ownership must have the vision to know *why* they are implementing open-book management and to know in what direction they plan to take the company. Major emphasizes the need for a company's leadership to be committed to the program for the long haul. He feels that if a company starts to implement open-book management, but then abandons it, the work environment will be much worse off than if the company had never attempted it in the first place.

Major also emphasizes the need for company leadership to be flexible and patient, pointing out that any company implementing open-book management will have a lot of growing pains. Accordingly, executives must not expect the impossible from open-book management; they must not expect it to work perfectly at first. Says Major, "You will make a lot of mistakes along the way, but you have to be willing to stay the course." That means management and others (including trainers, team leaders, and game designers) who take part in open-book management must be totally committed to the program, but also willing to make changes along the way.

NAS leadership also recognizes the need to include others besides top management in the open-book management effort. For example, Tom Yarger agrees that open-book management should be championed by someone high enough in the company to ensure a continuing, long-term commitment, but he also believes that if one person is assigned the job of managing the program, he or she might attempt to do too much. He believes, instead, that open-book management works much better when various duties are distributed among a number of different people. Noel emphasizes the need to get every worker committed to the program as well, noting that peer pressure to contribute to the company's success is a major motivation.

On an operational level, Major advocates communicating financial information to employees as clearly as possible. Anyone planning to make presentations—financial executives and employees alike—must be able to communicate and prepare before meetings, he advises. As many financial executives would agree, it is often very difficult to hold people's attention when talking to a group of any size about such dry material as financial numbers. Presenters, especially those formally trained in accounting or finance, should avoid using acronyms or technical terminology, because 99 percent of their listeners would not understand. Presenters must talk in everyday terms and focus on their audience.

Presenters must also help their audience understand exactly how to use the information. Employees must be able to interpret and apply the information they receive to specific actions that can improve their performance.

Role of Financial Executives

Tom Yarger thinks financial executives play a very critical role in open-book management. Without their enthusiastic support, it would be very difficult to implement effectively. However, supporting open-book management might pose a challenge for many financial executives. He feels the typical finance person might be too rigid, too numbers-oriented, and too concerned with payback, which may explain why open-book management often ends up in the human resources (HR) area of most companies. Human resources staff typically have a greater interest in and desire for these types of programs. A partnership between finance and HR might be a good thing, if a company had a finance person and an HR person who were both interested in pursuing open-book management.

Major notes that his own temperament is not typical for an accountant, because he needs a good deal of human contact to be satisfied at work. Perhaps that explains why he enjoys doing HR-type work and interacting with employees about open-book management.

Major feels financial people can also have a very difficult time with open-book management because the approach requires them to justify themselves and their work to the entire company. Noel Yarger adds that once employees gain a greater understanding of the business, they ask more and more pointed, tough questions. Thus, financial executives involved with the open-book management program must prepare to be challenged and to meet those challenges appropriately. If financial executives are to have credibility with employees who are not trained in finance, they must take the time to be mentors—to teach and explain. The financial executive must understand that the open-book process involves a lot of growing pains and must practice consistency and patience in the give-and-take the process requires. Executives who come from more autocratic, closed working environments may have difficulty explaining themselves and their company's actions.

Noel Yarger also points out that the financial executive must be able to engender trust and communicate information. Open-book management's success can be threatened by employees' suspicion that management is cooking the books. Thus, it is critical that the company select a financial executive who is widely viewed as trustworthy.

Case Summary

All the top executives and managers at NAS enthusiastically support open-book management and consider it a fundamental element of the company's culture. NAS does not attempt to quantify costs or benefits, but both active owners believe open-book management has helped the company grow and prosper. NAS implemented open-book management when it was a profitable company, and management believes the approach has made NAS even more profitable. Although managers can't point to specific financial results, they are firmly convinced the benefits of a more motivated and productive workforce *far* exceed the costs of operating open-book management programs and the risks of information leaking to competitors or customers.

Because the company had been using aspects of open-book management informally for years, there was no specific start-up date or difficult transition. Opening the books was more of a natural evolution for a company that treats its employees with respect and encourages them to develop their personal as well as professional potential. Given this evolutionary development, NAS has discovered what is probably true for all companies: The program changes over time as the company adapts and modifies it to meet ongoing challenges.

Without question, enthusiasm and commitment to open-book management stem directly from the two active owners, Noel and Tom Yarger. They actively participate in open-book management activities and encourage the NAS controller, Mike Major, to share information about the company's financials and to initiate programs that involve more employees in presenting monthly figures. Note that Major's interests may not be typical of most financial executives—he actively engages in human resources issues, enjoys educating NAS employees, and willingly shares information about company finances. Open-book management programs would still function at NAS if Major was not involved. A more conventional financial executive might not find work at NAS as satisfying as Major does, he points out.

NAS leadership notes that a company's owners and key executives, including its financial executives, must be firmly committed to open-book management, strongly enough to get through the difficulties and challenges open-book management presents over the long run. As many employees as possible should be involved in conducting the program, and management must encourage commitment to open-book management among all employees, advises NAS. Only with this involvement and commitment can the program achieve its fullest potential for the company as a whole and for each individual employee.

People Interviewed

Noel Yarger, President

Tom Yarger, Vice President

Michael A. Major, Controller

John Yarger, Management Consultant

Larry Bigsby, Estimator

Tim Bragg, Union Steward

Doug McCoige, Production Coordinator

Tony Mejer, Sign Painter

Jerry Smith, Lead Painter

Susan Grontkowski, Account Manager

7

Physician Sales & Service, Inc.

A CEO thinks, "I showed my employees the financial information, I'm an open-book company." The reality is, the employees don't care. I don't believe that they care if they see the financials and know if you're making money or not. They only care relative to what it means to them.

The reason we became an open-book company is the employees own the company. I had to share information so they knew if their investment was good or bad. And I felt I owed that to them because they were shareholders. If I had just said, "I'm going to be an open-book company because it feels good and I want them to know what I make, and it's an issue of trust," I don't think you'll accomplish anything. There has to be a financial incentive. They either have to have gained from sharing open-book or not have gained.

Patrick C. Kelly, Chairman and CEO,
Physician Sales & Service, Inc.

Company Background

Physician Sales & Service, Inc. (PSS), is a public company based in Florida that distributes medical supplies, pharmaceuticals, x-ray supplies, and equipment to doctors' offices, nursing homes, and hospitals. It was started in 1983 by Patrick C. Kelly, Bill Riddell, and Clyde Young. Riddell and Young had worked with Kelly previously as salesmen for a medical supply company. A fourth investor was a businessman named Tom Underwood. Kelly and friends believed they had a better idea for PSS: focus on selling exclusively to physicians, and provide fast delivery and a high level of overall service.

Kelly, Riddell, and Young mortgaged their homes for a total of $40,000 in start-up capital. But this money and the $60,000 contributed by Underwood were soon exhausted. During the first few months, the company grew very rapidly—almost too rapidly. Kelly says, "We grew fast because everybody else who was working at the other company [where he had worked] all wanted to come over. And the company exploded real quickly. We ran out of our credit line. And our investors and our banks were saying, 'No, you're growing too fast. You're burning up your capital too quickly.' That's what drove us to become an employee-owned company."

Kelly and his associates decided to look internally for capital. They had a goal of $150,000, but they actually raised $167,000 by selling preferred stock to their employees. The preferred shares carried a fixed annual return but were convertible into common stock after three years. Kelly felt a strong stewardship obligation to his employee-shareholders and created his open-book culture almost immediately. But that was long before the "open book" moniker was applied by John Case to this type of environment.

During its first year of operation, PSS generated net sales of $1.9 million and earned a net income of $50,000. The future was bright and things were looking up—but rapid growth continued to put serious pressure on the company coffers and the bottom line. This was to be an ongoing problem for PSS long into the future.

Kelly now jokes about PSS' banks "firing" them for growing too fast, but, at the time, it was no laughing matter. PSS' hypergrowth caused two severe banking crises that tested the company's ability to stick to its ambitious plans and even survive. In an often-quoted tale, Kelly describes how, after one bank terminated their relationship, he and his employees buried a casket in Kelly's backyard containing bank loan documents and bank giveaway items such as pens and notepads. They erected a tombstone and each corporate employee threw a handful of dirt into the grave. The burial plot exists to this day. Kelly now adds pragmatically, "The rest of the story: I didn't bury them at sea, which is what one of our employees wanted me to do. 'Cause I wanted to be able to dig it up in case I ever have to kiss that bank's a— again."

Company CFO David A. Smith offers this assessment of PSS' bank problems:

> We've been in and out of eight banks. You scare a bank when you're a growth company because you're not as focused on profits as they would be, you're more focused on growth. Even though you're controlling your assets and your people well, the bank wants you to have a bottom line to limit their risk on the debt. To a growth company, every dollar on the bottom line is a dollar not invested in growth. You're looking 5, 10 years out when the bank is looking at today. So we sacrificed earnings for our aggressive growth. But today we are reaping the benefits of our historical growth with profits that can be invested in new growth opportunities.

Even with a past replete with watershed events, these banking crises are remembered by Kelly as PSS' worst moments: "[O]ur banks told us to leave twice in a row, and being able to bridge over to new banks required a level of profitability we didn't have." Today Kelly is unequivocal in identifying the one single factor that led the company through these two potentially ruinous crises: "This company got saved because it was *open book*—twice."

CFO Smith came on board in 1986 but in an operations position. Smith had been the Coopers & Lybrand audit manager on the PSS engagement, and Kelly lured him—Smith says "tricked" him—to join PSS. Smith describes it as follows:

> PSS was by far my smallest client. But they had a great vision, a great idea about how they wanted to grow the business. They were starting to look at mergers, which was my background with Coopers & Lybrand. Patrick [Kelly] and Bill Riddell tricked me into coming on board—"tricked" in the sense that they were $5 million in sales, they were my smallest client, and they wanted me to go into what was unnatural for me with my background in accounting and finance. I transferred to St. Petersburg as the operations manager. At that time, we had four locations and they kind of threw me into it right away. I started driving trucks, purchasing product, and going out on sales calls, which really gave me a feel for the business.

> During my tenure as operations manager of the St. Petersburg branch from 1987 to 1989, we doubled the business.

Subsequently, Smith was called on for some tough operational assignments. He moved to Waco, Texas, in 1989 to take over the management of a recent strategically important PSS acquisition. Part of Smith's responsibility was to instill the PSS culture in his new Texas employees. Says Smith, "That was tough. Texans have mighty big egos."

The work that Smith did in Texas turned out to be critical for PSS' future. It was in Texas that PSS, under Smith's direction, competed head-to-head in a sort of "fight to the finish" with Taylor Medical, Inc., another medical supply company with the same ambitious national goals as those of PSS. Smith explains as follows:

> In 1988, Taylor Medical raised $3 million in venture capital. They said they were going to go national with their company and that scared us, which is why in 1989 we raised $2 million in venture capital from Tullis-Dickerson. Now, we took that money and went into their breadbasket, which was Texas. That's where they were making all their profits. They took their money and grew out West and in the Northeast, and they never came into the Southeast. It was very scary in that initial phase because their goal was the same and they had raised more money than we had, but we took our money and went after them.

Eventually, PSS won out over its tough Texas rival. PSS acquired Taylor Medical in 1995 in a transaction valued at some $57 million, and created what the company calls the "First National Physician Supply Company," a goal that had been set by Kelly in the late 1980s. PSS widely publicized this achievement on the front of its 1996 annual report and in other venues.

Following his very successful stint in Dallas (then PSS' most profitable location), Smith was brought back to corporate headquarters to help get PSS ready to go public.

> We spent about a year getting corporate ready to be a public company. You need both financial reporting capabilities and financial models that tell the story of the company. Our same-store sales models and branch operating profit models are what helped rein-

force our cultural and growth story. We went public in May of 1994 and successfully completed a secondary offering in 1995.

In its initial public offering (IPO), PSS issued 5.1 million shares at a price of $3.67 (adjusted for a subsequent three-for-one stock split). The company's stock price climbed rapidly following the IPO: to $6 per share in October 1994, $12 per share in April 1995, $20 per share in December 1995, and to its high of $33 per share in mid-1996. Since then, the stock has fallen to 1995 levels. At the end of June 1997, the price was hovering around $19 per share. With a total of 34.5 million shares outstanding, PSS has a market capitalization of around $650 million. Figure 7.1 is a graph of PSS' daily closing stock price from the IPO date through June 1997.

From PSS' modest first year sales of $2 million in 1983, sales have grown at a compound rate of 52 percent per year. Net sales increased by 43 percent from fiscal 1996 to 1997. But profits have been erratic and somewhat elusive over PSS' 14-year life. Net income reached a high of

Figure 7.1
PSS Stock Price from Initial Public Offering through June 1997

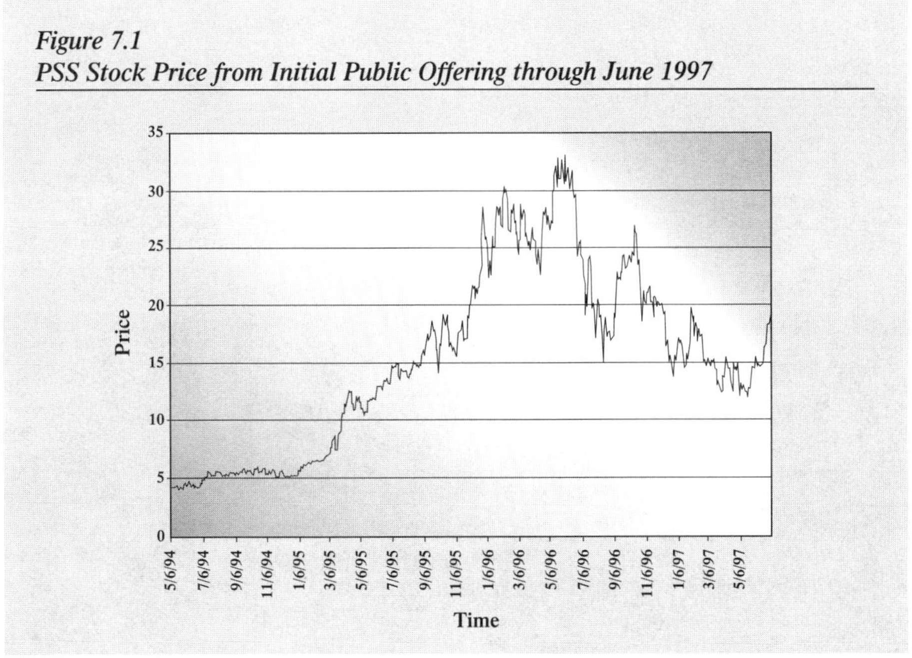

$4.4 million in fiscal 1997. PSS' worst year was in fiscal 1991, when it had a net loss of $496,000.

The net income figures tell only part of the story because reported net income has suffered from PSS' conscious hypergrowth policy, as explained by Smith earlier. In a sense, the company is sacrificing current profits for a long-term strategy of creating wealth through growth and strategically positioning itself to be a dominant player in its industry. Figure 7.2 presents a graph of PSS' net sales and net income from 1986 to 1997. It shows that sales have increased consistently at a strong rate while net income has been relatively small in relation to sales, and highly volatile.

According to Smith, there are over 200 millionaires working for PSS, from executives to truck drivers. These are generally people who started with PSS early on, received stock when the company was private, and then saw their stock holdings explode in value when PSS went public. The PSS story is one of enormous wealth creation and opportunity. But the PSS story is also one of a company culture anchored in

Figure 7.2
PSS Net Sales and Net Income, 1986–1997

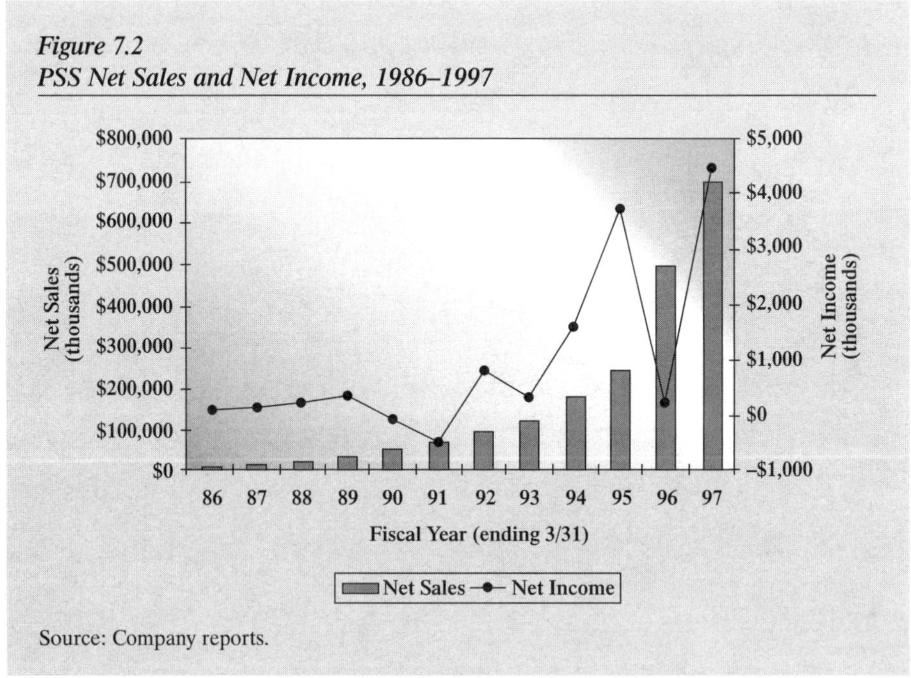

Source: Company reports.

trust and openness. This culture goes far in explaining the deep roots of open-book management at PSS.

The PSS Way

> I was hired by PSS out of college to drive a truck in Tulsa. I was making $900 a month. My route was from Tulsa, Oklahoma, to Springfield, Missouri, every day. It's probably about a three-hour drive. I had many conversations with my father, where he said, "What the hell are you doing driving a truck when we paid all this money for you to go to a private university?"
>
> I drove a truck from November to March. Then I came inside and started working as purchasing agent and, in six months, I went to Dallas. At that time, Dallas was probably one of our largest branches. I was in Dallas for a year as a purchasing agent. Then I went to Baltimore as operations leader (manager). I went from $900 a month to $4,000 a month in 16 months. *Then, what did your Dad have to say?* He bought stock in the company.
>
> Brian Rolling, PSS Branch Operations Leader

> When PSS first started in 1983, a driver in Jacksonville who didn't even have a high school education came to work for PSS and was loyal to the company. Now Pat Kelly back in those days didn't have a bonus program, so he gave shares of stock. At the time, they were worth 33 cents. Do you know how much that guy is worth now? He's worth over $10 million. This is a guy who didn't have a college education, who didn't really think he'd ever have any kind of a future. Pat turned around and made him a multimillionaire.
>
> Rob Blackmore, PSS Branch Sales Leader

To understand PSS, one has to first understand Pat Kelly. Kelly is the ultimate self-made man. He grew up in the Richmond (Virginia) Home for Boys after having been placed there at age five with his older brother. Kelly wore hand-me-down clothes until he was 17, when he received his first pair of new pants. After failing out of college, he ended up in Vietnam as a buck sergeant but was responsible for "issuing all the weapons north of Da Nang." Following his military tour, he returned to college and earned a degree in biology in two-and-a-half years with a place on the dean's list each semester.

Kelly's first job after college was with a large medical supply company, working mostly in the warehouse. Kelly had never envisioned himself in sales ("Too shy," he says); nevertheless, he ended up as a sales representative after 16 months with the company. In his first month as a sales representative, he had *negative* sales (returns exceeded sales), but eventually he not only succeeded in sales but wound up as sales manager for the company. He moved on to another medical supply company as a division manager and became its marketing vice president three years later. Around this time, Kelly came up with the then-revolutionary ideas that became the cornerstone of PSS—ideas that grew into almost three-quarters of a billion dollars in value within 14 years.

In 1997, Kelly was one of 11 recipients of the Horatio Alger Award. The award is bestowed by the Horatio Alger Association on individuals who "have achieved extraordinary success despite challenging life circumstances." The association says the award recipients have "sent a resounding message to the nation: that the American Dream is alive and well; honesty, hard work, and determination can triumph over all obstacles." Other 1997 award recipients were Ted Turner, actor James Earl Jones, and author Mary Higgins Clark.

Open-book management at PSS is merely an extension of the PSS culture, which, in turn, is a reflection of the Pat Kelly way of doing things. The following are several manifestations of this culture:

- **New Hires.** "Part of the advantage we have is we hire very inexperienced salespeople. Our industry is a very mature industry with very mature sales reps who have a breadth of knowledge but also certain ways that they do business. By starting new from scratch, we were able to change the way business was done within our own company. So our sales force is not focused on getting the order but on teaching, and on showing new products, and at the same time taking an order for other products. They show up more regularly and they provide better service than our competition."
  David Smith

- **Open Communications.** "That's what really attracted me to PSS, is that you have an opportunity to work with a group of people your own age. You get around them and you get the energy going, and once you get established, you definitely feel the openness. You can pick up the phone and call Pat Kelly if you wanted to, or Dave Smith, or [president] John Sasen. It didn't matter who you were or where you were, you could just pick up that phone. It was always instilled from the beginning, from the time I walked through the door." Rob Blackmore

- **Grievance Procedures.** "Part of the culture of our company is you can bypass anybody in this company, go over anybody's head at any point in time, and come directly to me. You can go over my head and go directly to the Board of Directors. Nobody will ever take retribution against you. So today, literally once or twice a week, I will get a telephone call from somebody in this company if they feel they got maligned or they weren't treated fairly [by a manager]. They'll come to me.

  "We'll try to bring the two back together again. Sometimes the manager, let's say, is very adamant that this individual did wrong in whatever, and I can't save the individual. I'll try to interfere on their behalf but sometimes I can't save them. But if I clearly think the manager is making a bad decision, we will then offer a position to that person in another branch of PSS.

  "Believe it or not, it normally ends up in the employee's favor. *That's my job, to protect the employees.*" Pat Kelly

- **Employee Input.** "We always tell the leadership of this company: We will not fire you; your employees will fire you. They'll come right out and say, 'Get the bum out of here.' Because they recognize this leader is not bringing value and driving profitability. If you're an employee of a location and you're not getting a bonus and you're hearing twice a year at picnics and national sales meetings [that] everybody else is, you start to say 'Why can't my management get us there?' I can tell you the past three months in doing the forecast, I've showed up at three locations, and literally the employees met with me and they fired their management, on the spot."

Pat Kelly

- **Income-Earning Potential.** "From my parents, it was always a personal issue—how much money you make or how much your family is worth, things like that. Money was always sort of on the back burner. You don't really talk about it. You earn it, you spend it, you have fun with it but you don't really flaunt it. When you come to PSS, it's like everybody's flaunting it. And it was pretty much what everybody talked about. What are your numbers, where you're at, how much money is the branch making. It's all over the place. I mean it's money, money, money."

  "So you hear that story (about the multimillionaire truck driver), especially a young guy coming out of college in a marketplace where there's so much unemployment and so many layoffs, and so much discontent—you work for such a great company where financial information is just wide open and you hear all these great stories about people making so much money. If you didn't have that oneness, if you didn't have that culture, I don't think you would really have that same push across the country.

  "You might hear it locally, but you probably wouldn't hear the story about the sales rep who's 24 and making $100,000 a year and driving a brand-new Porsche. Every month, we're shown the top [sales] writers in our company. And every now and again, there's a couple of them who are 25, 26, 27. A gentleman out of New Jersey—I believe he's 25 or 26 years old—made $70,000 back in January, in *one month*.

  "It just blows you away and that's part of our culture. You hear that story, and as a sales leader, I go out to my sales reps and I say, look what this guy can do. He's your same age. Why don't you get out there and do it? You can make it happen."

  Rob Blackmore

- **Creativity Week.** "All the new leaders in PSS get on a boat with me and go down the Intercoastal Waterway to Miami. They have to read three books. And the books are *A Whack on the Side of the Head: How You Can Be More Creative, The Goal,* and *The Seven Habits of Highly Effective People.* They read those three books ahead of time and we discuss them in the morning. I'm the teacher. Three of these new leaders are the students.

"That afternoon, they go over 25 problems we've had as a company. Major mistakes we've made. They try to problem solve it in a case study and they come up with solutions. I tell them what actually happened, so I'm passing on the culture of the company too: how it happened and how we solved it at that time. Sometimes it's different than what they came up with. So that's the end of the first day. The next day I have three new students come on the boat and the three students from the prior day now become the teacher. And I just help moderate.

"Every year, these 30 or 40 new leaders in the company get to really understand the culture of the company. They get to understand clearly our goals and articulate them. And the 25 problems—we have no policy manual—so this is our way of communicating, don't make this mistake. *We* made this mistake. So they learned the mistakes through solving the problems themselves. But after I've spent two days with them in close quarters, I clearly have an understanding of their capabilities, their strengths, or weaknesses. I clearly know if they know me. And we spend two days together in camaraderie from the standpoint that now, we're friends." Pat Kelly

- **On the Spot.** "When I do 'on the spot,' I literally ask them questions about their company and their business. When I or the regional vice president go to a branch to inspect it, we call all of the employees together on the spot and say, 'I'm going to find out if y'all are playing the "Challenge" [monthly knowledge game] and if you're learning.' And I then get each employee to pick a number from 1 to 100 and as they pick the number, there is a question about the company. If they know the answer, I pay them $20 on the spot. And I'll give them at least two chances to answer the question." Pat Kelly

"Jim Stallings (executive vice president) has a list of about 100 questions. We'll gather right out here in this little open area, and he asks questions, 'What was the operating profit of PSS last year?' That was a tough question. Jim says, 'Well then, where can you find that?' We happened to have a financial statement sitting out right there and someone grabs it and says, 'Right here.' So he gave him 50 bucks.

"That was a hard one but there are some easier ones in there: What is PSS' return policy? You know, we'll take anything back. Right. Fifty dollars."
Brian Rolling

- **Dumb Questions.** "I carry with me $2 bills all the time. You can check with the Federal Reserve Bank. I'm probably the number one user of $2 bills in America. And the $2 is to encourage the employees to ask dumb questions. And as they ask questions, I pay them two bucks. They're allowed to literally ask me *anything* and I tell them straight at the front end, you can ask me my salary, you can ask me anything you want about this company and I will tell you. Unless I've signed a confidentiality agreement that says I can't. Or unless I'm breaking SEC rules, I can't. I'll tell you anything else. And if I can't tell you, I'll tell you why I can't tell you. So understanding that, here's $2. And I start answering questions. Now, I could get up there and say, 'Here are the salaries of the officers.' But you know, they've stopped asking me what the salaries are. It's just . . . knowing they could ask me is why the trust issue is there."
Pat Kelly

Open-book management was never imposed on PSS. It grew naturally out of a culture of trust and candor—a culture that has existed at PSS from the company's humble beginning in 1983. It is a culture that reflects in all major aspects the personal philosophy of Pat Kelly. Kelly mentioned that he will answer any question unless there is a confidentiality agreement on the subject or if it would be a violation of SEC rules. Thus, the operation of an open-book management system in a public company must be somewhat different. We will explore those differences later.

The PSS Challenge Meetings

> We designed a game board like the "Family Feud." We split up the group into two teams, red and blue. They're asked questions such as, "Who is PSS' largest vendor?" Let's say today Abbott is. So they answer Abbott for 40 points. If they answer Johnson & Johnson, they get 30. There are three or four answers and they build the points up.
>
> They play it every month but on a different area. One might be on manufacturers; the next one might be understanding our customer; it could be understanding accounts receivable, understanding inventory control, or [understanding] the very culture of the company. There are 12 lessons they learn in a year. They play it as a team and get points. They get to hold those points and they're put on a board. They keep the tally for the year. And they get to turn those points in for gifts. Pens, sunglasses, radios, coolers, stuff like that. So they have fun and they learn about the company. But they must also attend 10 of these to be in the bonus program.
>
> Pat Kelly

A core of the open-book management program at PSS is the PSS Challenge monthly meetings. Part of the meetings occur off-site, at a bowling alley, for instance, or a miniature golf course. The purpose of the Challenge meetings is threefold as follows:

- To encourage employees to learn about various aspects of the business side of PSS.
- To give updates on the progress that the particular branch is making toward earning a bonus.
- To encourage camaraderie and team spirit at the branches.

Kelly explains how the PSS Challenge meetings are described to new employees:

> We don't hire just truck drivers. We want you to learn about what's going on, to understand how to make a bonus here because we've

> seen that the branches that make bonuses have very little turnover. The people stay in the company and want to prosper. [We also want people to] come together as a team and have fun. So it's competition and have fun. That's the process of how we've been able to drive our productivity. And our productivity is the highest in the industry.

PSS management is candid in saying that the company does very little formal training in understanding the branch's financial statements. When asked about how much of such training PSS actually gives its employees, Kelly responded as follows:

> Not a lot, other than the monthly PSS Challenge meetings. But I guess I *would* say we do it a lot because 12 times a year employees come and they're incentivised for coming to these meetings. So they definitely get extensive training if you understand that they get at least an hour a month, a minimum of 10 times a year, to get their bonus.

CFO Smith views training as informal and part of the normal routine at the branch:

> We don't have Financial Accounting 101 as a training course. It's not a formal process; it's an informal process. Each individual employee is going to be different. Some people are going to pick this up easily, some people will never want to pick it up. They'll go along with whatever the plan is or they might have some ideas on how to make things better. But they won't want to understand how depreciation works. They'll want to understand how their area can help get a bigger bonus.

The informal training happens continually at the branches but is more directed during the Challenge meetings. Smith describes the P&L (profit and loss) portion of the Challenge meetings, which usually occurs after a "Family Feud" competition:

> In the P&L meeting, we take the budget results and compare it to the actual results. Normally, the operations manager is going to lead the discussion because that person is a business manager. And they'll compare by line or by area where we're off or where we're ahead.

> And if it's interest expense, we can start talking about why interest is up. We're not collecting our receivables [in a] timely [manner]; we've got too much inventory.

The Challenge meetings are not just about education and problem solving. Remember that one of Kelly's objectives in these monthly meetings is to foster a spirit of togetherness that will further the ability of the branch employees to work as a team. Branch Operations Leader Rolling explains it this way:

> For our last Challenge meeting, we met here at the branch at 5:30 p.m. This time we went through the "Challenge" game here at the branch and after we got finished I said, "Let's go out to the parking lot," and I didn't tell them where we were going. They all followed me to this little pool hall up the street and we had a pool tournament. I gave out 100 bucks for the first prize and 50 bucks for the second team. We had dinner and shot pool and drank beer.
>
> Everyone mixed and got to know each other on a personal level outside of work, where everyone's guard can come down. That's what it does. We had a new truck driver. His name is Wayne, and Wayne delivers for Brennan, who is one of our salespeople. And those two had never talked outside of work. I came back the next day and, you know, sometimes you hear people talk about other people. Wayne says, "You know Brennan is really a great guy," because they got to meet each other. That's what the Challenge does—above and beyond educating people about . . . I think the topic was accounts payable and accounts receivable.

By all accounts, the Challenge sessions are very valuable to individual employees. Dale Staudinger, a branch warehouse leader who has been with PSS for about a year, has these observations:

> The first time, it [the Challenge] shocked me. What the heck is this? But they just made me feel right at home: "Hey everybody, this is Dale. We just hired him last month."
>
> We started playing right along into the way the game goes. To me it's not a game. It's educating you about the company. It's not necessarily who's better than who, it's you using the company information to give you more knowledge. I got a couple of the answers right my first meeting.

> I've learned about accounts receivable, accounts payable, history of the company itself. Basic things like that.

For rank-and-file employees to be interested in somewhat arcane concepts such as receivables-days or inventory-days is surprising. And the interest is not sparked by the chance to win nominal prizes in a contest. What really motivates the employees is the prospect of earning a significant bonus based primarily on net profits, but also on other measures such as asset-days.

The PSS Bonus Plan

> Most companies have employee bonuses based on productivity and on earnings. The employees typically get a bonus based on their salaries. If you've got so much salary, you get a percentage of that salary back in bonus. Ours is different. Ours pays bonuses equally. We don't care if you're a truck driver making $18,000 a year or you're the manager making $60,000 a year. When that bonus is divvied up, you both get *the same check.*
>
> Pat Kelly

Kelly strongly believes that open-book management will work only if the employees have a financial stake in the outcome. The PSS bonus plan is what ultimately rewards employees if their branch does well financially. The fiscal 1997–98 version of the plan is described in a brochure that uses a baseball metaphor to communicate the facets of the plan (figure 7.3).

To earn the full bonus, an employee must attend at least 10 of the 12 PSS Challenge meetings per year, and sales representatives must achieve their gross profit forecast in dollars. The bonus is calculated as follows:

1. The first hurdle is a single in baseball parlance: the branch earns a 5 percent net profit rate on sales. Five percent of the excess of actual profit over the 5 percent rate goes into the branch's bonus pool.

Figure 7.3
Employee Bonus Program (front)

Field of Dreams '97

Fiscal Year 4/97 - 3/98
Branch Incentive Program

Everyone plays...
Operations, Sales Reps, and Leaders....It's a Game where everyone's efforts are counted!

Everybody's a Valuable Player!

Here's how to win big...

Field of Dreams '97

Are You in Shape to Play?

Last year, PSS paid out the largest bonuses ever! Many PSS'ers shared in the profits. It's a team goal based on overall bottomline net profits.

GUIDELINES

1. No *Pool* without the single base hit.
2. Sales reps must achieve their GP$ forecast.
3. Pay out mid-year and year-end. Must be employed 6 months prior to payout.
4. Inventory pick-up limited to 3% COS total.
5. You must attend (10) PSS Challenge Meetings per year to get 100% of your Team Bonus.
6. Asset Days = Last Quarterly Average.

See the PSS baseball diamond for more information!

PSS® Physician Sales & Service

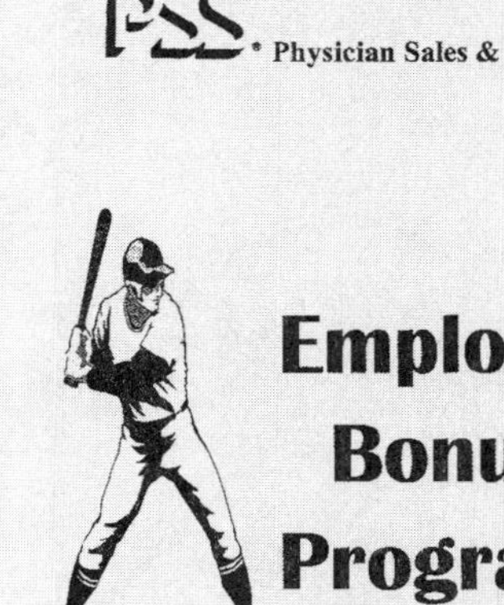

Employee Bonus Program

Field of Dreams '97

Figure 7.3
Employee Bonus Program (back)

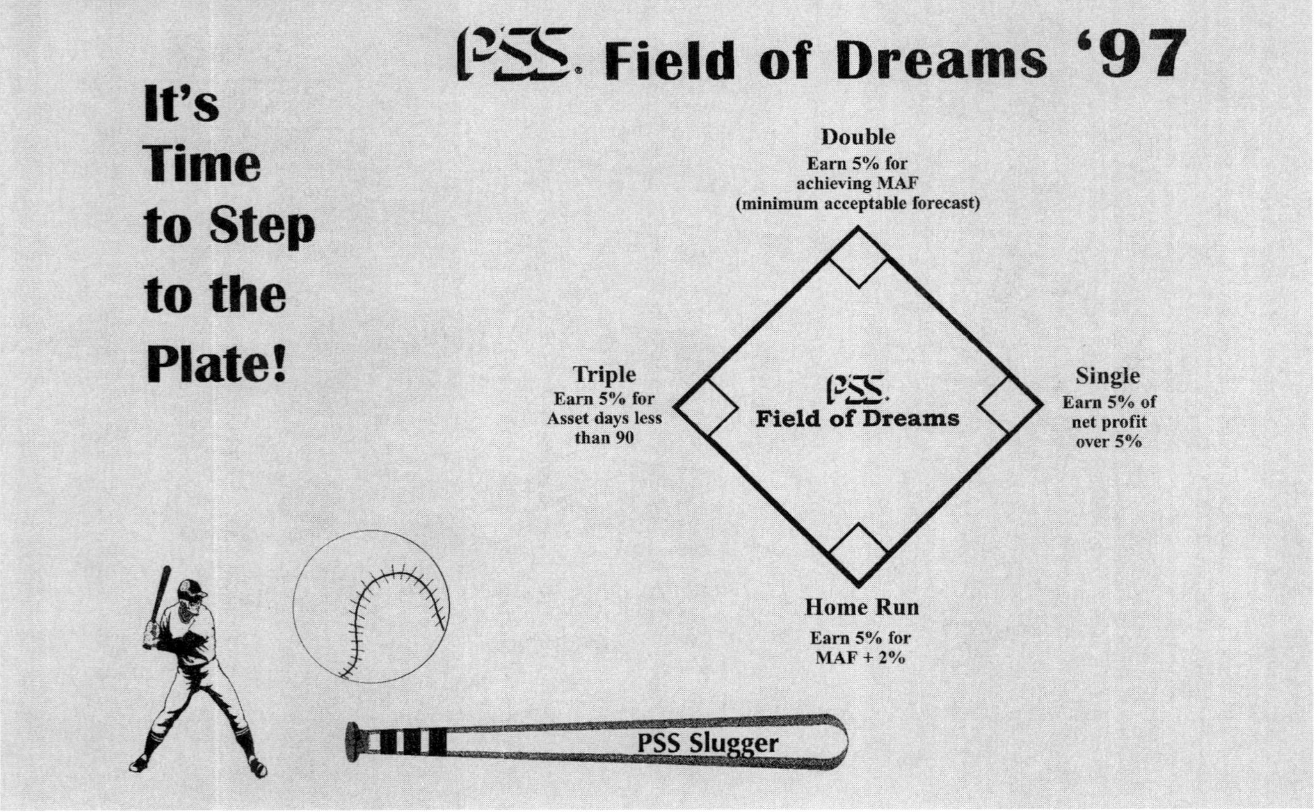

PSS Field of Dreams '97

It's Time to Step to the Plate!

Double
Earn 5% for achieving MAF (minimum acceptable forecast)

Triple
Earn 5% for Asset days less than 90

PSS Field of Dreams

Single
Earn 5% of net profit over 5%

Home Run
Earn 5% for MAF + 2%

PSS Slugger

2. Next the branch can hit a double by achieving its minimum acceptable forecast (MAF) in addition to the single. This will result in another 5 percent of the excess over the 5 percent hurdle rate going into the bonus pool.
3. A branch can then earn a triple if its asset days for the last quarter are fewer than 90. A triple gives the employees another 5 percent of the excess profit for the bonus pool. (Asset days for a quarter are average branch assets divided by net sales times 90. This number represents how long it takes assets to be converted into cash, on average. A high asset-days statistic means that the branch has too much money tied up in receivables and inventory.)
4. A home run is earned when net sales exceed the MAF by 2 percent. Another 5 percent of profit excess goes into the pool.

Figure 7.4 gives an example of the computation of a branch bonus, using information for a hypothetical branch.

This lucrative bonus program drives open-book management at PSS. Kelly comments as follows:

> In the process of building a team concept, we must share financial information because we pay over and above operating profit of 5 percent. The employees can earn 20 cents of every dollar over and above that, and it comes back to them equally. So they've got to know where they are, they've got to know where their profits are, they've got to know what they're doing.
>
> We pay the bonus twice a year, only so it stays visible to them. You can't pay it earlier than that because one month you can have a great month and next month have a poor month.
>
> The largest check we've ever paid was $9,300. So $9,300 is a significant amount to a truck driver who's making $18,000 a year.

One might question the wisdom of splitting the bonus equally among all branch employees. A $5,000 bonus is 20 percent of the base pay of an employee drawing $25,000 per year but only 7 percent of the pay of a sales representative making $75,000. Does this situation cause problems or friction in the branch? Rolling says, "No. Every employee

Figure 7.4
Illustration of Branch Bonus Computation

Suppose that Branch A with 25 employees earns a net profit of $800,000 on net sales of $10 million, with a minimum acceptable forecast (MAF) of $9.5 million and asset days of 85. This is a home run for Branch A, and the branch bonus pool will be calculated as follows:

- **A Single.** Branch A passes first base because the branch earned a net profit in excess of 5 percent of net sales: $800,000 is greater than $500,000 (5 percent × $10 million) by $300,000. Five percent of that excess goes into the bonus pool: 5 percent × $300,000 = $15,000.
- **The Single Becomes a Double.** Branch A passes second base because it achieved the MAF. So another $15,000 goes into the bonus pool.
- **The Double Becomes a Triple.** The branch passes third base with its asset days fewer than 90. A third $15,000 goes into the bonus pool.
- The Triple Becomes a Home Run. Finally, Branch A hits a home run because its net sales exceeded the MAF by 2 percent. A fourth $15,000 goes into the bonus pool.

So Branch A has $60,000 in its bonus pool to be split evenly among its 25 employees. Each employee who attended the minimum number of PSS Challenge sessions (10 of 12) would receive a bonus payout of $2,400.

As in baseball, the branch can progress to the next base only after passing the previous one. For example, if Branch A's asset days were 92, only $30,000 would go into the bonus pool instead of $60,000. It would lose $15,000 for not achieving the asset days, and would not be eligible to receive the last $15,000 for exceeding MAF by 2 percent.

in this branch has been a truck driver, so everyone knows how hard that person works also. All the boats rise in a flood, you know."

Open-book management and the bonus program are inseparable at PSS. Open-book management without the bonus program would result in disinterested employees with no immediate stake in their branch's results. And the bonus program without open-book management could create frustrated, distrustful employees who don't know what it would take to earn their bonus and might not believe the final results anyway.

The bonus program has worked well for PSS. One significant advantage is that, once targets have been set, the program allows senior management to concentrate on the few branches not performing up to par and on expansion. Kelly explains it this way:

> If you give some of those profits back to the people who are driving it, guess what they will do? They will sustain it. A branch that has been successful in hitting a bonus over two to three years, they're on cruise control. I don't have to visit them. I don't manage that company. I don't have to spend any time there. The employees drive the profitability of that branch. They know the rewards are there.
>
> After I get my 5 percent return, every dollar over and above that the employees get 20 percent, the management team gets 20 percent, the shareholders get 60 percent. They're on cruise control. So they're managing it for us for the stake. This allows me then to go invest in a company in Dallas, and one in Salt Lake, and one in Seattle. And that's why today PSS is a billion-dollar company. Because we've been able to do that—where the people drive the profitability.

In the previous discussion of the PSS Challenge meetings, CFO Smith described a P&L phase of the meetings in which the focus might be on interest expense exceeding budget. Smith elaborates as follows:

> Interest is off because we have too much inventory. Well, why do we have too much inventory in stock? It could be a lot of reasons. One, purchasing isn't quite up to speed or salespeople have asked us to bring in products that aren't moving. You have to motivate the salespeople to move those products out so that we have the right number of inventory days. Or we brought a product in that everybody said was going to sell and it hasn't sold. We need to do a sales program to get rid of it, or we need to start calling manufacturers to return product.
>
> Anyway, the team comes up with an answer that solves *their problem.* Not corporate coming to the team and saying, "Get your interest cost down." The team itself comes up with an answer because they're going to be compensated on their performance to this budget. So they are motivated to come up with their own answer. Corporate gets involved or management, regional or vice presidents

get involved when, after a few months, the team's plan hasn't worked.

It may be puzzling to some observers how the sharing of information under open-book management could cause a PSS truck driver, for instance, to have a positive impact on company profits. How would the truck driver *use* the information to improve the company's bottom line? The answer lies in PSS' extensive use of the team concept and "the sharing piece," discussed in the next section. Smith talks about how, within the branch team environment, solutions to operating problems are a communal effort:

> They get to get down to the nth degree of detail from how much we pay each other to how much gasoline they're using per truck to where they're over budget per line item like freight, electricity, or telephone, or are people abusing the telephone, or do we have a territory that's not producing and do we need to talk to that person and get them producing.
>
> It's almost like an internal policing force. They talk to their own people and say "Look, you're not pulling your weight in this area. You've got to help us out here." So it's a lot easier to manage that group also because they have all the information. They also can help create entrepreneurial solutions. They can make their job easier and more efficient to do and create more profit on the bottom line if they know that their job is costing or their area is costing so much money and it's over budget or if it's on budget. And *they're* doing *their* job so they know they *could* do it better, they know *how* to do it better.

As soon as it's sent to the branch, all branch financial information is available to all branch employees: sales detail, expense detail, salaries, and detailed forecast information. Sales information is posted on the wall daily, and the other figures are reported monthly. The employees need this information to track where they are for the semiannual bonus. But very little company-level information is reported to the branch because PSS is a public company.

Open-Book Management in a Public Company —The Sharing Piece

> In November (1996), one of our investor analysts wrote that we weren't going to achieve our quarter. We *did* end up achieving our quarter. But we watched our stock literally fall from $22 down to $14 because of the analyst's report.
>
> We had always communicated to our people what revenues were, and we communicated on a monthly basis. But we became more aware that it might potentially cause problems. So therefore it's a real issue of how we can communicate to our employees. Really it says to us that we have to be careful as a public company.
>
> Pat Kelly

The problems of using open-book management in a public company are delicate and sensitive. Most PSS employees are shareholders in the company. Obviously, it would be impossible for PSS to share overall company results with its employee-shareholders in a way that benefits them as company insiders and risks SEC rule violations. But another equally serious matter is information leaks. PSS has some 4,000 employees. If only one of those employees leaked company-level information to the outside, it could have serious repercussions.

In our discussions with PSS management about how open-book management is practiced, Kelly and Smith emphasized that the bonus program is the main financial incentive and that the open-book disclosures are directed toward that end, even though PSS also maintains an ESOP program and an employee stock purchase plan. In addition, Kelly placed $1 million of PSS stock into a special pool to be distributed among employees who attend 10 of 12 Challenge meetings during the year.

After one year of service with PSS, employees can divert up to 10 percent of their pay into the ESOP. Accordingly, employees who draw a constant annual salary of $30,000 and who began putting 10 percent of their salary into the ESOP in 1994 (the IPO year) would have about $15,800 in the ESOP three years later. Of this, $6,800 is appreciation on the PSS stock, representing a compound annual return of 34 percent.

With these plans in place and promoted throughout the company and with the dramatic gains in PSS share value, employee attention will naturally be drawn to the PSS stock price. Yet the open-book focus remains on individual branch results, and very little financial information at the company level is reported to all employees. Smith notes the following:

> We used to tell our people what our monthly sales were on a consolidated basis. We sort of stopped doing that because the information might start leaking out to the public. So what we've now focused on is just giving each individual branch their numbers. And if we set a record or if there's some event that is significant, we'll tell them that one event, like we hit a record in sales for the month. But we won't tell them what our quarter-to-date number is or any consolidated data.
>
> As a public company, the process has become more difficult because we would truly like to share every number of the consolidated corporation with our employees to get them excited about the overall company because they have stock in the ESOP, they have their investment in the 401(k)—so they feel good about their company overall. But we're limited in what we can and can't say with the SEC and the insider trading rules.

So is it realistically possible to practice open-book management in a public company? Kelly says yes, and the solution is what he calls the sharing piece, which is basically all information at the branch level:

> On open-book for us today, the only piece that we share with the employees is the sharing piece. I don't stand up in front of them today and say, "This is what I make in salary." I stopped doing that even before we went public. Today it doesn't matter. They can pick up the newspaper in Jacksonville and read what I make, and the other officers of the company. But it was clear they are only interested in the open-book piece that affects *them.* I mean it's just the way the world is. Fortunately for us, the employees are in it for gain. That's the American way.

Open-book management at PSS is constructed around the sharing piece. But the company firmly believes that any branch employee can benefit the branch operations by having access to the sharing piece. Staudinger, the warehouse leader, compares his experience with information at PSS to his previous career in the Marines:

> It gets you more, what would you call it, branch-minded. You know, hey, if we're going to succeed as a branch, everybody's got to come together. If you want a bonus, turn the heater off just a little bit early, save that money on the gas bill. In the Marine Corps, it was *spend it.*

The sharing piece gives employees greater awareness of the bottom line, and that awareness shows up in unexpected ways; as Rolling says, "It really shocks salespeople when a truck driver comes up and says, 'Hey, I was looking at your numbers and they're a little low.' It puts people on the spot."

The sharing piece ultimately loops back to the company's incentive plan. Kelly offers some insights for other companies on open-book management, the sharing piece, and incentives:

> Tie an incentive package together for your employees in the certain parts of your business that drive productivity. At least share that information with them. And in doing that, you're going to be able to drive a lot more money for all the owners and everybody else running the company. And they can do it simply. What in each company drives productivity? Therefore, the process of driving productivity drives profits. Each business has got to decide.
>
> You could be in manufacturing: productivity could be making the product right the first time. In driving that part to be successful, as those gains come in place with your employees, there should be a mechanism for an open-book approach to rewarding them. They know what's going to be produced, they know the level of productivity, and as it increases they get rewards. It could be in distribution like us, reward on sales, or profitable sales. There are many ways to reward. And if they just focus on that, get the employees bought in, the rest of it will come naturally.

It's clear that Kelly believes that whether a company is public or private is irrelevant to the success of open-book management. For him, success comes from deciding on that company's unique productivity drivers and tying open-book incentives to those drivers. PSS would like to disclose all financial information to every employee—that's what the company's culture would dictate. But as a public company, PSS can disclose only the sharing piece in open-book fashion, and for PSS, that's fine.

The CFO's Role

> In the early days before we had a CFO, I was the CFO, chief marketing officer, everything. And we were something like 18 months into our formation before we had a full-time CFO. But ultimately the role of the CFO in these monthly meetings became the communicator to the employees of what financially we were doing. And it got so boring. To communicate financial information to employees is clearly a struggle on the employee's part to grasp what is being communicated to him.
>
> But as the company grew, the local management team does it for the local branch now. So once we got that big, the CFO's role [in open-book management] became really diminished.
>
> Pat Kelly

The CFO's role is diminished because open-book management at PSS is best viewed in the context of each branch. The CFO's role is critical to the branches, but in an indirect way with respect to open-book management. The importance of that role is evident in the areas of branch performance issues and information availability.

The CFO is intimately involved in tracking the performance of each branch and intervenes when needed. Smith explains his view of branch operating performance and his CFO role:

> It's a bell curve. You have a bell curve with 65 branches. You have 6 to 10 that aren't performing. You have 6 to 10 that are blowing it out. And you have 40-something that are in the middle that you're trying to push further to the right than to the left of the big bulge in the bell, because where you spend your time managing is in that middle 40. You're trying to implement new programs and tweak the

operations to get that middle 40 to move further to the more profitable group.

You leave the good ones alone and only make yourself available if they need you. The bad ones, no matter what you do, you're not going to really be able to turn them enough to compensate for the loss if they get really off track. So it's the middle 40 that you're spending all your time on.

When things are veering off track at a branch, Smith prefers to let the branch team members work out their own solutions. He acts as a facilitator to help the branches deal with their own problems. But as a former branch manager himself, he has little patience for excuses. Here Smith explains how the discussion would progress in a branch "town hall" meeting held after a new plan has been devised:

Because we have a new plan at that point in time, we talk about why the first one didn't work, just like we talked in the first meeting about why the forecast didn't work. And we talk about what we're going to do as a team and a unit to correct it.

Sometimes, managers come back and say, "I never should have signed off on that forecast—it was unrealistic." To that, Smith has the following reply:

[T]hat's a terrible answer. That's unacceptable. The reason it is not legitimate is because we set the forecast based on their input, not some number contrived at corporate. This isn't a forecast of what we might do if the stars align. This is a forecast of what we can do with the resources we have in play, with the people and talents of the branch, and with the marketplace we have.

Our normal parameter for PSS is growth. So these forecasts include growth. But our managers and our people are expected to grow and they're not expected to be comfortable with where they are.

For branches that are seriously off track, corporate intervention is swift and powerful:

We've got our hit list. You don't want to be visited twice by corporate. The suits show up. Actually, the first meeting is not a bad

> meeting because we try to say, "OK, you tell us what's wrong," meaning to the branch, you tell us what you *think* is wrong.
>
> And you could have everything from competition, to a change in the customer base, to a loss of a contract, to the manufacturers aren't supporting them, to we've lost two or three key people because of marriage or sickness or doing something else, or whatever. Our [employee] turnover's very low, but if you've got 65 branches, you're going to see as you go across the country every possible reason the business could go off track.

When branches remain off track even after Smith and associates have worked with them, changes in branch leadership usually occur. Kelly referred to that earlier as employees "firing their management." Smith elaborates, as follows:

> The employees will call us and say, "Look, this person is not leading us, they're not bringing the value to us to help us get back on track." When your employees can clearly see what needs to be done and management is not taking that action to get it done, then you know you have a problem because management has lost credibility with employees.
>
> You have to step in and make a change, or sometimes it's the employees who are off base. You have to bring in a plan that looks attractive to employees and to management, and have confidence built back up in management. And sometimes you have a great manager who just isn't doing well in the location and you move him or her.

As CFO, Smith runs the finance and accounting function at corporate headquarters. In PSS' incentive-based open-book environment, the timely flow of financial information to the branches is especially critical. Recently, Smith implemented a new system for the dissemination of the branch monthly financial statements that could serve as a model for efficiency and effectiveness. PSS calls this the A-Team Net.

PSS headquarters maintains the company's general ledger in an Oracle database. Branch information is downloaded into individual

Microsoft Excel spreadsheet files after each monthly closing, one file for each branch. Then branch management logs onto a special secure intranet connection. The branch Excel file is downloaded from the corporate server to the branch workstation's hard drive. The file is complete with a set of powerful macros that not only automate the process of printing the monthly statements but also allow the manager to see the general ledger detail for any number appearing on the statements down to exact posting information. Via macro execution, this information can be sorted in order of decreasing amount, for instance, to allow the manager to examine only the largest items. If travel expense is over budget, the manager can execute a macro that displays all postings to travel expense for the month. Another macro reorders the postings by amount of the charges instead of by date (the default). All this information is in the one self-contained Excel spreadsheet for that branch, which is a very large file of one to two megabytes. After download, the branch has immediate access to its full general ledger on its own computer and the ability to manipulate the display of the data in virtually any way possible.

Early experiments with using CompuServe persuaded PSS to set up its own intranet connection because transfer of the massive Excel files was too slow and there was too much potential for "traffic jams." With its own dedicated connection, the system is highly efficient. A printout of a typical branch's monthly general ledger detail will run a hundred pages or more. Before, these thick printouts were shipped overnight to the branches from headquarters. Now the branches download their own general ledgers immediately and can conveniently manipulate the display of the information to facilitate decision making.

For a public company with $1.3 billion in projected 1998 sales, PSS operates a very lean finance and accounting function at corporate headquarters. This example of using state-of-the-art technology in a cost-effective way to further improve the open-book management culture at PSS is typical of the creative problem solving that PSS shows in all areas of its business. And it helps to explain how PSS continues to exhibit extraordinary growth in apparent defiance of the laws of gravity.

7

Case Summary

It would be almost impossible to imagine PSS without open-book management. Pat Kelly and his team have imbued PSS from the beginning with a culture of trust, openness, and respect that literally could not exist without an open-book environment. In good times, opening the books and tying healthy incentives to performance has led to even greater growth and success. But as stated earlier, Kelly believes that open-book management literally saved the company:

> We had to take pay cuts twice, and the last time there were 525 employees who took pay cuts. The pay cuts varied from 3 percent for truck drivers all the way up to 20 percent for the senior management of the company. And no one left. We went five months under these pay cuts, and no employee left the company because of those pay cuts.
>
> They understood *why* we had to do it. We communicated it and there was trust—he's been telling us all these years where we are, what we're doing, sharing it with us; we're equity owners, we're part of this. So when it came time, the difficult issue was at hand, the pay cuts were in place, and the employees didn't leave. That was the benefit, it was significant at the time and it wasn't that long ago. It was five years ago. Five years ago this company was $50 million in sales. Next year we're going to a billion dollars. If we had not passed that point in time, we might not be where we are today.

As PSS has shown, open-book management can work very well in a large, public company, if management chooses the sharing piece carefully and links it with strong financial incentives. Kelly enthusiastically recommends open-book management across the board:

> I would encourage any company to be open book. Like I said, you don't have to expose everything. But enough where the employees feel they've got a stake in the organization, they've got a share in the organization. You don't have to disclose everything.

People Interviewed

Patrick C. Kelly, Chairman and CEO

David Smith, Chief Financial Officer

Brian Rolling, Branch Operations Leader

Rob Blackmore, Branch Sales Leader

Dale Staudinger, Branch Warehouse Leader

Plow & Hearth, Inc.

Open-book management is an extension of our quality efforts. It is one of the tools we use to be a quality organization. In and of itself, I am not sure if open-book management would really accomplish much if it were not in a context of an overall total quality management type of philosophy.

Peter G. Rice
President and Co-founder, Plow & Hearth, Inc.

Company Background

Plow & Hearth, Inc., is a national mail order company specializing in "products for country living." The company was a true "kitchen table" start-up when it was founded as a small retail store in 1980 by Peter and Peggy Rice. The catalog operation was begun in 1981 and conducted from a barn on the Rices' farm. In May 1994, the company moved the catalog operations from a temporary facility in Orange, Virginia, into the current headquarters located on a 38-acre site in Madison, Virginia. The new 120,000-square-foot warehouse was completed at a cost of \$3.25 million. A 5,000-square-foot retail store operates in an upscale shopping center in Charlottesville, Virginia. It shares the center with specialty retailers such as Talbots, Barnes & Noble, Blue Ridge Mountain Sports, Britches, and Laura Ashley.

Peter Rice is responsible for two prior start-ups. He started the highly successful Blue Ridge Mountain Sports, outdoor outfitters, while a graduate student at the University of Virginia's Darden Graduate School of Business Administration in the 1970s. Blue Ridge Mountain Sports was one of the East Coast's first specialty stores offering backpacking and outdoor adventure equipment. Although he sold his interest when he began Plow & Hearth, the company remains extremely successful and now has 10 stores concentrated in the Mid-Atlantic region. Rice left Blue Ridge to co-found a kayak manufacturing company in Kentucky. Phoenix Kayaks still exists, although Rice has since sold his interest.

For fiscal 1996, Plow & Hearth sales were almost $32 million, with all but about $1 million from the national catalog operation. The earnings before interest and taxes (EBIT) in 1996 were 8.5 percent of net sales. For specialty retail catalog companies an EBIT of 8 percent is generally viewed as exceptional performance; 5 to 6 percent is considered good performance. Since its humble beginnings, the company has had rapid growth (figure 8.1). The company received a spot on *Inc.* magazine's list of the 500 fastest growing companies in America from 1986–1989. When the company made the *Inc.* list for the fourth

Figure 8.1
Gross Mail Order and Retail Sales in Millions

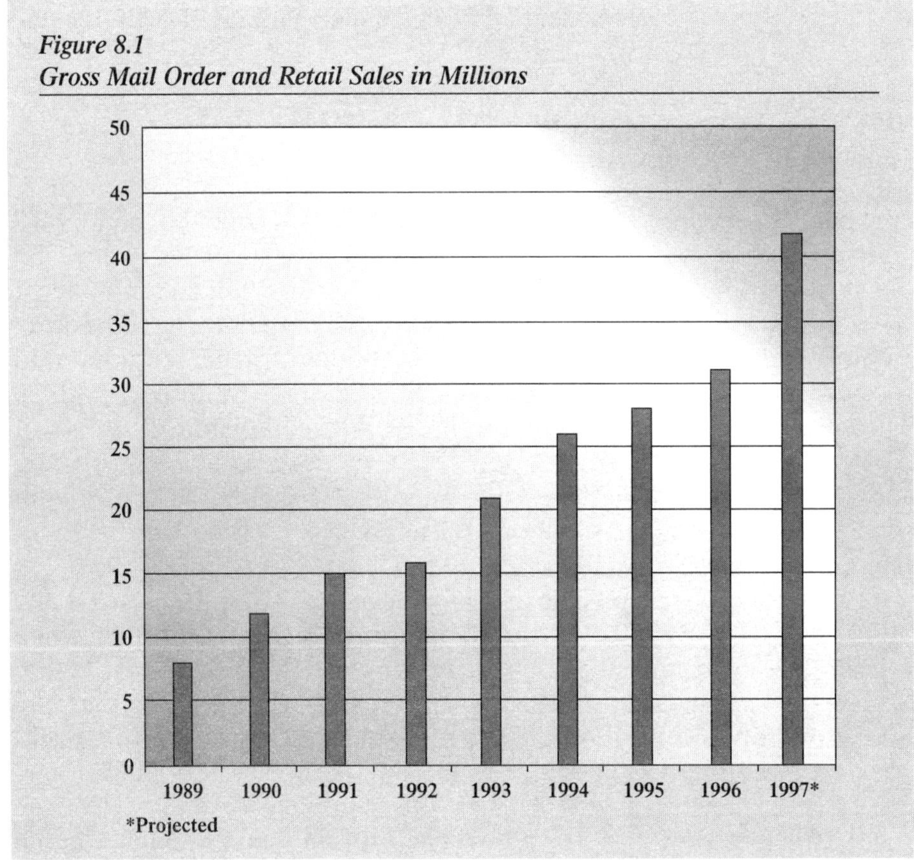

consecutive year in 1989, it joined an elite handful of companies. For that year, Plow & Hearth was number 454, with a sales growth of 642 percent. In 1997, the company will mail more than 20 million catalogs and projects sales of over $38 million. The growth in sales has been fueled by the trend among Americans toward a "more informal, country style of living." As Rice has noted, "Country living is a lifestyle—a state of mind as well as location."

The company has made several acquisitions that have broadened its product line and enhanced its sales growth. In 1983, Plow & Hearth purchased the customer list and computer system of The Warming Trend, a Vermont catalog company specializing in woodstove and hearth products. In 1985, the company purchased Green River Tools, a Vermont-based gardening catalog company. Additionally, Plow & Hearth acquired Kemp & George, a home furnishing catalog company, in 1990.

Plow & Hearth publishes four seasonal catalogs each year. Items in the catalog include hearth and fireplace accessories, outdoor furniture, functional clothing and footwear, practical lawn and garden tools and products, decorative lawn and garden accessories, problem-solving products and gadgets, and bird- and nature-related products. The company currently has more than 1.3 million mail-order buyers, of whom over 325,000 made a purchase in the past 12 months. In 1997, the company expects 556,000 telephone calls and anticipates shipping 460,000 orders. The company describes its customers as people who "generally have a love for the outdoors, a demonstrated concern for the environment, and an appreciation for high-quality products that are functional in nature."

Recognition has come to Rice for his retailing prowess. In 1992, he was selected by *Target Marketing* magazine as one of America's 100 Most Influential Direct Marketers. The Virginia Retail Merchants Association recognized him as its Retailer of the Year in 1995.

Company Culture

Plow & Hearth began as a family business. The original group included Peter and Peggy Rice; Peggy's sister, Marty, and her husband, Buzz VanSantvood; and Steve Wagner. As the company has grown since

1980, every effort has been made to maintain a family-type environment. The company has been very successful at hiring and retaining a highly motivated and skilled workforce. Employees are referred to as "associates"—a term that puts people on an equal footing. Currently, the company employs 72 full-time and 50 part-time associates. During the peak 1997 holiday season, Plow & Hearth anticipates having approximately 350 associates. About 12 of the associates are among the 45 stockholders of the company.

The tone set by Rice continues to foster a sense of family among associates. Rice has an open-door policy, he knows the names of the associates, and they feel very comfortable in telling him if they are upset or bothered by something. As an avid outdoors person, he leads associates on bicycle rides across the Virginia countryside and takes them kayaking. Associates note how Rice and the other managers are approachable and are often seen in the operating units. Most of the management team is home-grown. Associates are provided plenty of personal growth opportunities to match the growth of the company. There is a real sense that Plow & Hearth will succeed by operating as a partnership with all its stakeholders: customers, associates, stockholders, suppliers, and the community in which it operates.

An example of the company's partnership with the community is its Two for One program. In this program, Plow & Hearth, working with the Virginia Forestry Department, plants two seedlings for every tree used in the production of its catalogs. This program has been responsible for the reforestation of more than 100 acres of Virginia land. The company instituted this practice because it does not use recycled paper for its catalogs. After much investigation, management concluded that color photographs of the products in the catalog could not be rendered attractively on currently available recycled paper.

The adoption of a new mission statement also illustrates the company culture. Previously, the Plow & Hearth mission statement read:

> We will profitably build our company by anticipating and meeting the needs of our customers while delivering unparalleled service and high-quality, unique, functional products through our direct marketing and retail efforts.

One day Rice asked one of the associates to describe the company's mission. The associate was honest with Rice and said, "Peter, I don't know. You guys developed that statement in a management meeting and I cannot remember it." Rice then asked, "Why are we here?" An associate provided this reason: "We are really here for customers, for associates, and for profits. And we are here to be world-class in all three." In this somewhat informal manner the mission statement was simplified under the acronym of "CAP," which stands for "customers, associates, and profits." According to Rice, the company's strategic plan is "driven off of CAP and the desire to be a world-class organization."

Quality-Driven Culture

Plow & Hearth became involved in the total quality movement in 1990 when Peter and Peggy Rice attended the Malcolm Baldrige Quest for Excellence presentation in Washington, D.C. According to John Whitlow, Vice President of Human Resources, the company's effectiveness is attributed to a structured, total quality management process that is called quality improvement process (QIP). The company's QIP benefited from instruction provided by two vendors—Federal Express (a 1990 winner of the Baldrige Award) and Quad/Graphics, the printer of its catalog and a company included in the book, *The 100 Best Companies to Work for in America.* Federal Express conducted a one-day course for Plow & Hearth, and Quad/Graphics led a two-day program.

The QIP steering committee was established to oversee the company's quality efforts. In turn, the QIP steering committee designates corporate action teams (CATs) as needed to undertake specific quality projects. Plow & Hearth also surveys associates and customers, and the information is used to improve specific processes. Dawn Mahoney Cottrell, Vice President of Finance, noted the following:

> We survey our associates and our customers, then communicate the feedback to everyone. It's a complete loop: gathering data, listening to what people say, finding which areas need improvement, and then empowering associates to make changes and follow through. Then we resurvey to make sure the improvements have taken place. Through education and training, and by sharing information, they [associates] feel a sense of ownership and involvement in making changes.[1]

The company annually administers a 33-item associate satisfaction survey (figure 8.2). Questions 1–13 focus on leadership and questions 14–33 on the overall work environment. In addition, the company has a service quality index (SQI) of 12 measures related to customer service that are tracked weekly (table 8.1). Each metric has its own tracking bulletin board in the lunchroom. Each board includes the goal for that metric, an explanation of the metric, a monthly chart, a weekly indicator, and either a green or a yellow flag. A green flag indicates that the goal has been met for the previous week, and a yellow flag indicates that it has not been met. When the weekly results are posted with a yellow flag, a cross-functional team of management and line associates from different departments, designated as service quality index advocates, must research what occurred in the process to prevent the company from meeting the satisfaction goal. The advocates' team writes an explanation, which is posted on the bulletin board, and indicates what is to be done to meet the goal the next week.

Each catalog states the company's "spirit of country living," which is: "if for any reason, at any time, you are less than 100 percent satisfied with a product you have purchased from us, you may return it for exchange or full refund." In describing the spirit of country living, the catalog contains this statement:

> Like owners of the "old-fashioned" country store, we believe in treating our customers like our neighbors and friends. We offer only products we use or would use ourselves, we offer them at fair prices, and we guarantee them without conditions. That's the spirit of country living we practice at Plow & Hearth.

As Cottrell stated, "When merchandise returns were analyzed several years ago, we found out that most of them were the result of poor product quality. So we started quality control at the receiving area and worked more closely with our vendors to eliminate problems." That effort has reduced returns and translated into savings or an increase in net sales. As part of its QIP, the company began in 1993 the Plow & Hearth's Partners in Quality Program. This program recognizes vendors "who have provided exemplary vendor services to Plow & Hearth for at least three years." The company publishes *The Vendor Connection,* a newsletter for Plow & Hearth suppliers. In the fall 1996 issue, the newsletter listed 15 vendors who had been recognized thus far by the

Figure 8.2
Survey/Feedback/Action 1995

		Total			
		1992	1993	1994	1995
	Base	percent	percent	percent	percent
1	I feel free to tell my manager what I think.				
2	My manager lets me know what's expected of me.				
3	Favoritism is not a problem in my work group.				
4	My manager helps us find ways to do our job better.				
5	My manager is willing to listen to my concerns.				
6	My manager asks for my ideas about things affecting my work.				
7	My manager lets me know when I've done a good job.				
8	My manager treats me with respect and dignity.				
9	My manager keeps me informed about things I need to know.				
10	My manager lets me do my job without interfering.				
11	My manager provides leadership and support to the QIP.				
12	My manager emphasizes quality improvement and customer satisfaction.				
13	My manager uses quality improvement techniques, tools, and processes in my work group.				
	Leadership Index 1-13:				
14	My manager's boss gives us the support we need.				
15	Upper management lets us know what the company is trying to accomplish.				
16	Upper management pays attention to ideas and suggestions from people at my level.				
17	I have confidence in the fairness of management.				

Figure 8.2
Survey/Feedback/Action 1995 (Continued)

		Total			
		1992	1993	1994	1995
	Base	percent	percent	percent	percent
18	I can be sure of a job as long as I do good work.				
19	I am proud to work for Plow & Hearth.				
20	Working for Plow & Hearth will probably lead to the kind of future I want.				
21	I think Plow & Hearth does a good job for our customers.				
22	All things considered, working for Plow & Hearth is a good deal for me.				
23	I am paid fairly for the kind of work I do.				
24	Our benefit programs seem to meet most of my needs.				
25	Most people in my work group cooperate with each other to get the job done.				
26	There is cooperation between my work group and other groups at Plow & Hearth.				
27	In my work environment we generally use safe work practices.				
28	Rules and procedures do not interfere with how well I am able to do my job.				
29	I am able to get the supplies or other resources I need to do my job.				
30	I have enough freedom to do my job well.				
31	My work group is involved in improving service to customers.				
32	The 1995 Survey/Feedback/Action concerns were addressed satisfactorily.				
33	I believe the QIP is resulting in positive changes at P & H.				
	Company Index 14-33:				
	Overall Average 1-33:				

Table 8.1
Service Quality Index

Week of: March 23, 1997–March 29, 1997

Standard	Score (percent)		Weight		SQI Score
On-time shipment	99.74	×	10	=	9.97
Fulfillment accuracy: order entry	98.00	×	10	=	9.80
Fulfillment accuracy: warehouse	95.00	×	10	=	9.50
Returns turnaround	100.00	×	6	=	6.00
Initial fill	100.00	×	10	=	10.00
Product satisfaction*	70.00	×	10	=	7.00
Customer satisfaction turnaround	99.00	×	6	=	5.94
Average speed of answer	100.00	×	5	=	5.00
Nonabandoned calls	100.00	×	9	=	9.00
Merch/IC/Inbound turnaround	100.00	×	5	=	5.00
Returns accuracy	100.00	×	10	=	10.00
Ship/Loss damage	95.00	×	9	=	8.55
	Service Quality Index				95.76

* The goal for this metric is that 100 percent of products to the customer are satisfactory. However, a customer may return merchandise for any reason for exchange or a full refund, and this metric is affected by the company's liberal return policy.

Partners in Quality program. The importance of this effort to the company's bottom line is revealed in the following facts: in each of the company's four catalogs, more than 300 vendors are represented; approximately 400 products are chosen for each catalog from well over 2,000 items considered; and the cost of space allocated to the average item in a recent catalog was $8,000, which includes production and marketing costs (postage, paper, list rental, printing, and photography).

The company's QIP has benefited greatly from the leadership of Whitlow, Vice President of Human Resources, who joined the company in 1993. Whitlow had previously worked in human resources at BellSouth Corporation and at Martha Jefferson Hospital in Charlottesville, Virginia. While at BellSouth, he taught in its leadership institute. He brought to Plow & Hearth experience in human resources, organizational development, and training. Whitlow has developed and taught numerous training workshops on a variety of management-related topics for Plow & Hearth associates. He has developed a 40-hour leadership institute, which is offered in modules over a six-week period. The program focuses on team-building skills and a variety of leadership issues. All full-time associates have now completed the company's leadership institute.

In 1993, Plow & Hearth applied for the U.S. Senate Productivity and Quality Award for the Commonwealth of Virginia, which is similar to the Malcolm Baldrige National Award. The USSPQA was established in December 1982 by the U.S. Senate to foster awareness of the need for productivity and quality improvement, as well as to recognize organizations at the state level that demonstrate results. The Commonwealth of Virginia began its process in 1982 and has the longest continuously running award program in the United States. (Interestingly, all the 1996 Baldrige award winners had previously won a USSPQA in their state.)

Plow & Hearth was a finalist for the USSPQA in 1993 and received the Medallion of Excellence in 1994. The citation for Plow & Hearth reads as follows:

> The medallion winner...in the private sector category has a well-integrated quality effort. They have created a unique approach in mail order catalog services and have involved many employees in training. Their top management leads their culture change. Their measures focus on process improvement. They have a strong customer focus and excellent supplier relationships.

Since receiving the USSPQA, the company has served as a quality training site for a group from the Federal Executives Institute, which is an executive training facility for senior-level executives from the federal government. Those sessions have involved telling the Plow & Hearth story. Also, Whitlow's human resources operation has become a profit center. Drawing on his experience with Plow & Hearth, he now spends about 20 percent of his time consulting with other organizations.

Open-Book Management

> Open-book management was an easy fit for our culture because that is the way we have always operated; it just formalized it all.
>
> Dawn Mahoney Cottrell
> Vice President of Finance

Plow & Hearth has a long history of sharing financial information with associates. In fact, no one could put a finger on when the company began doing it. Cottrell joined Plow & Hearth in 1989, and she has been sharing financial information in various ways with associates since that date. Rice stated that the company had shared financial information before Cottrell joined, but "she really made sure it happened on a regular basis." In the early years, Cottrell shared financial information on a semiannual basis at the company meetings held with all associates. At the company meeting coinciding with the end of the fiscal year, which corresponds to the calendar year, the annual financial results were shared with the associates. In an effort to make the annual financial statements seem less abstract, Cottrell described her approach at the company meetings as follows:

> Annually, I picked a product and brought it to the company meeting and went through the income statement line by line showing the impact of this product on our income statement. For example, if we sell the product for $10, I would remind them that we get 2 percent returns, so that is taken off whatever number we sell. I traced the product all the way to the bottom line indicating what the product cost us and what the various expenses were until we got to what we have on the bottom line for the product. This is a more meaningful way to explain to associates what net income means.

When Cottrell presented the 1996 financial statements, she did not use this approach because the associates had by then been trained through the open-book management courses, which are discussed in a later section.

In recent years, the company started having monthly huddle meetings with managers, who are accompanied to the meeting by an associate. In these meetings, the financial statement variances from the previous month are discussed. Managers have to report on the variances for which they are responsible and must explain why they are over or under budget. They also complete the "open-book management huddle meeting score card" (appendix), which gives the financial benchmarks for the month. This form is taken back to the department and discussed with the associates in each work group. It is also posted in the lunchroom.

Although financial information has been shared with associates for several years, "open-book management" was not used to describe the process until recently. Plow & Hearth started referring to this initiative as open-book management about the time that they were applying for the USSPQA in 1993 and 1994. It was also during these years that Rice came across Jack Stack's book, *The Great Game of Business,* which, he stated, "really appealed to him." Rice provided this overview:

> I am a very competitive person and I have always been involved in sports, so that the analogy in Stack's book really hit home. It is absolutely true, if you don't know how to score in a game, you are just going to be running around the field. So kind of typical of the way we've done things is, if we see a good idea, we do not study it very long. We just figure we are going to do this because it makes great sense.
>
> We had been looking at open-book management and were figuring out how to make it work here at about the time that we had our first really crummy year. In 1995, the pressures applied by the bank were very tough. We had told everybody about the budget, and we would have monthly reviews as well as our quarterly reviews, but those did not seem to mean anything to people in terms of what they had to do with their job security. When we started making some of the decisions that we had to in 1995, it came as more of a shock to people than I had expected it would. What we did is to say that we needed to accelerate the program so we started having weekly meetings with everybody filling them in on what exactly happened that week. And, obviously, everybody appreciated it immensely. It is something one needs to do anyway, but we began at

that point to think about training for our associates on the income statement, and we started our huddle meetings.

1995: A Defining Year for Open-Book Management

In 1995 Plow & Hearth had a challenging year, which in retrospect enabled the company to make considerable progress in its open-book management initiative. Despite a national trend in 1995 toward a softening market for catalog sales and rising costs for catalog production, the company ended the year with sales growth. However, during the year some difficult decisions had to be made. External factors facing the company included a 60 percent increase in paper prices and a 14 percent increase in postage. Along with these factors, sales from the spring/summer 1995 catalog did not materialize as expected. The company had included a number of new products in that catalog and had done some prospecting by renting mailing lists to expand the distribution of its catalog and to increase sales. Renting the mailing lists increased costs. Also, at this time the company was undercapitalized, and the bank placed additional covenants on the company's line of credit. Additional capital was raised from stockholders, but when sales did not develop as planned, the company had a severe cash-flow problem. Frequent meetings were held with the associates to explain the financial situation.

When the situation did not improve, the company had to lay off people. Everybody took time off without pay, and everyone's salary was reduced. When it was all over, the company had gone from about 89 to 65 associates. All of this was a new experience for the company, which had a history of growth. As Cottrell observed, "We shared the financial woes with the associates through weekly meetings telling them exactly where we stood. Everyone was involved in brainstorming with their department to try to determine how costs could be reduced." At the meetings, associates reported what they were doing to save money for the company and offered suggestions to further reduce costs. For example, it was suggested that the company do more mailings with the U.S. Postal Service, which provides boxes at no charge, rather than use a private express mail carrier. (This suggestion was tested and implemented.)

Another suggestion was that everyone pay $30 a month toward their benefits.

As 1995 ended, the company had successfully met the challenges, and open-book management had become more firmly embedded in the company's culture. Accordingly, it was decided that open-book management would be a theme for the company during 1996. The following statement was posted on a bulletin board near the lunchroom to remind everyone about the theme:

> Open-book management involves educating and involving all employees in the financial management of the business in order to maximize profitability, to enhance the quality of work life, and to promote the overall business success of the company.

Training

To reinforce the theme, specific training in open-book management was initiated. Although financial information had been shared with associates for a number of years, many of them did not know what the numbers meant and how their work affected the numbers. Hence, the company began offering two new training courses in 1996: Open-Book Management I and Open-Book Management II. The technical course content was written by Cottrell, and advice on the instructional process was provided by Whitlow.

The first course teaches associates how to read and fully understand a portion of the Plow & Hearth income statement. This course, which takes three hours, focuses on revenues, gross margins, cost of goods sold, marketing margins, and explains how these relate to Plow & Hearth's business operations. A case study called Limelite, Inc. takes a product (limelite) from the Plow & Hearth catalog and traces the product through the Plow & Hearth income statement to the marketing margin line item. Open-Book Management II, which takes four hours, builds on the first course and focuses on concepts of fixed expenses, variable expenses, income before interest and taxes, and net income. This course also utilizes the case study introduced in the first course, and in both courses the associates from different departments work in groups of two on the case. Both courses include a discussion of the company's application of open-book management and of how this management practice affects associates' departments and positions within the company. All full-time associates are required to take both courses.

The next level of open-book management training is a course called "The Profit and Cash Game: Developing Business Literacy." This is a business simulation game that has participants manage the financial aspects of a company. The game is highly interactive and competitive, and teaches business finance and budgeting skills. This three-hour course is taught by Cottrell. All associates are required to take this new course.

In this course, the "Profit and Cash Game"[2] is played in teams of five associates with two teams to a course. Teams compete to see which comes closest to meeting the financial goals set at the outset of the game. The play proceeds in a way that one might visualize in "Monopoly" or other board games. The players on each team take turns rolling the dice, advancing on the board, and drawing cards that contain business decisions. The objective is to teach the associates to think like owners and to see the big picture of running a business. The intended learning outcomes include the following:

1. Profit is not the same as cash.
2. A company cannot operate without cash.
3. Companies increase profits by increasing sales and controlling or lowering cost.
4. Companies increase cash by speeding up collections on sales and by avoiding unnecessary cash outlays.

The game encourages teamwork and introduces participants to huddle meetings at which the team assembles information from the business decisions that they have made to prepare their company's financial reports. Financial ratios and percentages based on the financial statements are also calculated. One of the deficiencies with the game is that it is based on rolling the dice, allowing chance rather than judgment to determine business decisions. However, as Cottrell noted, "There are a lot of similarities in the game to what happened to Plow & Hearth in 1995, like increases in cost and having to negotiate with the banker." Cottrell has indicated that once all the associates have completed the profit and cash course, the company would like to offer a course on the balance sheet and cash-flow statement.

A focus meeting with five Plow & Hearth associates revealed the impact that open-book management has had on the company and its operations. The associates emphasized the importance of the program, and especially of the open-book management classes, to their understanding of the larger context of their work and to the way they do that work.

With regard to the program's overall importance, one associate said the following,

> I have never worked for a company that is open about the financial information like Plow & Hearth. In other jobs, I never knew what was going on. It was just a place to go. You did not feel a part of the company. I think it is ridiculous to run a company any other way than to just be open, totally open about what is going on and making people feel engaged in the bottom line. You feel that you are responsible for what is happening to the company and it is not only the president who is responsible.

Specifically, associates stressed the significance of the open-book management courses to the program's success. One associate put it this way:

> The company had always shared financial information with us, but we did not have as good an understanding of what it all meant as we do now. Since taking the courses, when we have a meeting and they share the financial information, I am able to understand more of what they are talking about.

Another associate remarked as follows:

> I think accounting in general is kind of dry stuff, but when you can apply it specifically to what you are doing every day-in and day-out and how you can make improvements in the bottom line, it starts to become a lot more interesting and real to you.

The associates reported that, as a result of open-book management, they have a much clearer understanding of the company, its business, and how their own work contributes to it. One associate noted the following:

> Plow & Hearth has always been very customer focused. That has always been what has driven our business. I don't think we really

> thought about profit that much until we started doing open-book management. It just really matched with our focus on the customer and now everybody just thinks about it more and probably the single biggest benefit is that it is all on our minds. It is not just the customer, but it is how we can also be profitable. Now everybody talks about EBIT. That is part of our culture and that is how we talk to each other.

Another associate agreed: "The focus on profitability just permeates the company at every level. When you understand the financial statements, you realize the company did not just deliberately cut our pay in 1995 because they wanted to do it, but it was a matter that they had to do it."

The program's success might best be gauged by the effect it has had on associates' approach to their own work. Here are three examples described in the focus meeting:

> I have been on a team where we are trying to reduce returns because we have done studies and it costs us around $25 each time an item comes back. The team meets on a weekly basis, and we look at how we can change the copy or pictures in the catalog or something because we know that impacts the bottom line.

> I don't think we really ever took into account what it costs to run a business. I think employees try to keep the costs down. They don't waste like they ordinarily would.

> In the warehouse, the team leaders are very involved in setting up budgets and working on the budgets with the warehouse manager. They are not keeping us in the dark. We know how much money we have to spend, how many people we can hire, and it is very open.

Bonus Plan for Associates

When Cottrell came to work for Plow & Hearth in 1989, the company had a bonus plan but it had not been formalized. As she noted, "If we had profits, the Board of Directors would designate a sum to be shared with the associates." According to Rice, "The bonus was discretionary; it was after the fact and, therefore, it was not a motivator." In 1995, the associates took a salary reduction, and in 1996 the company did not give raises. Going into 1996, the Board of Directors stated that if the company at year-end hit EBIT of 3 percent, the reductions in salary would be restored. Also, earnings above 3 percent EBIT would be shared—20 percent would go to associates and 80 percent would be retained in the company.

As previously indicated, 1996 was a good year for the company: it earned 8.5 percent EBIT, and bonuses averaged about 17 percent of an associate's salary. Once the company knew that the 3 percent EBIT was going to be made, it restored for each associate an amount equal to the salary reduction. In the first pay period in January 1997, another 5 percent was paid out to associates, with the balance distributed in March 1997.

At the monthly meeting in early February 1997, Rice told associates that a bonus plan was in the works for the year, and as soon as it was finalized it would be explained to them. For 1997, the compensation committee of the Board of Directors has set a goal for the company of 5 percent EBIT. The bonus plan, which has limits prescribed in it, is based on exceeding that target.

Recent Changes

In addition to the monthly huddle meetings with managers, the company holds monthly meetings and quarterly town hall meetings with all associates. At the monthly meetings, Cottrell discusses the company's financial affairs in general. During the quarterly town hall meetings, a more extensive discussion of the quarterly financial results occurs. At the town hall meetings in 1996, Cottrell added a new twist to open-book management by having associates explain some of the line items on the income statement. For example, at one of the town hall meetings an associate discussed the line item for import duties by taking a rubber boot that Plow & Hearth imports and discussing why the company imports it, what it costs, and what the company pays in import duties. The associates making the presentation have a good learning experience, and their fellow associates seem to appreciate the fact that one of their peers is making the presentation. In 1997, Cottrell is continuing the practice of having associates assist her in explaining the financial statements at the quarterly town hall meetings.

Change has also occurred in the monthly huddle meeting—variances are now reported and discussed. The company is reconsidering how to report the variances when the comparisons are made for year-to-date information and how to explain variances that are the same from one meeting to the next. Also, Cottrell has assigned many budget line items to other members of the management group so that they now have some responsibility for preparing the budget.

Reflections on the Implementation of Open-Book Management

Cottrell explains the success of open-book management at Plow & Hearth by first noting the importance of the company president's involvement:

> I have been involved with some companies where the president would not allow the financial information to be shared. The implementation of open-book management at Plow & Hearth would not be possible without the total support of the president, Peter Rice, and his willingness to have the associates know the financial results and his support of the training necessary for them to understand the information.

Without his support for teaching associates about the company's money-making methods and about accounting, open-book management would not work.

However, she noted, "We should have begun the training on the income statement that was done with the two open-book courses long before we did. We had the company meetings of all the associates and went through the financial statements, and probably only 10 or 20 percent of the associates understood what we were discussing," because they had not yet learned about the income statement. In addition to doing the basic training sooner, she stated that the company probably should have used a generic game such as "Profit and Cash" before the income statement training. Cottrell also noted that she would have liked to have made better pairings among the groups that worked on the case study in the open-book management courses.

As Vice President of Finance, Cottrell's role in implementing the open-book management at Plow & Hearth has been that of "chief financial educator." Cottrell, a CPA, studied accounting as an undergraduate, then earned an MBA and worked with a Big Six accounting firm and in industry as an assistant controller before joining Plow & Hearth. She has tried to seize every opportunity for associates to learn how the company makes money. In her opinion, the chief financial officer must have an "organizational focus as well as an accounting and finance one." She noted the following:

> I think you can be too much either way. You can be an accountant who loves the financial details but you are not able to see the big picture. You must understand the long-term strategy of the company. I see my role as keeping my eyes and ears open as to what is happening in the industry and within the company. I must be able to gauge what is happening in the industry and understand it with my accounting and finance background.

Cottrell went on to say, "I see the financial person's role as being really good with financial information, but being even better at managing and coaching people and understanding things other than just the structured, financial data." The chief financial officer (or in her case, the vice president of finance) must be "able to balance the creative part of the position and the structured analytical part." One of Cottrell's colleagues pointed out that "she has the blend of all the best CFOs with whom I have ever worked."

When asked if there is any concern about anyone in the company giving financial information to someone outside the organization, Cottrell stated that "they have never been too concerned about that. And we figure, what if the company's financial information is disclosed outside the company? What can competitors gain from that?"

Case Summary

Plow & Hearth implemented open-book management in the context of its quality effort. President Peter Rice views open-book management as an extension of that initiative. In 1995, Plow & Hearth faced a number of challenges in its business. Frequent meetings were held during that year with associates to brainstorm ways to reduce costs. Coming out of that difficult experience, the company strengthened its commitment to open-book management and made open-book management a theme for the company in 1996. Three courses were developed to teach associates how the company makes money and what the income statement is. All associates have taken the first two courses, and, indications are that they have a much better appreciation of what it takes for the company to be profitable.

Without the strong support of Peter Rice, open-book management would not have taken hold as it has. Also, Dawn Mahoney Cottrell, Vice President of Finance, has been committed to sharing financial information and to offering training courses in accounting for all associates. Training for open-book management is part of the overall training program led by John Whitlow, Vice President of Human Resources. In summary, open-book management has now become a vital part of Plow & Hearth's culture.

People Interviewed

Peter G. Rice, President

Dawn Mahoney Cottrell, Vice President of Finance

John H. Whitlow, Vice President of Human Resources

Associates in focus group: Elizabeth M. Colvin, Customer Satisfaction; Susan L. Couch, Inventory Control; Carolyn S. Crawford, Returns Processing; Christopher W. Duncan, Marketing; and Nora Anne Shifflett, Receiving.

Endnotes

1. "Managing 'Total Quality,'" in "Operations and Fulfillment Think Tank," *Operations and Fulfillment* (March/April 1994): 57. (Panel in which Dawn Mahoney Cottrell participated.)

2. "Profit and Cash" (Kansas City, MO: Capital Connections, Inc., 1996).

Appendix

Plow & Hearth, Inc.
Open-Book Management
Huddle Meeting Score Card

Month ________________

KEY INDICATORS:

	SPRING 199_	SPRING 199_	SUMMER 199_	SUMMER 199_
Sales per book	$________	$________	$________	$________
Catalog cost per book	$________	$________	$________	$________

	FALL 199_	FALL 199_	HOLIDAY 199_	HOLIDAY 199_
Sales per book	$________	$________	$________	$________
Catalog cost per book	$________	$________	$________	$________

	YTD 199_	YTD 199_
Sales/payroll	$________	$________
Sales per full-time equivalent	$________	$________
Cost per call	$________	$________
Cost per box shipped	$________	$________
Initial fill	$________	$________
Inventory turnovers	$________	$________

	MONTH ACTUAL	MONTH PROJECTED	PRIOR YEAR ACTUAL
Call summary	$________	$________	$________
Order summary	$________	$________	$________

INCOME STATEMENT ITEMS:

	YTD 199_ ACTUAL	YTD 199_ BUDGET
Sales	$________	$________
Returns	$________ percent	$________ percent
Cancels	$________ percent	$________ percent
Cost of goods sold	$________ percent	$________ percent

	YTD 199_ ACTUAL	YTD 199_ BUDGET
VARIABLE:		
Salaries—fulfillment	______ percent	______ percent
Net shipping (income)/expense	______ percent	______ percent
Telephone—fulfillment	______ percent	______ percent
TOTAL VARIABLE:	______ percent	______ percent
OTHER INCOME:		
List rental income	$______	$______
TOTAL FIXED EXPENSE:	$______	$______
EARNINGS BEFORE INTEREST & TAXES $______		$______
BALANCE SHEET:	199_	199_
Cash	$______	$______
Inventory	$______	$______
Accounts payable	$______	$______
Line of credit borrowings	$______	$______
ANNUAL PROJECTIONS:	FORECAST	BUDGET
Sales	$______	$______
Net sales	$______	$______
EBIT percent	$______	$______
Bonus Pool	$______	$______

Update on action plans:
Cost of backorder ______________________________
Initial fill ______________________________
Cost of return ______________________________
Cancellation team ______________________________
Discount team ______________________________
New Action plans: ______________________________

Springfield ReManufacturing Corp.

I wasn't brought up to study history as a way of determining what the future was going to be. I was always taught to reinvent the future.... For 14 years we have been on this incredible odyssey of opening up our books. Not only have we opened up our books, but we have opened up an educational process to bring people up to speed to learn about business.[1]

Jack Stack
CEO of Springfield ReManufacturing Corp.

Introduction

The story of Jack Stack, CEO of Springfield ReManufacturing Corp., has become almost legendary in contemporary business lore. It is the story of how he and his partners transformed a struggling division of International Harvester into a profitable, $100-million company and, in the process, invented a powerful new philosophy for doing business—open-book management. The basics of this philosophy are simple in concept but require a comprehensive new vision of the structure and function of business organizations: Bring intelligence into the workplace, teach employees to see the big picture, provide incentives, and distribute wealth. Stack now travels extensively, spreading his open-book philosophy to *Fortune* 500 executives and to young entrepreneurs alike. In addition, more than 3,000 visitors have traveled to Springfield to witness open-book management in action and to attend SRC's bimonthly "huddles," in which employees, managers, and executives construct financial statements in assembly-line fashion. They watch as representatives from SRC's growing number of spin-off divisions supply their particular numbers to the statements and present good and bad news that will affect the corporation's bottom line and, therefore, everyone's quarterly bonus.

It is an extraordinary process to witness, and many visitors who see this side of open-book management can't wait to return home and emulate it in their own organizations. Who wouldn't be impressed when employees work together, with high energy and enthusiasm, to improve the company's bottom line? But once visitors leave Springfield and think about all the changes that must occur before they can have their own company huddles, questions begin to arise. Will SRC's version of open-book management work for them? Will it succeed in a large, unionized, conservative company or in a new high-tech venture as well as it does at SRC? What changes are needed to make it work, and how long will it take to yield positive results? What if open-book management doesn't succeed? Will the company be worse off for having tried but failed? Stack and other SRC executives are convinced that open-book management can help *every* company, as long as employees know the rules of the game, are involved in the action, know how to keep score, and have a stake in the outcome. Stack is so convinced of open-book management's value to other companies that he has bet SRC corporate profits on it by creating a separate division, The Great Game of Business, to spread the word.

Clearly, Stack and other SRC staff members have a vested interest in spreading the gospel about open-book management. But what are outsiders to make of Stack and his story, amid the growing amount of adulation he receives in the popular business press and his near-cult status among other believers who have successfully adopted SRC's practices?[2]

This case describes certain features of SRC's current use of open-book management and SRC executives' assessment of its prospects for working in other companies. The case, therefore, is not just about SRC or about Jack Stack—both of those stories have been told many times. Instead, it will examine why open-book management succeeds at SRC and will discuss the attractions and challenges of implementing its techniques in other organizations. The aim is to help financial executives determine whether open-book management is just another passing fad or, as author John Case suggests, "the coming business revolution."[3]

The Genesis of Open-Book Management

SRC was a small, precarious division of International Harvester (IH) in 1983 when Jack Stack and 12 other IH managers decided to take the company private in a leveraged buyout. Facing 22-percent interest rate payments, the loss of its major customer, and the possibility of employee layoffs, Stack decided to share the company's financial problems with every employee. He held nothing back, opened up the books, conducted a lot of meetings, and described what was needed in financial terms for the company to pull through and survive.[4]

Irene Schaefer, executive at large with SRC's corporate staff, started as a shipping and receiving clerk with SRC in 1979, while it was still a division of IH. She witnessed firsthand the transition to open-book management. She recalls that SRC had no cash when it started and that making payroll was a real challenge. Each day, she notes, people watched how much they sold, how much they bought, and how much they could spend. There were just over 100 employees, and everyone was learning how to run a business without any money. She says, "Open-book management...was the only way we were going to survive."

Stack and his co-owners staked the future of SRC, and their own fortunes, on two simple functions: communication and education. According to Schaefer, communication was a problem at SRC before the buyout:

> When we were International Harvester it was very, very evident that we had walls. Production didn't talk to purchasing, engineering, or accounting. We were in our own little world. And very quickly after SRC formed, those walls came down.

One of Stack's first moves toward dismantling the walls was to move the controller into production, where he taught factory supervisors about the importance of improving financial statements, if only to meet requirements of the company's loan. Supervisors then passed along what they learned to rank-and-file employees. Meanwhile, the human resources manager served as a production manager and taught employees about the employee relations side of the business. By shifting into different areas in this way, SRC managers experienced firsthand different facets of the business, and SRC's production employees were exposed to different types of managers.

The result was an expansive, invigorating learning experience, in which all employees gained a fuller understanding of every facet of the business, as well as its problems and its progress. This understanding, in turn, helped instill an all-for-one spirit throughout the company, in which employees and executive staff came to see every function of the business as mutually supportive and mutually rewarding.

Such an organizational style is far different from what Stack had started with at IH. Stack says that when he worked at IH, he was never taught about the business as a whole—what makes it work and what needs to be done, in financial terms, for it to succeed. Although he was entrusted with hundreds of millions of dollars of machine tools, for example, he never knew the financial implications of allocating fixed costs.

As SRC gained stability and began to prosper, its management team came to realize not only that it had saved a business enterprise, but that it was pioneering a radically innovative and successful strategy for running a business. SRC's ability to rely on employees to reduce costs, meet delivery deadlines, and develop new products and markets convinced Stack that techniques developed at SRC out of desperation could help every company improve its performance, in good and bad times alike. As SRC has continued its pioneering work during the past 15 years, it has refined open-book management into a definitive set of principles and procedures and, more recently, has formalized the approach in a set of products, consulting services, and training aids marketed as "The Great Game of Business" by the SRC division of the same name.

Open-Book Management at SRC Today

Schaefer cautions that open-book management is not supported across the board by all SRC employees. No matter what management approach a company chooses, there will always be some employees who just want to come to work, put in eight hours, and go home. They don't care if the company is making money or losing money, as long as they have a job; and they never seem to realize that if the company continues to lose money, they are not going to have a job. There are such employees at SRC and at every company—very good people in terms of skills and perhaps some of the best workers. They love it when they receive a bonus check, but they never get into the whole game.

Although open-book management is not a condition of employment at SRC, every new hire is informed that SRC is an open-book company. In a series of interviews, prospective employees meet first with a human resources person, then with their supervisor, and finally with a panel of three SRC employees who are looking to see how well the prospective hire will do in the company. These panels usually consist of two peers and one supervisor/manager. During the meetings, prospective employees often realize they will not fit in at SRC and take themselves out of the process.

After employees are hired, they go through an orientation at the factory level. About two or three months later they receive a corporate orientation, which includes a half-day exposure to open-book management concepts and another half-day of training with the Yo-Yo workbook (see page 33). The book is written at a sixth-grade reading level and introduces basic accounting and business concepts in very understandable terms. A year or so after this orientation, new hires attend one of SRC's monthly two-day seminars—the same one that visitors attend in Springfield. Managers and salaried employees go through the seminar as well, but much sooner after they begin work.

Perhaps the most important part of SRC's open-book management program is the staff meetings, or huddles. Huddles are held every week across the corporation to update monthly and quarterly budgets and compare actual results with the forecast. On Wednesday morning, SRC holds division-level huddles to disseminate the week's numbers. Each of the corporation's 1,000 employees who is working that day is required to attend the meeting—a requirement that imposes a definite cost in lost production time. The meetings may last from 15 to 30 minutes, depending on the supervisor's speed in presenting the numbers or on the issues that arise. The meetings are structured, disciplined, and focused on the most significant issues.

Every other week, pre-staff meetings are held on Tuesday afternoons so divisions can get their numbers ready for the Wednesday morning, corporate-level staff meeting. In this huddle, chaired by Stack or, in his absence, a senior-level manager, division representatives come together to report their numbers, update the budget and variances, and talk about new ideas, surprises, or anything else that might be newsworthy. After the meeting, the corporate-wide numbers are taken back to the divisions, and a manager or supervisor personally informs every person in the division about the latest corporate numbers. The HR staff conducts post-huddle audits to ensure that every employee has been informed.

Denise Bredfeldt, President of BizLit, Inc., an SRC subsidiary, says the weekly huddles are the principal way SRC provides ongoing business literacy education to employees. She wrote the *Yo-Yo* workbook and believes the weekly huddles cement the concepts presented in the book because people are exposed to new financial issues every week. When Stack attends the meetings, he usually takes the first 10 or 15 minutes to provide something educational to the gathering. He might pick up the *Wall Street Journal,* talk about a particular article, and describe how the scenario would play out at SRC. Or he may discuss a trend in SRC's cash-flow statement or balance sheet and ask employees how they are going to fix it. Thus, the huddles do much more than just bring the numbers together; they gather people together for informal, but crucial, communication. It is important for everyone to know, for example, that a subsidiary has lost a major customer, because that customer may be the customer of another subsidiary and the problems that ended the relationship might be preventable in the future.

Much of the information that is spread through huddles could be communicated electronically, but both Bredfeldt and Schaefer believe there is immeasurable value in communicating results person to person. Also, SRC goes through a more detailed and participative annual planning process than most companies. Each fall, managers meet with groups of employees to set the coming year's goals and to formulate, rank, and fold objectives into a detailed budget plan. Management establishes the yearly bonus, and the company pays it in quarterly installments as targets are met.[5]

SRC's bonus plan ensures that everyone throughout the company has a common goal. Bonuses are based on the same number (such as sales, production, and purchasing) at each plant, division, and functional area. However, SRC does differentiate between levels of payment. Hourly employees earn bonuses of 13 percent of their annualized income, including overtime. Exempt and management personnel receive 18 percent of salary because they are not paid overtime but work on evenings or weekends. There is also a special "top gun" award for outstanding achievements. This award is determined by the board of directors and is given to five or ten people a year.

People throughout the organization take on responsibility for the numbers. Management's main role is to provide constant and highly visible feedback. This feedback occurs through the weekly huddle process and, as a result, SRC's workforce is highly informed and exceptionally business literate. Everyone is part of the team, and the numbers help unify the organization to aim for the same target. The huddle process gets everybody talking about the same issues and shows them that they need each other to be successful, that there are names and people behind the numbers. When SRC plays games that involve accounting numbers, it provides a very human aspect to the accounting system.

Stack describes the importance of financial statements to the success of open-book management in vivid terms:

> We began to realize that we had to spread ourselves out, and all we had to do was look at the business differently than we had before; and we couldn't disregard all the messages that the financial statements were telling us. Financial statements are a crystal ball to tell you what you need to know in order to survive. And if you don't listen to them, somewhere down the line something is going to happen to you.

Over the past 15 years, SRC has changed the layout or format of its financial statements at least a dozen times, either to simplify them or to break out things that people have wanted to see in more detail. These formats are designed to help people manage the business better; they are not geared to outsiders, nor are they designed to meet reporting requirements. Currently, the huddles focus on income and cash-flow statements but spend very little time on the balance sheet. Stack notes that SRC's critical number is usually *not* the level of profits, although achieving the designated target number will improve profits in the long run.[6]

SRC is focused on improving the return on total assets and other key ratios, and SRC managers and executives are working to bring people to a level of financial literacy that will allow them to run the business by looking at these ratios. Because the return-on-total-assets ratio is the critical number that drives the bonus, people will want to learn how to improve that ratio. The goal, according to Stack, is for all employees to look at the company as though they were outside investors. That degree of understanding has probably penetrated to the mid-management level.

Schaefer and Bredfeldt are working on visual aids to educate employees on the shop floor. Their goal is for employees to understand that turning over assets more quickly earns them more money and makes the company more attractive to the investment community. Schaefer points out, however, that the finance side of open-book management is just a part of the process, and not even the key part. In her view, running the business by the numbers "keeps the business whole, but without the customer, the supplier, or the employee, there is no business."

Schaefer notes that people play a lot of different games at SRC, not all of which relate to the bonus program. SRC also plays games that relate to safety, which continues to be a very important issue in the company. Until a few years ago, the record for SRC as a corporation was 170,000 hours without any time lost because of accidents. Then the general manager of the heavy-duty division designed a series of games that focused on safety. That division then went for more than two years—1.8 million hours—without a lost-time accident. At the half-million mark, the division had a parade, in which the production manager, quality manager, and controller wore costumes and marched around the factory. At the 1-million mark, the division had a 24-hour celebration. Schaefer reports the general manager wanted to start a different game after that because he was afraid he would open up a closet and find a person who had been hurt on the job months earlier.

When the division played the game, the general manager kept saying it would pay off. SRC did not have to invest much money in the game, but the reduction in lost work hours saved the company well over $100,000 in workers' compensation, insurance rates, and similar items.

SRC is constantly developing and playing new games, which requires a great deal of effort and creativity. However, the employees interviewed believe games are crucial for maintaining energy and enthusiasm, as well as for providing the incentives people need to attain certain goals. They also say celebrating success with parties and rewards is very important.

Will Open-Book Management Work at Other Companies?

Stack and the rest of his SRC management team are convinced open-book management will work in other companies, given certain commitments and conditions, but that it will pose challenges that most firms have never before encountered. Even SRC faces daunting challenges in implementing open-book management in some of its own subsidiaries.

SRC recently acquired a business that had been run as a totally closed organization—the owners shared nothing with employees. Understandably, the employees didn't trust the new management team from Springfield, in part because the original owners, who still work in the company, told them that open-book management wasn't going to work, that it was simply a façade. But in just a month, attitudes began to change as Schaefer went into the factory and began to educate employees about the financials. Now, she reports, employees know there is a cash problem and, more important, that it is their problem, not just SRC's.

According to Schaefer, SRC's system or one like it could help any company:

> I think every company should run this way. And if they don't, how do the small incremental improvements happen? Unless you're talking to people and teaching them to understand how to make money or how they are losing it, they can't make improvements. And it's the small incremental differences that add up to a big difference. I think every company has to go for it: union, nonunion, or private.

She notes that the implementation of open-book management depends first and foremost on trust. The effort to educate and build trust must be ongoing because open-book management's success depends on being open about the numbers, about what numbers are projected to be, and about what needs to be accomplished in financial terms. She discusses this aspect of open-book management at SRC:

> I'm not going to say people don't bag their numbers. When they give a forecast, they might put a little fluff in there once in a while.

> But for the most part, when we go through the numbers, you trust that everyone is looking throughout their organizations and figuring out their numbers. Even before that, you have to trust one another.

One might wonder whether the number of meetings and the level of interpersonal communication at SRC are necessary for open-book management to work. But as Schaefer observes, the essential element in a successful open-book program is the genuine commitment to share information, which starts with the business owners and top executives. If the key people are unwilling to share, especially if they have something to hide, they probably shouldn't start an open-book program.

As an example, Bredfeldt relates her experience of going into one company and talking to them about open-book management. She used the Yo-Yo workbook to get them started, and employees began asking some very pointed questions. There was a high level of mistrust and lack of credibility within the company because the owners were hiding things—they had formed a leasing company and were leasing cars to themselves through the company at a profit. At the same time, they were telling employees how badly the company was doing. The owners' deception was discovered, and they almost lost the business.

Jay Burchfield, former president of The Great Game of Business, also notes the importance of total commitment to open-book management among an organization's top people if the program is to work. If the CEO is not an enthusiastic supporter, he says, "you might as well forget it"; but with the CEO's active involvement, open-book management can work in every department and in every organization. In his view, the major task—and major challenge—for company leadership is to be continually creative, to find new games, to keep raising the bar, and to keep evolving. "The most difficult part is having the creativity of your leadership staff to continue the evolution of it and not let it stagnate."

Bredfeldt agrees that company leadership is critical to implementing open-book management, but she observes that much more is involved: The commitment to open-book management must be pervasive throughout the company, and that commitment must be rooted in the key functions of communication and education. Specifically, when asked whether SRC's commitment to open-book management would continue were Stack to leave the company, she noted the following:

> People say that we are only successful because of Jack. Well, that really gets him rocking, because open-book management is a system and a process, and the financial part is one small piece of it. Everyone thinks that all they have to do is open the books and everything will be okay. That is just not true. You still have to communicate, you have to teach people about it, you have to make them understand it, you need to have ways to bump their careers and make them grow through it, you've got to give them some incentive to want to do it or they are going to leave you. If you don't do these other things you can share numbers all day long and nobody cares, nobody knows what to do with them. A lot of people say they are an open-book company, but all they do is stick their income statement on the wall. The truly successful companies are doing many of these other things; they are not just sharing the numbers.

Stack concurs with the notion that open-book management involves pervasive and dynamic commitment, but he still places responsibility for this commitment with the CEO:

> I believe that the whole role of the CEO is to teach.... The message that the CEO sends when he gets involved in training is to tell the organization that things are constantly changing. It supports the message of continuous improvement and it enhances the idea that the person who has the educated workforce is going to have the dynamic company.

Stack himself emphasizes the need to focus on financial statements and to develop a viable bonus plan, if open-book management is going to work in other companies. In Stack's mind, the message contained in financial statements is the real great game, and he loves playing it. Doing all the things to improve the financials on a daily basis in manufacturing, purchasing, and sales is the hard part, and that is why he spends so much time educating and motivating employees. The accounting side is really very black and white—the company cannot walk away from the messages that the numbers send, and the messages in certain key financial ratios are clear and must be addressed.

For Stack, a lot of other popular management tools, such as market share, customer focus, and total quality management, are passing fads. But open-book management is not, because it is tied directly to financial statements, and the financials tell it all. For example, the proponents of market share argue for a dominant position in a particular sector, but the financial statements indicate that if most receivables are tied up in one market or with one customer and there is a downturn, the company can get burned. With this concern in mind, Stack intentionally diversified SRC by encouraging and funding new start-up businesses.

Stack argues that if executives are going to be honest with people, they have to bring the financial marketplace to them; they have to show them what is required to survive. The financial statements do that in no uncertain terms. SRC's management team does not talk about market share, but it does indicate what will happen to key ratios if sales and profit targets are not met. In Stack's words, "The financials translate the stories of people into numbers."

Stack feels strongly that open-book management must be anchored in a viable, well-designed bonus plan to reward employees' involvement in running their business. Stack has written about problems associated with variable-pay and profit-sharing plans, as opposed to bonus plans like SRC's.[7] Under traditional profit-sharing plans, the company puts a percentage of profits into a pool and distributes the money to employees at the end of the year. When companies use this type of plan, employees usually don't think or act any differently, and the plan does not motivate them—they just receive money at the end of the year without really knowing why. They may even come to expect it or depend on it as part of regular compensation.

Stack identified four essential elements of a good bonus plan: (1) clear, understandable goals that are accepted and set democratically; (2) frequent feedback, usually on a weekly or daily basis; (3) a structure that encourages people to work together to achieve goals; and (4) targets that are challenging to reach. According to Stack,

> A good bonus program draws people into the process. It drives the value of the company by educating people, not with formal training programs but through the work they do every day on the job. It gives them the tools they need to make and understand decisions. It provides them with business knowledge they can use to enhance

their own standard of living and job security as they're making a measurable difference to the company as a whole.... It's not a gift and it's not an entitlement. It's payment for a job well done.[8]

SRC's management team believes that open-book management can be successful in any organization, but implementing it in certain organizations might pose specific challenges. For example, open-book management might be especially challenging in privately held, family-run businesses in which owners have shown no desire to share information in the past, Schaefer observes. Obviously, management can use profits for many things, such as building the organization, distributing bonuses, or increasing long-term security. But if owners or top executives hide the financials, employees will probably think the worst—that profits go right back into their pockets.

Bredfeldt thinks that open-book management works best in small to mid-size companies because "it is very hard to change the direction of a large ship." In other words, an entitlement attitude may be more prevalent in a large company because employees may have received a particular benefit or annual wage increase year after year. Open-book management brings a lot of changes to a company, and it may be more difficult to change old, entrenched attitudes. In her experience, most large companies begin open-book management by conducting a pilot study using a small group setting, so they can work out the bugs before rolling out the program to thousands of employees.

Stack believes, without hesitation, that there are no limits to where open-book management can succeed. He is convinced the approach suits larger companies with global operations and high-powered MBAs as it does SRC, which is located in the relatively small and isolated midwestern town of Springfield. As evidence, he lists major companies, such as Kodak, Southwest Airlines, and Harley-Davidson, that have implemented various features of open-book management, although they might call their programs by a different name. The only bad candidates for open-book management are companies whose owners or executives are not totally forthright about the business, Stack stresses.

Stack acknowledges that once people learn more and get a taste of playing the game, they become hungrier and more ambitious. "These people are often a company's best employees, and they have to be fed or they leave." SRC accommodates its best people by providing

.ıoney for new ventures. Allowing ambitious employees to ɞ ᴧ businesses also enables younger employees to move up in the orgɑ ıization.

As Stack puts it,

> The mountain is to build a good company. It is not to build just the product or just to have good quality or top-dog service. It's to take off and elevate the company—to teach people how to build strong lives. Then the good products and the good ideas will follow.

The Role of Financial Executives

Financial executives play an important, and sometimes pivotal, role in any company's conversion to open-book management. The implementation of open-book management will place new, intense demands on financial staff and executives, requiring them to reconceive their function within the organization. SRC management notes that by far the most challenging of these new demands is that of learning—and being willing—to communicate with other employees to a greater degree than ever before.

Although conversion to open-book management may be initiated by the CEO, the total organization will continually push finance people to communicate once the program gets going and employees buy into it. In Schaefer's view, there is really no way to stop the communication process once people realize that they have been given access to financial information and that this information will affect what they do as well as how big their bonuses are.

Schaefer thinks a lot of controllers and finance executives would be extremely uncomfortable with the level of employee involvement open-book management requires, mainly because employees are watching them and constantly questioning their numbers, especially if the actual results don't meet the forecast. Bredfeldt describes how she and other SRC employees pressured their accountant when open-book management was first initiated:

> I was not the only person who challenged the accountant. There were several people challenging him. And I don't think accountants

> like to justify where they put different transactions and how they code the accounts. They don't like someone coming in and saying, "I don't want it in this particular account, I want it in that account."

In the current system, the person ordering a particular item specifies the account it affects. Thus, SRC staff accountants don't have to decide where to record transactions, which eliminates a lot of the pressure accountants used to face. Because everyone tracks their own numbers on a daily basis, they rely less on accountants for financial information. Accountants receive information from employees, rather than vice versa.

Bredfeldt provides an interesting perspective on the role of financial people during SRC's huddle process:

> I don't think that accounting controls the numbers. Operational and sales people control the numbers. They are the ones who ought to stand up and say that such and such is going to happen. The accountant is more of a backseat driver, and if he notices something awry, then he should speak up. We pass much more responsibility further upstream.

Bredfeldt notes that companies should recognize from the outset the need to restructure the accounting function within the organization. Too many companies start the process of converting to open-book management by turning to the accounting people for the numbers because of their more traditional role in organizations, she observes.

According to Stack, many financial people are unwilling to concede they don't have all the answers to questions about improving a company's financial performance. Many of them believe they are the only people with financial skills in the company, so they think giving away financial information will only produce chaos, he reports. But if financial executives really want to enhance productivity, they must realize that open-book management works because it relies on people *working together* to reach a common goal, Stack observes. In other words, financial executives must give others the tools they need to make sound business decisions.

Once financial people accept they are not the repository of financial wisdom, they will, it is to be hoped, get into the spirit of the game of business, as Stack envisions:

> I would love for financial people to be cheerleaders. I think they should be supporting the team and should be motivators and spectators at any given business. In very few organizations do we have the opportunity to coexist between a team and a spectator's support. Financial people can give us our dreams; they can tell us the routes we have to take to get there.

Burchfield relates an experience he had with a CFO that illustrates the difficulties that may await financial executives unwilling to accept their redefined roles. Burchfield was CEO of a bank that was implementing open-book management. Before the implementation, the CFO had handled all the budgeting and provided all the financial information. However, when Burchfield decided to involve everyone in the financial planning process, the CFO became concerned that he was losing his responsibility, his power base, and his standing as financial expert because he had to share financial information with lower-level staff. According to Burchfield,

> It created a rather difficult work environment for our CFO, and he was reluctant to do the things that I asked. And if I hadn't been so adamant, he never would have. And he still didn't do a very good job at it. I still had to go back to him every day, every week, every month and get him to get the reports out to everybody and get him to communicate, get him to be involved in teaching. But he hated it; absolutely hated it.

The CFO was excellent in his job, Burchfield notes, and had been a loyal employee for 30 years; but, like many other financial people, he believed that financial information should be kept closely guarded by the people who understand it best. And he felt he was the person who understood it best—even better than Burchfield and other senior officers of the bank because they didn't have the background, experience, or education in finance.

As the bank's performance improved dramatically under open-book management, however, the CFO finally came around. But Burchfield says it took nearly five years, and getting him actively involved in the new system was "like pulling teeth." Given this experience, Burchfield cautions that a reluctant CFO can significantly impede the effective implementation of open-book management.

Bredfeldt notes that apprehension about financial staff and nonfinancial employees working together more closely is a two-way street. Accountants and financial staff may be suspicious of open-book management, because it requires them to openly provide information to employees, whom they suspect may not understand it or may misuse it. However, she notes that employees in nonfinancial areas may have similar misgivings about accountants, suspecting them, for example, of secretively fabricating many of the numbers included on financial statements and tax returns. Speaking of production employees, she says,

> They don't have a great respect for what goes on. I didn't until I went back to school and learned about debits and credits and ledgers. After that I came out with a new respect for what accountants did. Even so, they tend to hide everything; everything is so secretive. It's no wonder that factory people will speculate the worst about them.... If they could break out of that mold and explain why they have to do certain things a certain way, then people would understand that they are not just making up rules, that there is a lot more to it.

Bredfeldt thinks this mutual wariness could be overcome if production employees were paired with accounting people to work on certain tasks, so each could understand the other's role.

Stack thinks financial executives reluctant to commit to the open-book management process should confront their basic fears about misuse of information and mistrust of people's motives. The theories of open-book management are filled with common sense ideas, he claims, such as providing all employees the tools and training they need, and keeping a current scorecard of how the company is performing. However, financial people may simply not want to give up control over an area they have dominated for years. Many of them truly believe people will use proprietary information for their own betterment and that customers who obtain certain information will use it against the company. For some reason, these fears encumber financial people more than others.

After financial executives have overcome these elemental impediments, many of them face another challenge that may be even more difficult to overcome—simply learning to communicate with employees who lack financial training. According to Schaefer, it was SRC's good fortune that one of its first controllers was a "people person" who could meet this challenge without much difficulty:

> He could talk English. He could speak the same language that the folks on the floor spoke. Those who don't talk in laymen's terms are out of place with the rest of the organization, and the operations people are not going to make a difference in financial performance. I think they have to have a certain personality, but if they don't, factory operations people will push them to the point that they will start to come around. But again, we still have people in those positions who speak a different language, and that makes it very hard for the rest of the people around them.

But even financial executives who aren't naturally blessed with the talent for communicating will be amply encouraged to develop it, Schaefer remarks. One division controller, for example, could never communicate in everyday language: "He just couldn't loosen up." The operations people spent hours and hours with him, actually teaching him to speak in laymen's terms. They did not let up on him, and they did not allow themselves to be intimidated by his use of accounting jargon. They demanded to learn what the numbers meant in words they could understand, and, ultimately, they prevailed.

Given such communication difficulties, financial executives may not be the best ones to conduct the training programs to help employees understand the information they receive. Burchfield, in fact, believes strongly that financial people should not train employees. He suggests that CFOs lead the training program and provide moral support and assistance in training the trainers, but CFOs and other financial executives simply have too much difficulty communicating in basic language and concepts to be effective as trainers themselves.

Bredfeldt expresses similar concerns about financial people who attempt to conduct business literacy training. She feels financial people will probably fail because they forget that most people don't use business language every day. She recalls one CFO who was extremely rigid and would not teach the trainers what they needed to know. This person was eventually replaced by someone from outside the organization who was willing to provide the information the trainers needed.

Any financial executive intending to provide training must be able to interact well with people. Bredfeldt believes the trainer should typically be someone from within the company, rather than an outside consultant. The person should be extremely patient and good at explaining concepts and information. Also, the trainer must be someone who can talk to people and not look down at them. These skills are more critical to successful training than a background in accounting or finance, Bredfeldt claims.

However, if finance people are responsive to open-book management but have a problem teaching and communicating, they can take courses in interpersonal skills—courses that will help them interact with people more effectively, Schaefer points out. Although finance people are rarely expected to teach and communicate with employees in more traditional companies, these activities are critical in an open-book company; financial executives must develop the skills they need to successfully carry out these responsibilities.

Another problem that many financial people have with open-book management is their need for tangible and quantifiable results. To Schaefer, open-book management is more of a concept or philosophy than a specific, measurable activity. Of course, if financial results improve shortly after the company implements open-book management, financial people will be thrilled and may then join the bandwagon. But more often than not, especially in the early years, a company will experience incremental improvements, along with a growing excitement as people get more involved and realize they can make a difference in their company's financial performance. This excitement will eventually spread to the finance staff, who will then want to be a part of the process rather than just sitting on the sidelines.

Given the special demands open-book management places on financial staff, not every finance person can fit comfortably into an open-book company, cautions Schaefer. Some, she says, may never come to consider the task of teaching factory workers how the income statement works as anything other than ludicrous. There are two kinds of finance people: those who can change and those who are stuck in a conventional mind-set, and those who resist new ideas and programs will not survive in an open-book management organization, Schaefer asserts.

Even worse, they may undercut the process by withholding information that production people must have. It is more likely, however, that really negative people will take themselves out of the company, especially if everyone around them continues to push them for information. This tension may be particularly problematic when a CEO wants to stick with a finance person who has been with the company for years, but who is now holding it back from achieving all that it could under open-book management. Burchfield advises CFOs who are going to get involved with open-book management to visit an organization that practices it and to spend some time with the CFO, learning how it works and what their role will be.

He also notes that the financial executive is not always the stumbling block to successful open-book management implementation. More vexing are those cases in which the CFO is actively interested, but the CEO may be doubtful. He observes that CEOs are very competitive and can be convinced once they see the results that open-book management can bring about, but many CEOs resist because they think it may be just another passing fad.

Burchfield believes otherwise:

> Open-book management is a way of managing and leading people and making people rise to a higher level of productivity. It's not just the financial part of it, but open business, open everything.

Case Summary

A number of clear and consistent messages emerge from discussions with SRC executives. First, they emphatically stress that open-book management encompasses much more than just opening up the books to employees. Rather, it embodies a philosophy for doing business that involves trusting and caring about people, providing incentives and opportunities for employees to advance, sharing wealth, and celebrating success.

Second, although SRC executives feel strongly that open-book management can benefit any company in theory, it forces companies to engage in activities and practices they may not be comfortable sustaining. For one, owners and executives must be entirely open about company finances. If they have something to hide, it will come out, and the credibility of the open-book management program—and management's intentions—can be destroyed. Furthermore, an organization's top people must be fully committed to open-book management because its success requires tremendous effort. It takes a great deal of creative energy and goes far beyond just opening the books or posting the income statement on a bulletin board. Companies must design new and challenging games; hold frequent meetings to share information; carefully target goals and give proper incentives to achieve them; make opportunities for advancement available for ambitious employees; and celebrate successes on a company-wide basis.

Top executives must also realize the need to be actively involved in the program themselves, and they must be involved pervasively. Executives who think their efforts are best placed in strategic areas or that they can delegate open-book management to specialists at lower levels in the company are cautioned against implementation.

SRC executives highlight the special demands placed on financial executives in an open-book management organization, and they caution that some finance people will have difficulty meeting these demands. CFOs or other finance executives may not be the best people to conduct training in business and accounting literacy because they may talk above those who lack their specific training. They might also think they are the only ones qualified to make important financial decisions.

Financial people often are cautious and guarded by temperament, and thus may have difficulty adjusting to the open environment open-book management requires, say SRC executives. Financial staff often fear losing control over an area they have dominated, or fear the repercussions of other employees' gaining deeper insight into their area of expertise.

Financial executives tend to be especially troubled by the thought of proprietary information falling into the wrong hands. While SRC executives acknowledge that this potential exists, they believe the benefits of distributing knowledge to employees far exceed these risks. In general, they feel finance people should be more open to the new challenges and new excitement that open-book management offers and should join the celebration rather than sit on the sidelines.

Open-book management's success may hinge on whether it reinforces or contradicts the core beliefs of the CEO, of other leading executives, and of the organization's culture. At its core, open-book management gives people top priority and assumes that people want to improve, are able to change, are willing to learn and assume responsibility, and are motivated to reach higher goals.

SRC has been able to sustain open-book management because it lives this philosophy on a daily basis. As Schaefer says, open-book management is a way of life at SRC. Its success at other companies requires no less of a commitment.

People Interviewed

Denise Bredfeldt, President, BizLit, Inc.

Jay Burchfield, President, The Great Game of Business[9]

Irene Schaefer, Executive at Large, SRC Corp.

Jack Stack, CEO, SRC Corp.

Endnotes

1. Jack Stack made these statements during an interview and presentation in Waltham, Massachusetts, on June 23, 1997.
2. Even the *Wall Street Journal* has toasted Stack's success ("Company Wins Workers' Loyalty by Opening Its Books," Dec. 20, 1993: B1–2). The article notes that the value of SRC's stock had increased from $.10 to $18.60 and clearly attributes the rise to open-book management. The stock price had grown to more than $38 per share, presplit value, in 1996.
3. See John Case, *Open-Book Management: The Coming Business Revolution* (New York: HarperBusiness, 1995), for a description of SRC.
4. See Jack Stack with Bo Burlingham, *The Great Game of Business* (New York: Doubleday, Currency, 1992), for a full discussion of Stack's background and SRC's early experiences with open-book management.

5. See Jack Stack, *The Great Game of Business,* for specific details about SRC's planning process.

6. Jack Stack, "The Problem with Profit Sharing," *Inc.* (November 1996): 67–69. Stack notes that SRC had 21 different targets in the past 14 years, including debt-to-equity ratio, inventory accuracy, and the current ratio.

7. *Ibid.,* 67–69.

8. *Ibid.,* 68–69.

9. Burchfield was president of The Great Game of Business at the time of the interview but no longer holds that position.

10

Conclusion

In the 21st century, third-wave corporations, as they deal with increasing and inevitable change, will come to realize that open-book management is "an idea whose time has come." They will find that to empower employees, they must share a broad array of financial and other information with them; and these companies will learn that information in the hands of employees is a powerful incentive. Without such sharing of information, the alignment of employee goals with those of the company is probably not achievable to the degree required of a world-class organization. CEOs who lead their companies through the adoption of open-book management may find themselves proudly proclaiming before shareholders that they are an open-book company, as did Patrick Kelly, founder and CEO of Physician Sales & Service. Kelly began his company's 1997 annual meeting of shareholders by stating, "PSS has always been open book." This declaration is a strong testament to the importance Kelly places on open-book management. It would be hard to imagine his opening the shareholders' meeting by saying, "PSS has always used activity-based costing" or "PSS has always used the balanced scorecard." Our examination of seven companies that have successfully adopted open-book management reveals that the approach is more than just a management practice or accounting phenomenon: It is a corporate culture.

The great motivational researchers—McGregor, Maslow, Argyris, Herzberg, among others—laid the foundation for open-book management with their research into employees' need for esteem, achievement, and responsibility. But perhaps a missing piece in the effort to draw out higher levels of employee performance has been the very simple but powerful notion of information sharing—the systematic dissemination of a wide array of financial and other information that employees can use to do their jobs more profitably. How can management expect employees to be concerned about the bottom line if they (1) have no knowledge of the bottom line and (2) have no idea of how their own actions can affect the bottom line? Steve Wilson, the colorful founder of Mid-States Technical Staffing Services, uses a sports analogy: "How can you put together a team if the players don't get to see the playbook? If the players don't know all the rules of the game, and the coach is trying to educate them move by move: 'No, don't do that—you'll be out of bounds.' And the player's saying, 'Where the hell is out of bounds?' 'Don't worry about it. I'll tell you when you get close.'" In open-book cultures, employees think like owners, even if they own none of their company's stock, because they understand the big picture.

To compete successfully in the 21st century, companies will have to continually achieve higher levels of productivity. Bob Collins, CEO of GE Fanuc, envisions accomplishing this goal with a workforce of "go-to" people—the people you turn to when you face a tough business situation. Empowerment through open-book management should groom more employees to become "go-to" people, and thus give a firm the capacity to continually improve productivity.

Probably the greatest obstacle to implementing open-book management is the fear of information sharing: "What if our competitors know how much we make?" or "They'll run us out of business if they find out our costs." But, surprisingly, this was not a particular concern at any of the study companies. The seven companies are all doing well financially, and many sense that perhaps the competition would be intimidated by their strong numbers or wouldn't know what do with the numbers anyway. Dennis Zimmerman, CEO of ComSonics, has another view of this concern: "Most people I know in the management world share financial information with their golfing buddies, with their attorney at the country club, or even when they are talking with their doctor or dentist.... Or, if Dun & Bradstreet calls, [management] shares the financial information with them. Yet the employee on the workbench building the product is going to have a lot more impact on how successful the business is than the golfing buddy, attorney, doctor, or Dun & Bradstreet." Pat Kelly has seen CEOs who are concerned more about their employees, not the competition, having the information: "The biggest obstacle [prospective open-book companies] have is the CEO—in overcoming the fear of the knowledge of the employees' knowing what's going on." Open-book management is like the proverbial genie-out-of-the-bottle: You can't put it back in again. Once employees have tasted open-book management, they are not likely to settle for anything less. As an employee of Mid-States Technical put it, "I would just feel totally left out" at a company that didn't practice open-book management.

Open-book management is nothing less than a seismic shift in a company's culture. For the shift to happen, the CEO must be the primary open-book champion, and the CFO, a secondary champion. In each of the study companies, this support was there. The shift to open-book management cannot merely be farmed out to a task force, with the CEO and CFO having only incidental involvement. The result will not be real open-book management but perhaps some variation on gain sharing that masquerades as open-book management.

The CFO's role in an open-book company is dramatically different from the norm. Dawn Mahoney Cottrell, CFO of Plow & Hearth, views the CFO of an open-book company as the chief financial educator, responsible for ensuring that employees understand the information shared. A traditionalist CFO who cannot deal with disclosing sensitive financial information or who perceives a loss of control will probably play a destructive role in the open-book management process and will have to resign if open-book management is to work.

Effective training is absolutely essential to open-book management; otherwise, employees will not understand the numbers and—even more important—will not know how to affect the numbers. The study companies approached training in different ways. Some conducted formal training courses; others used informal methods, such as company newsletters or competitive games. When open-book management is first implemented, however, extensive formal training is necessary to bring employees up to speed. After the initial implementation, informal training may be sufficient to keep existing employees current and to bring new employees up to speed quickly.

What about educating our CFOs of the future, especially as they pursue undergraduate and graduate business degrees? The topic of open-book management crosses traditional boundaries within the business school curriculum because it encompasses organizational behavior, strategy, and management accounting. It should be addressed in the current business school curriculum, and it may take an interdisciplinary teaching effort to give it proper coverage.

Each study company had a lucrative incentive plan linked to profit numbers. The plans differ widely in how they are structured, but they all contained a well-publicized formula based on open-book numbers. Employee interest and attention are focused on attaining bonuses, and so employees are naturally drawn to the open-book numbers that will determine the size of their incentive pay. Companies felt free to alter the compensation formula periodically to accomplish strategic objectives. None of the study companies made extensive use of discretionary bonuses.

Empowerment took a variety of forms at the study companies. Employees at Mid-States Technical and Plow & Hearth "own" an expense line item. GE Fanuc makes extensive use of High-Involvement Workforce teams that are empowered to solve almost any problem encountered on the factory floor. Empowerment focuses employee attention on what individuals and teams can do to improve the company's numbers. But empowerment also has the advantage of giving employees greater business awareness so they understand when tough decisions must be made, as in the case of a layoff. When a layoff did occur at ComSonics, employee reaction was more along the lines of "What took you so long?" During a financial crisis at PSS, employees took a short-term pay cut, and no one left the company because all understood why the cut was necessary.

Whether a company is publicly held or unionized doesn't seem to hurt the prospects for open-book management. As a public company, PSS must ensure that it conforms to SEC rules, which has not been difficult, only somewhat delicate. North American Signs has established an effective open-book system while meeting the requirements of its union contract. Union representatives are happy with the outcome.

But open-book management is not for every company. It requires an extraordinary commitment on the part of senior management, especially the CEO and CFO. There is no such thing as "open-book management lite." A company is either open book or it's not. Either a high degree of trust exists between management and employees—or it doesn't. A company either shares its information regularly, routinely, and thoroughly—or it doesn't. It trains the employees, empowers them, and rewards them—or it doesn't.

Certainly, there is considerable latitude with respect to the information shared, but it must be extensive enough to warrant the use of the term "open book." It should probably include disclosures of sales and profits, unless there is a very good reason for excluding these numbers.

Companies may want to avoid sharing salary or wage information (as did most of our study companies), but there shouldn't be too many other restrictions. And the CEO should be prepared to deal with the inevitable question, "If we're open book now, how much do you make?"

The fruits of open-book management are many. The alignment of employee goals with company goals should and will show up in a stronger bottom line. Steve Wilson benefited financially from open-book management when his profitable company was acquired by a much larger company, because the culture of openness helped assure the purchaser that there were no hidden problems. CEOs can reduce their stress levels by the delegation of responsibility that accompanies open-book management. Employees tend to find their jobs more satisfying—they are more involved and can shape their own destinies.

Open-book management is likely to play a major role in propelling the business world into the next millennium. With a business-literate, empowered, and highly motivated workforce manning the front lines, open-book companies will make formidable competitors indeed.

APPENDIX A

Interview Protocols

Company Background, History, and Environment

1. Briefly describe the parameters of your company—size, industry, products, markets, and history.
2. How did you hear about open-book management?
3. Why did you think open-book management was right for your company?
4. Whose idea was it to try to implement open-book management in the company?
5. When did your company begin to implement open-book management? Describe the status of your company when you began open-book management implementation.
6. How far along are you in your open-book management implementation plan? Describe the various stages of open-book management implementation that your company has undergone.

Role of the Financial Executive

1. What are the financial executive's responsibilities in your company with respect to open-book management?
2. Are special skills required of a financial executive in an open-book management company? If so, please describe.
3. How much information is shared with employees?
4. Who determines the information to be shared?

5. What information is not shared?
6. How do you expect employees to use the information you share with them? Describe specific ways in which employees have used the financial information to improve the company's performance.

Training and Education

1. Generally describe the open-book management training process.
2. What information is regularly communicated to employees?
3. How is this information communicated to employees?
4. Who attends the training sessions?
5. Who presents the training?
6. What is the frequency of training?

Implementation Issues

1. How did the company get past the concerns of disclosing confidential information to employees and the risk of disclosing information that could benefit competitors and, if a publicly held company, nonshareholders?
2. What are the biggest obstacles to successful implementation of open-book management?
3. What type of support is needed from top management for open-book management?
4. What is the best way to implement open-book management?
5. What would you do differently if you were initiating open-book management again?

Incentives and Bonus Plans

1. Generally describe your open-book management incentives and bonus plans.
2. How have you tied incentives to performance?
3. How do you communicate to employees the results of performance on an ongoing basis?
4. What are the key facets of your bonus plan?

Results

1. How has open-book management affected the performance of your company?
2. Can the results of implementing open-book management be quantified?

APPENDIX B

References

Albrecht, Karl. *The Northbound Train.* New York: AMACOM, 1994.

Case, John. *Open-Book Management: The Coming Business Revolution.* New York: HarperBusiness, 1995.

Case, John. "The Open-Book Managers," *Inc.* (September 1990): 104–113.

Case, John. "The Open-Book Revolution," *Inc.* (June 1995): 26–43.

Derber, Milton. *The American Idea of Industrial Democracy, 1865–1965.* Urbana: University of Illinois Press, 1970.

Falconi, Robert R. "Too Many Cooks Spoil the Books," *Financial Executive* 11 (November/December 1995): 15–16.

Flynn, Gillian. "Workforce 2000 Begins Here," *Workforce* (May 1997): 78–84.

Forbes, Ted, and Isabella, Lynn A. *GE Fanuc North America A, B, C.* Charlottesville: University of Virginia Darden School Foundation, 1993.

Gardner, John. *On Leadership.* New York: The Free Press, 1990.

GE Fanuc *Times* (May 1997).

Hope, Jeremy, and Hope, Tony. *Competing in the Third Wave.* Boston: Harvard Business School Press, 1997.

"Managing 'Total Quality'," in "Operations and Fulfillment Think Tank," *Operations and Fulfillment* (March/April 1994): 56–60, 64–69. (Panel in which Dawn Mahoney Cottrell, Vice President of Finance, Plow & Hearth, participated.)

McGregor, Douglas. *The Human Side of Enterprise: 25th Anniversary Printing.* New York: McGraw-Hill, Inc., 1985.

Morris, Gerald F. "Owning the Numbers," *CFO* (March 1995): 72.

Naisbitt, John. *Megatrends.* New York: Warner Books, 1982.

O'Brien, Timothy L. "Company Wins Workers' Loyalty by Opening Its Books," *Wall Street Journal* (December 20, 1993): B1–2.

Plotkin, Hal. "Jig May Be Up on Fantastic Stock Multiples from Roll-up Acquisitions," *Inc.* (February 1997): 22.

Randolph, W. Alan. "Navigating the Journey to Empowerment," *Organizational Dynamics* (Spring 1995): 19–32.

Seidman, William, and Skancke, Steven L. *Competitiveness: The Executive's Guide to Success.* Armonk, NY: M.E. Sharpe, Inc., 1989.

Senge, Peter M. "Communities of Leaders and Learners," in "Looking Ahead: Implications of the Present," *Harvard Business Review* (September/October 1997): 18–32.

Shenkir, William G., and Barton, Thomas L. "A New Small Business Order," in *Performance Management in Small Businesses.* New York: International Federation of Accountants, 1996.

Sherman, Stratford. "Bringing Sears into the New World," in "From the Front," *Fortune* (October 13, 1997): 183–184.

Stack, Jack. "The Problems with Profit Sharing," *Inc.* (November 1996): 67–69.

Stack, Jack, with Bo Burlingham. *The Great Game of Business.* New York: Doubleday, 1992. (Revised Currency paperback edition in 1994.)

Stern, Robert N., and Comstock, Philip. *Employee Stock Ownership Plans (ESOPs): Benefits for Whom?* Ithaca: New York State School of Industrial and Labor Relations, 1978.

Szabo, Joan C. "Using ESOPs to Sell Your Firm," *Nation's Business* (January 1991): 59–60.

Toffler, Alvin. *The Third Wave.* New York: Bantam Books, 1980.

U.S. Senate. Senator Long of Louisiana speaking on "Another Successful ESOP Company." Proceedings and debates of the 98th Congress, 1st sess. *Congressional Record* (21 April, 1983), vol. 128, no. 52.

Volard, Sam V., and Brennan, Tim. "More than an ESOP—ComSonics, Inc.," unpublished paper (1988).

APPENDIX C

Annotated Bibliography of Selected Books and Articles

Books

Case, John, *The Open-Book Experience.* Reading, MA: Addison-Wesley, 1998.

The book contains lessons from over 100 companies that have successfully transformed themselves. The case studies include every example of open-book management—scorecards, compensation plans, and programs that provide business literacy training.

Case, John, *Open-Book Management: The Coming Business Revolution.* New York: HarperBusiness, 1995.

This book contains many anecdotes about the benefits of open-book management and identifies specific companies and individuals who advocate open-book management. Case describes basic principles and writes in an informal, journalistic style, typical of *Inc.* and *Fortune*. The book is fairly comprehensive, but Case is clearly partisan in his presentation of open-book management material.

McCoy, Thomas J., *Creating an "Open Book Organization."* New York: AMACOM, 1996.

The author provides an "integrated approach" for transforming an organization such that "employers think and act like business partners." The book presents a number of short case studies illustrating how companies have become open-book. The book also describes different incentive plans and the nature of empowerment.

McGregor, Douglas, *The Human Side of Enterprise: 25th Anniversary Printing.* New York: McGraw-Hill, Inc., 1985.

This book provides much of the conceptual underpinning for open-book management. McGregor discusses Theory X and Theory Y assumptions and presents the principles of participative management and gain-sharing plans.

Schuster, John P., Jill Carpenter, and M. Patricia Kane, *The Power of Open-Book Management.* New York: John Wiley, 1996.

The authors, all consultants, present a detailed, step-by-step approach to implementing open-book management. The book provides an introduction to open-book management concepts and benefits, but is more of a how-to guide for potential implementers. Success stories predominate.

Shenkir, William G., and Thomas L. Barton, "A New Small Business Order," in *Performance Management in Small Businesses.* New York: International Federation of Accountants, 1996.

The authors argue that a "new small business order" holds the key to small business success in the future. A promising component of that new order is empowerment accounting. Open-book management is presented as a respected version of empowerment accounting.

Stack, Jack, with Bo Burlingham, *The Great Game of Business.* New York: Doubleday, 1992. (Revised Currency paperback edition in 1994.)

This book presents the most comprehensive case study of open-book management and describes principles that Stack has implemented at SRC, perhaps the most successful open-book management company. The book also illustrates Stack's personal growth as an open-book management chief executive. The book includes many important insights on open-book management from an insider's perspective.

Articles

Davis, Tim R.V., "Open-Book Management: Its Promise and Pitfalls," *Organizational Dynamics* (Winter 1997): 7–20.

Davis presents a balanced view of open-book management and discusses the factors needed for a successful implementation. Davis traces the origins of open-book management and describes ten principles that should be followed. He also discusses the difficulties and potential concerns of open-book management.

Falconi, Robert R., "Too Many Cooks Spoil the Books," *Financial Executive* 11 (November/December 1995): 15–16.

Falconi, a financial executive, concludes that open-book management is more fad than revolution. The article describes his difficulties in trying to educate nonfinancial executives and managers about accounting and paints a very negative view of open-book management.

Fierman, Jack, "Winning Ideas from Maverick Managers," *Fortune* (February 6, 1995): 66–80.

Jack Stack, CEO of Springfield ReManufacturing Corporation, is one of the "maverick managers" featured in the article. The author presents a quick, condensed summary of Stack's success.

Lee, Chris, "Open Book Management," *Training* (July 1994): 21–27.

Lee describes how to empower workers, discusses the advantages of open-book management, and briefly describes successes in different companies.

Stack, Jack, "The Problem with Profit Sharing," *Inc.* (November 1996): 67–69.

Stack describes the flaws of most variable pay plans and explains why the bonus program used at SRC is more effective.

Stendardi, Edward J., and Thomas Tyson, "Maverick Thinking in Open-Book Organizations: The Challenge for Financial Executives," *Business Horizons* (September/October 1997): 35–40.

The authors critically examine the arguments Falconi raises against open-book management. They identify companies that have been successful with open-book management and challenge financial executives to be open-minded about open-book management.

ACKNOWLEDGMENTS

This research project has benefited greatly from the help of a number of people. The authors are indebted to the chief executive officers, chief financial officers, and all the others in the seven companies in this study for being so candid in telling their open-book management stories. They always gave their complete cooperation.

The authors are grateful to Tony Crunk for his invaluable editorial assistance.

Tom Barton would like to recognize the following students at the University of North Florida (UNF) who ably and conscientiously assisted him in either this study or earlier related research: Janet Dahlseid, Elvie DeGuzman, Samantha Hill, Melissa Humphries, Wyndee Joseph, Keely Mitts, Jerry Mucha, Mike Price, Arianna Raguinan, Emily Speyerer, Erica Stafstrom, and Terah Tyre. He thanks Pat Cagnassola for her excellent work in transcribing many hours of interview tapes and Rosa Price for her effective design and execution of the Chapter 1 timelines. He also thanks the members of the UNF Research Colloquium for their constructive questions and observations in the early stages of this work. He is especially grateful to Earle Traynham, Dean of the College of Business Administration at UNF, who has been most supportive of this and other research efforts.

Bill Shenkir thanks Laura Lengowski, who did an excellent job in transcribing the interviews for three of the cases and in preparing numerous tables and exhibits. He thanks his colleague, Professor Andy Ruppel, who has brought to his attention articles and videos on open-book management. He is grateful to Dean Carl Zeithaml of the University of Virginia's McIntire School of Commerce and his staff for support of his research projects, particularly in providing the excellent students to work as research assistants. Over the past three years, at one time or another, the following students have worked as his research assistants and spent some time on open-book management. They are Tom Contiliano, Duane Carling, David Davick, Barbara Hutchinson, Sara Kenny, Deborah Parkinson, Gregory Pope, Rick Singh, Tara Zimmerman, and Mohammed Vaid. Finally, he thanks his wife, Missy, for her constant support of all of his professional endeavors and, in particular, for telling him about Plow & Hearth's implementation of open-book management after her investment club's visit to the company.

Tom Tyson thanks the St. John Fisher administration for their continual support of his academic and practice-oriented research. He thanks his 1997 MBA students for engaging in discussion regarding the controversial aspects of open-book management. He specially thanks Professor Ed Stendardi for his contributions to a co-authored paper on open-book management and Ann Lomax for promptly and professionally transcribing taped interviews.

Finally, the authors would like to thank the FERF staff and the Advisory Committee. Their support was constant and superb. Jim Lewis, Bill Sinnett, Janet Hastie, and Rhona Ferling were extremely helpful in completing the project on schedule. Also, the Advisory Committee, led by Bob Schuler, kept the authors mindful of the timetable and was supportive all along the way.

ABOUT THE AUTHORS

Thomas L. Barton is Professor of Accounting and KPMG Peat Marwick Fellow at the University of North Florida. He holds a Ph.D. in accounting from the University of Florida and is a CPA. Dr. Barton has over 25 professional publications, including research articles in *Barron's, Decision Sciences, Abacus, Advances in Accounting, CPA Journal,* and *Management Accounting.* He received the Lybrand Silver Medal for his article, "A System is Born: Management Control at American Transtech." He is the co-author of the *AccKnowledge* software package and three other software products for educational use. Dr. Barton is the creator of the Minimum Total Propensity to Disrupt (MTPD) method of allocating gains from co-operative ventures. This method has been the subject of several articles in *Decision Sciences.* He is also a recognized expert in the application of management controls to highly creative activities. Dr. Barton has taught over 75 professional development seminars and has extensive consulting experience with a wide cross-section of organizations in the public and private sectors. Dr. Barton is the recipient of several teaching awards for his undergraduate and graduate work. He was a winner of the State University System of Florida's prestigious Teacher Incentive Program (TIP) award in 1994, the program's inaugural year.

William G. Shenkir is the William Stamps Farish Professor of Free Enterprise at the University of Virginia's McIntire School of Commerce. He served as dean of the School from 1977 to 1992. His teaching and research interests are in management accounting and accounting policy. He has produced more than 50 professional publications in leading academic and practitioner journals, made more than 70 presentations before professional and academic organizations, and edited or co-authored four books. From 1973 to 1976, he served as a technical advisor and project director at the Financial Accounting Standards Board. Dr. Shenkir has served as president of the American Assembly of Collegiate Schools of Business and as a vice-president of the American Accounting Association. He has been on numerous committees of the American Accounting Association, AICPA, FEI, IMA, and the Virginia Society of CPAs. He was a member of the Board of Directors of Dominion Bankshares Corporation and the Deloitte & Touche Academic Advisory Board. He is currently on the Board of

Directors of First Union National Bank of Virginia, Maryland, and Washington, D.C., and on the Corporate Banking Committee. He has taught executive development programs for personnel from industry, government, and accounting firms. He is a CPA and has consulted with a variety of organizations.

Thomas N. Tyson is Professor of Accounting at St. John Fisher College in Rochester, New York. He is a Certified Management Accountant and an Enrolled Agent with the Internal Revenue Service. Dr. Tyson's teaching and research interests are in current cost management issues, business ethics, and accounting history. He has published more than 30 articles in a variety of leading academic and professional journals and has made more than 40 presentations to academic and professional organizations. Two of his five *Management Accounting* articles, on bar coding and quality cost measurement, received Certificate of Merit awards. Dr. Tyson has conducted research studies for the Institute of Management Accountants, the Canadian Embassy, and the Academy of Accounting Historians. He recently served as Distinguished Visiting Scholar at La Trobe University in Melbourne, Victoria.